Congressional Elections

Campaigning at Home
and in Washington

Congressional Elections

Campaigning at Home and in Washington

Paul S. Herrnson
University of Maryland

A Division of Congressional Quarterly Inc.

Printed in the United States of America

Cover design: Ed Atkeson/Berg Design, Albany, New York

Library of Congress Cataloging-in-Publication Data

Herrnson, Paul S., 1958-
    Congressional elections : campaigning at home and in Washington / Paul S. Herrnson.
        p.   cm.
    Includes bibliographical references and index.
    ISBN 0-87187-973-5. -- ISBN 0-87187-972-7 (pbk.)
    1. United States. Congress--Elections, 1992.   2. Electioneering--United States.   3. Campaign funds--United States.   4. Political action committees--United States.   I. Title.
JK1976.H47   1994
324.9730928--dc20   94-33712
                                                                    CIP

In Memory of
Harry Perlman

Contents

Tables and Figures

Tables

Figures

Preface

Incumbents generally win both because of their own efforts and because many challengers find themselves in a "Catch-22" situation. Without name recognition, challengers and candidates for open seats have trouble raising funds, and without funds, they cannot enhance their name recognition or attract enough support to run a competitive race. This conundrum hints at a fundamental truth of congressional elections: candidates really wage two campaigns, one for votes and one for resources. The former takes place in the district or state that is being contested. The latter is waged primarily in Washington, D.C., where the political consultants, political action committees (PACs), and national, senatorial, and congressional party committees are located. The two campaigns are waged concurrently, but the candidates and their organizations must conceptualize the campaigns as separate and plot strategy for each individually.

My goal in writing this book was to provide a comprehensive description of congressional elections. The book focuses on congressional campaigns, but voters, candidates, governance, and campaign reform receive considerable attention. I have gathered information from candidates, campaign aides, party strategists, PAC managers, journalists, and other political insiders to describe their goals, strategies, decision-making processes, and roles in congressional election campaigns. I have also assessed the impact that these individuals and groups have on election outcomes.

The conclusion I draw is that the norms and expectations associated with congressional campaigns affect who runs, the kinds of organizations the candidates assemble, how much money they raise, the strategies they use, the level of public support they attract, and whether they win or lose. The need to campaign for votes and resources, in turn, affects how members of Congress carry out their legislative responsibilities and the kinds of reforms they are willing to consider. To some, these observations may seem intuitive. Yet they are rarely discussed in studies that focus on voting behavior and are usually overlooked in research that focuses on the role of money in elections. Although journalists and political consultants have commented on these issues, their observations are too anecdotal to provide a foundation for reliable generalizations.

This book systematically analyzes the campaign activities of the candidates, parties, and PACs that participated in the 1992 elections using personal interviews with and mail questionnaires from more than 360 House and Senate candidates and other political insiders. Campaign finance data furnished by the Federal Election Commission and election-related information collected from campaign organizations, party committees, and PACs round out the source material. This evidence supports the thesis that the campaigns candidates wage at home for votes and in Washington for resources have an impact on the outcomes of congressional elections. The activities of party committees, interest groups, campaign volunteers, and journalists are also important.

This project required the participation of many individuals and institutions. First and foremost, I am indebted to the hundreds of individuals who consented to be interviewed, completed mail questionnaires, or shared election targeting lists and other campaign materials with me. Their participation in this project was essential to its success.

The Graduate Research Board and the Center for Political Leadership and Participation of the University of Maryland provided financial support for the project. The Department of Government and Politics provided a supportive and stimulating environment in which to work. Students in my honors seminar on congressional elections assisted in preparing the questionnaire and collected detailed information from two dozen campaigns. Colleagues and graduate students participating in a study of PACs generously made some of their interview materials available to me. Kirsten Andersen, Chip Denman, Candice Kahn, Marie Gates, Michael Gusmano, Robert Tennant, and J. Toscano provided invaluable assistance during various stages of the study. Bob Biersack of the Federal Election Commission furnished information and feedback at several junctures. Chris Bailey and Jim Gimpel volunteered suggestions on various parts of the book. Stephen Salmore, Frank Sorauf, Ric Uslaner, and an anonymous reader reviewed the entire manuscript and offered many helpful suggestions. Brenda Carter and Jerry Orvedahl at CQ Press played a vital role in helping to prepare the manuscript. I am delighted to have the opportunity to express my deepest appreciation to all of them.

Finally, a few words are in order about the person to whom this book is dedicated. My uncle, Harry Perlman, did not live to see the completion of this book, but his contributions to it were critical. The construction jobs he gave me were the most important form of financial aid I received while pursuing my college education. His ideas about politics and philosophy helped me to appreciate the virtues of democratically held elections and to recognize the inferiority of other means of transferring political power. His unwavering belief that people can be taught to value what is good about their political system and to recognize its shortcomings was a source of inspiration that helped me complete this book.

Introduction

Elections are the centerpiece of democracy. They are the means Americans use to choose their political leaders, and they give those who have been elected the authority to rule. Elections also provide the American people with a vehicle for expressing their views about the directions they think this rule ought to take. In theory, elections are the principal mechanism for ensuring "government of the people, by the people, [and] for the people."

Different aspects of the electoral process give tremendous insight into the operations of our political system. Separate balloting for congressional, state, and local candidates results in legislators who represent narrow interests, sometimes to the detriment of the formation of national policy. Private financing of congressional campaigns, which is consistent with Americans' belief in capitalism, favors incumbents and increases the political access of wealthy or well-organized segments of society. Participatory primaries, which require aspirants to Congress to assemble an organization in order to campaign for the nomination, lead candidates to rely on political consultants rather than on party committees to contest their primaries and general elections. These factors encourage congressional candidates to campaign and members of Congress to legislate more independently of party leaders than do their counterparts in other democracies.

Congressional elections are affected by perceptions of the performance of government. Americans' satisfaction with the state of the economy and with the nation's foreign policy, as well as with their own standard of living, provides a backdrop for elections and a means for assessing whether presidents, individual representatives, or Congress as an institution have performed their jobs adequately. Issues related to the internal operations of Congress—such as the perquisites enjoyed by members—can have an impact on congressional elections. Conversely, congressional elections can have tremendous implications for the internal operations of Congress, the performance of government, and the direction of domestic and foreign policy. Major political reforms and policy reversals generally follow elections characterized by substantial congressional turnover.

1

One of the major themes developed in this book is that campaigns matter a great deal in the outcome of congressional elections. National conditions are significant, but their impact is secondary to the decisions and actions of candidates, campaign organizations, party committees, organized interests, and others who are involved in congressional elections. This comes as no surprise to those who toil in campaigns, but it is in direct contrast to what many scholars would argue.

In order to win a congressional election or even to be remotely competitive, candidates must compete in two campaigns: one for votes and one for resources. The campaign for votes is the campaign that generally comes to mind when people think about congressional elections. It requires a candidate to assemble an organization and to use that organization to target key groups of voters, select a message they will find compelling, deliver that message, and get the candidate's supporters to the polls on election day.

The other campaign, which is based largely in Washington, D.C., requires candidates to convince the party officials, political action committee (PAC) managers, political consultants, and political journalists who are the leaders of the nation's political community that their races will be competitive and worthy of support. Gaining the backing of these leaders is a critical step in attracting the money and campaign services that are available in the nation's capital and in other major urban centers. These resources enable the candidate to run a credible campaign back home. Without them, most congressional candidates would lose their bids for election.

This book presents a systematic assessment of congressional election campaigns that draws on information from a wide variety of sources. Background information on the more than 10,000 major-party contestants who ran for the House between 1978 and 1992 furnishes insights into the types of individuals who try to win a seat in Congress and the conditions under which they run. Personal interviews and survey data furnished by more than 360 candidates and campaign aides who were involved in the 1992 House and Senate elections allow for analysis of the organization, strategies, tactics, issues, and communications techniques used in congressional campaigns. They also provide insights into the roles that political parties, PACs, and other groups play in those contests.

Case studies of twenty-four House campaigns conducted in 1992 illustrate with concrete examples the generalizations drawn from the larger sample. These include many typical elections, such as Democratic representative David Price's overwhelming victory over challenger LaVinia "Vicky" Goudie in North Carolina's 4th district, as well as a few unusual contests, such as the open-seat race in Florida's 3rd district, which required both general election candidates to win a primary and a runoff before competing in the general election. A number of close contests, such as Democratic incumbent Vic Fazio's nine-point victory over Republican challenger H. L. "Bill" Richardson in California's 3rd district, are also discussed. Some races are included because of the role of scandal, which is often the cause of an incumbent's defeat. Seven-term incumbent Nicholas Mavroules (D-Mass.) lost his 6th district seat to Republican challenger Peter Torkildsen after being indicted on charges of bribery and influence peddling.

Most of the discussion focuses on House candidates and campaigns because they are easier to generalize about than Senate contests. Differences in the sizes, populations, and political traditions of the fifty states and the fact that only one-third of all Senate seats are filled in a given election year make campaigns for the upper chamber more difficult to discuss in general terms. Larger, more diverse Senate constituencies also make Senate elections less predictable than House contests. Nevertheless, insights can be gained into campaigns for the upper chamber by contrasting them with those waged for the House.

Interviews with party officials, which were conducted over the course of the 1992 election, give insights into the strategies used by the Democratic and Republican national, congressional, and senatorial campaign committees. Similar information provided by the managers of a representative group of PACs is used to learn about the PACs' contribution strategies. Campaign contribution and spending data furnished by the Federal Election Commission are used to examine the role of money in politics. Newspapers, press releases, and advertising materials distributed by individual campaigns furnish examples of the communications that campaigns disseminate. Collectively, these sources of information, along with scholarly accounts published in the political science literature, allow me to portray comprehensively contemporary congressional election campaigns.

The next five chapters examine the strategic context in which congressional election campaigns are waged and the major actors that participate in those contests. Chapter 1 discusses the institutions, laws, party rules, and customs that are the framework for congressional elections. The framework has a major impact on who decides to run for Congress, the kinds of resources that candidates, parties, and interest groups can bring to bear on the campaign, the strategies they use, and who ultimately wins a seat in Congress. Chapter 1 also focuses on the setting for congressional elections in 1992, which then-president George Bush referred to as a "weird" year in American politics but in the final assessment produced results that were not unusual in that most incumbents won.

Chapter 2 discusses candidates and nominations. It examines the influence of incumbency, national conditions, and the personal and career situations of potential candidates on the decision to run for Congress.

The chapter also assesses the separate contributions that the decision to run, the nomination process, and the general election make toward producing a Congress that is overwhelmingly white, male, middle-aged, and drawn from the legal, business, and public service professions.

The third chapter examines in detail the organizations that congressional candidates assemble to wage their election campaigns. Salaried staff and political consultants form the core of most competitive candidates' campaign teams. These professionals play a critical role in formulating strategy, gauging public opinion, fund-raising, designing communications, and mobilizing voters.

Chapters 4 and 5 discuss congressional elections from the perspectives of the major institutional suppliers of campaign money and services. Chapter 4 analyzes the goals, decision-making processes, and election activities of party committees. Chapter 5 focuses on the goals, strategies, and election efforts of PACs. These chapters demonstrate that Washington-based elites have a tremendous impact on the conduct of congressional elections.

Chapter 6 discusses the campaigns that congressional candidates wage in Washington in order to win the support of party committees and PACs. It also describes how candidates raise money from individuals in their own states, in Washington, and in the nation's other major political and economic centers.

The next three chapters focus on the campaign for votes. Chapter 7 discusses voters, campaign targeting, issues, and other elements of strategy. Chapter 8 focuses on campaign communications, including television, radio, direct mail, and field work. Chapter 9 covers the subject of winners and losers. It analyzes what does and does not work in congressional campaigns.

Chapter 10 addresses the impact of candidate-centered elections on the activities of individual legislators and on Congress as an institution. The final chapter discusses the highly charged topic of campaign reform. In it I recommend specific reforms and discuss the obstacles that must be overcome before meaningful campaign reform is enacted.

Chapter 1

The Strategic Context

Congressional elections, and elections in the United States in general, are centered more on the candidates than are elections in other modern industrialized democracies. This chapter discusses the candidate-centered U.S. election system and explains how the Constitution, election laws, and the political parties form the system's institutional framework. It shows how the nation's political culture and recent developments in technology have helped this system flourish. It also examines the impact of the political climate on elections. The 1992 election is analyzed to demonstrate that predictable events such as redistricting, highly likely occurrences such as the widescale reelection of House members, and transient, less predictable phenomena such as congressional scandals influence the expectations and behavior of candidates, political contributors, and voters.

The Candidate-Centered Campaign

Candidates, not political parties, are the major focus of congressional campaigns, and candidates, not parties, bear the ultimate responsibility for election outcomes. These characteristics of congressional elections are striking when viewed from a comparative perspective. In most democracies, political parties are the principal contestants in election campaigns, and the campaigns tend to focus on national issues, ideology, and party programs and accomplishments. In the United States, parties do not actually run congressional campaigns nor do they become the major focus of elections.[1] Instead, candidates run their own campaigns, and parties may contribute money or election services to them. A comparison of the terminology commonly used to describe elections in the United States and that used in Great Britain more than hints at the differences. In the United States, candidates are said to *run* for Congress, and they do so with or without party help. In Great Britain, on the other hand, candidates are said to *stand* for election to Parliament, while their party runs most of the campaign. The difference in terminology only slightly over-simplifies reality.

Candidates are the most important actors in American congressional elections. Most of them are self-selected rather than recruited by party organizations. All of them must win the right to run under their party's label through a participatory primary, caucus, or convention. Only after they have secured their party's nomination are major-party candidates as-sured a place on the general election ballot. Independent and minor-party candidates can get on the ballot in other ways, usually by paying a registra-tion fee or collecting several thousand signatures from district residents.

The nomination process in most other countries, on the other hand, usually begins with a small group of party activists pursuing the nomina-tion through a "closed" process that allows only formal, dues-paying party members to participate.[2] While the American system amplifies the input of caucus participants and primary voters, these other systems re-spond more to the input of local party activists and place more emphasis on peer review.

The need to win a party nomination forces congressional candidates to assemble their own campaign organizations, formulate their own elec-tion strategies, and conduct their own campaigns. The images and issues that they convey to voters in trying to win the nomination carry over to the general election. The efforts of individual candidates and their cam-paign organizations have a bigger impact on election outcomes than the activities of party organizations and other groups.

The candidate-centered nature of congressional elections has a fun-damental impact on virtually every aspect of campaigning, including who decides to run, the kinds of election strategies the candidates employ, and the resources that are available to them. It affects the decisions and activ-ities of party organizations, PACs, other interest groups, and journalists. It also has a major influence on how citizens make their voting decisions and on the activities that successful candidates carry out once they are elected to Congress. Finally, the candidate-centered nature of the con-gressional election system affects the election reforms that those in power are willing to consider.

The Institutional Framework

In designing a government to prevent the majority from depriving the minority of its rights, the framers of the Constitution created a system of checks and balances to prevent any one official or element of society from amassing too much power. Three key features of the framers' blueprint have profoundly influenced congressional elections: the separation of powers, bicameralism, and federalism. These aspects of the Constitution require that candidates for the House, Senate, and presidency be chosen by different methods and constituencies. House members were and continue to be elected directly by the people.[3] Senators were originally to be chosen by their state legislatures but have been selected in statewide elections since the passage of the 17th Amendment in 1913. Presidents have always been selected through the electoral college. The means for filling state and local offices were omitted from the Constitution, but candidates for these positions were and continue to be elected independently of members of Congress.

Holding elections for individual offices separates the political fortunes of members of Congress from one another and from other officials and does little to encourage teamwork in campaigning. A candidate for the House can win during an election year in which his or her party suffers a landslide defeat in the race for the presidency, experiences severe losses in the House or Senate, or finds itself surrendering its hold over neighboring congressional districts, the state legislature, the governor's mansion, and various local offices. The system encourages House, Senate, state, and local candidates to campaign using issues and messages that they perceive to be popular in their districts even when these issues and messages differ from those advocated by their party's leader. In 1990 many Republican congressional candidates took a "no new taxes" pledge which was diametrically opposed to the tax increase signed into law by their party's standard-bearer, President George Bush. In 1993 many congressional Democrats opposed the North American Free Trade Agreement (NAFTA), which was championed by Democratic president Bill Clinton. These acts of what some might label party disloyalty would be completely unacceptable under a parliamentary system of government with its party-focused elections, but they are entirely consistent with the expectations of the framers of the U.S. Constitution. As James Madison wrote in *Federalist* No. 46,

> A local spirit will infallibly prevail ... in the members of Congress.... Measures will too often be decided according to their probable effect, not on the national prosperity and happiness, but on the prejudices, interests, and pursuits of the governments and people of the individual States.

When congressional candidates differ from their party's presidential nominee or national platform on major issues, they seek political cover not only from the Constitution but also from state party platforms, local election manifestos, or fellow party members who have taken similar positions.

Federal and state laws further contribute to the candidate-centered nature of congressional elections. Originally, federal law regulated few aspects of congressional elections, designating only the number of representatives a state was entitled to elect. States held congressional elections at different times, used different methods of election, and set different qualifications for voters. Some states used multimember at-large districts, a practice that awarded each party a share of congressional seats proportional to its share of the statewide popular vote; others elected their House members in odd years, which minimized presidential candidates' abilities to pull some of their parties' House candidates into office on their "coattails." The financing of congressional campaigns also went virtually unregulated for most of the nation's history.[4]

Over the years, Congress and the states passed legislation governing the election of House members that further reinforced the candidate-centered nature of congressional elections at the expense of parties. The creation of geographically defined, single-member, winner-take-all congressional districts was particularly important in this regard. These districts, which were mandated by the Apportionment Act of 1842, encouraged individual candidates to build locally based coalitions. Such districts gave no rewards to candidates who came in second, even if their party performed well throughout the state or in neighboring districts.[5] Thus candidates of the same party had little incentive to work together or run a party-focused campaign. Under the multimember district or general ticket systems that existed in some states prior to the act and continue to be used in most European nations, members of parties that finish lower than first place may receive seats in the legislature. Candidates have strong incentives to run cooperative, party-focused campaigns under these systems because their electoral fortunes are bound together.

The timing of congressional elections also helps to produce a candidate-centered system. Because the dates are fixed, with House elections scheduled biennially and roughly one-third of the Senate up for election every two years, many elections are held when there is no burning issue on the national agenda. Without a salient national issue to capture the voters' attention, House and Senate candidates base their campaigns on local issues or on their personal qualifications for holding office. Incumbents stress their experience, service to the district, or seniority, while challengers attack their opponents for casting congressional roll-call votes that are "out of sync" with the views of local voters, for pandering to special interests, or for "being part of the problem in Washington." Open-seat races focus mainly on local issues, the candidates' political experience, or character issues.

In contrast, systems that do not have fixed election dates, including most of those in Western Europe, tend to hold elections that are more national in focus and centered on political parties. The rules regulating national elections in those systems require that elections be held with regularity, but the exact timing is left open.[6] Elections may be called by the party in power at a time of relative prosperity, when it is confident that it can maintain or increase its parliamentary majority. Elections also may be called when a burning national issue divides the nation and the party in power is forced to call a "snap" election because its members in parliament are unable to agree on a policy for dealing with the crisis. In contrast to congressional elections, which are often referenda on the performance of individual officeholders and their abilities to meet local concerns, these elections focus on the conditions facing the nation and the performance of the party in power.

Because the boundaries of congressional districts rarely match those for statewide or local offices and because terms for the House, the Senate, and many state and local offices differ from one another, a party's candidates often lack incentives to work together. House candidates consider the performance of their party's candidates statewide or in neighboring districts to be a secondary concern, just as the election of House candidates is usually not of primary importance to candidates for state or local office. Differences in election boundaries and timing also encourage a sense of parochialism in party officials that is similar to that in their candidates. Cooperation among party organizations can only be achieved by persuading local, state, and national party leaders that it is in their mutual best interest.

Although the seeds for candidate-centered congressional election campaigns were sown by the Constitution and election laws, roughly a century and a half passed before the candidate-centered system firmly took root. Prior to the emergence of this system, party organizations played a major role in most election campaigns, including many campaigns for Congress. Local party organizations, often referred to as old-fashioned political machines, had control over the nomination process, possessed a near-monopoly over the resources needed to organize the electorate, and provided the symbolic cues that informed the electoral decisions of most voters.[7] The key to their success was the ability to command the support of large numbers of individuals who were willing and able to persuade friends and neighbors to support their party's candidates. It was not until the demise of the old-fashioned machine and the emergence of new campaign technology that the modern candidate-centered system finally blossomed.

Reforms intended to weaken political machines played a major role in the development of the candidate-centered system. One such reform was the adoption of the Australian ballot by roughly three-quarters of the states between 1888 and 1896.[8] This government-printed ballot listed every candidate for each office and allowed individuals to cast their votes in secret, away from the prying eyes of party officials. The Australian ballot replaced a system of voting in which each party supplied supporters with a copy of its own easily identifiable ballot that included only the names of its own candidates. The Australian ballot, by ensuring secrecy and simplifying split-ticket voting, made it easy for citizens to focus on candidates rather than parties when voting. This type of ballot remains in use today.

State-regulated, primary nominating contests, which were widely adopted during the Progressive Movement of the early 1900s, deprived party leaders of the power to handpick congressional nominees and gave that power to voters who participated in their party's nominating election.[9] The merit-based civil service system, the product of another turn-of-the-century reform, further debilitated the political parties by depriving them of the power of patronage. The parties, which could no longer distribute government jobs or contracts, had difficulty maintaining large corps of campaign workers.[10] Issues, friendships, the excitement of politics, and other noneconomic incentives can motivate small numbers of people to become active in party politics, but they cannot motivate enough people to support a party-focused system of congressional elections.

Congressional candidates and the few congressional-district party committees supporting them also lacked the patronage or government contracts needed to attract large numbers of volunteer workers or to persuade other candidates to help them with their campaigns. By the mid-twentieth century the "isolation" of congressional candidates from one another and from their own party organizations was so complete that a major report on the state of political parties characterized congressional candidates as the "orphans of the political system." The report, which was published by the American Political Science Association's Committee on Political Parties, went on to point out that congressional candidates

> had no truly adequate party mechanism available for the conduct of their campaigns, . . . enjoy[ed] remarkably little national or local support, [and] have mostly been left to cope with the political hazards of their occupation on their own.[11]

Voter registration and get-out-the-vote drives were about the only area of electioneering in which there was, and remains, some cooperation among groups of candidates and party committees. But even here the integration of different party committees and candidate organizations—and especially those involved in congressional elections—was and continues to be short of that exhibited in other democracies.

The Federal Election Campaign Act of 1974 and its amendments (collectively known as the FECA) further reinforced the pattern of candidate-centered congressional elections.[12] The FECA placed strict limits on the amount of money parties could contribute to or spend directly on behalf of their congressional candidates. It further limited the parties' ability to raise funds that could be used to help congressional candidates by placing ceilings on individual contributions and an outright ban on corporate, union, or trade association contributions to the parties' federal accounts. Moreover, the FECA provided no subsidies for generic, party-focused campaign activity.[13]

The law's provisions for political parties stand in marked contrast to the treatment given to parties in other democracies. Most of these countries provide financial and in-kind subsidies to parties for campaign and interelection activities.[14] The United States is the only democracy in which parties are not given free television and radio time.[15] The support that other democracies give to parties is consistent with the central role they play in elections, government, and society, just as the lack of assistance afforded to American parties is consistent with the candidate-centered system that has developed here.

Lacking independent sources of revenue, many local party organizations are unable to play a dominant role in the modern cash-based system of congressional campaign politics.[16] Furthermore, the national and state party committees that survived the reform movements and changed election and campaign finance laws lack sufficient funds or staff to dominate campaign politics. Perhaps even more important, party leaders have little desire to do so. They believe a party should bolster its candidates' campaigns, not replace them with a campaign of its own.[17]

Political Culture

Historically, American political culture has supported a system of candidate-centered congressional elections in a number of ways, but its major influence stems from its lack of foundation for a party-focused alternative. Americans have traditionally held a jaundiced view of political parties. *Federalist* No. 10 and President George Washington's farewell address are evidence that the framers and the first president thought a multitude of overlapping, wide-ranging interests preferable to class-based divisions represented by ideological political parties. The founders designed the political system to encourage pragmatism and compromise in politics and thus to mitigate the harmful effects of factions. Although neither the pluralist system championed by the framers of the Constitution nor the nonpartisan system advocated by Washington has been fully realized, both visions of democracy have found expression in candidate-centered congressional campaigns.

Congressional elections test candidates' abilities to build coalitions of voters and elites from diverse individuals. The multiplicity of overlapping interests in American society has deprived the parties and candidates of the class-based support that exists for parties and their candidates in most other democratic nations. The lack of a feudal legacy in the United States and the relatively fluid social and economic structure discourage the formation of class-based parties.[18] The consensus among Americans for liberty, equality, and property rights, and their near-universal support for the political system further undermine the development of parties aimed at promoting major political, social, or economic change.[19]

Americans' traditional ambivalence about political parties has found expression during reform periods. The Populist Movement of the 1890s, the Progressive Movement that came shortly after it, and the rise of the New Left in the 1960s all resulted in political change that weakened the parties. Turn-of-the-century reformers championed the Australian ballot, direct primary, and civil service laws for the explicit purpose of taking power away from party bosses.[20] The reform movement that took hold of the Democratic Party during the 1960s and 1970s further weakened the control of party leaders by opening party conventions, meetings, and leadership positions to the increased participation of previously under-represented groups. The reforms, many of which were adopted by Republican as well as Democratic state party organizations, made both parties more permeable and responsive to pressures from grass-roots activists. They tremendously weakened what little influence party leaders had over the awarding of nominations. As a result, candidates, their personal supporters, and issue activists had a bigger impact on party affairs.[21]

Post-World War II social and cultural transformations undermined the parties even further. Declining immigration and increased geographic mobility eroded the lower-class ethnic neighborhoods that were an important source of party loyalists. Increased educational levels encouraged citizens to rely more on their own judgment and less on party cues in political matters. The development of the mass media gave voters less-biased sources of information than the partisan press. The rise of PACs, interest groups, and other forms of functional representation created new arenas for political participation and new sources of political cues.[22] The aging of the parties, generational replacement, and the emergence of new issues that cut across existing fault lines led to the decline of party affiliation among voters and to more issue-oriented voting.[23] These developments encouraged voters to rely less on local party officials and opinion leaders for political information.[24] Cultural transformations created a void in electoral politics that individual candidates and their organizations came to fill.

Current attitudes toward the parties reflect the nation's historical experience. Survey research shows that most citizens believe that parties "do more to confuse the issues than to provide a clear choice on the issues," and "create conflict where none exists." Half of the population believes that parties make the political system less efficient and that "it would be better if, in all elections, we put no party labels on the ballot."[25]

Negative attitudes toward the parties are often learned at an early age. Many school children are routinely instructed to "vote for the best person, not the party." This lesson appears to stay with some of them into adulthood. A month before the 1986 congressional elections, less than 10 percent of all registered voters maintained the candidate's political party would be the biggest factor in their vote decision. Candidates and issues ranked higher.[26]

Although American history and culture are unsympathetic toward the parties and extol the virtues of political independence and candidate-oriented voting, the electoral behavior of citizens does provide an element of partisanship to congressional elections. Roughly two-thirds of all voters are willing to state that they identify with the Democratic or Republican Party. About 60 percent of all self-identified independents hold attitudes and exhibit political behaviors similar to those of partisans.[27] In 1986, the same year in which so few registered voters stated that they planned to cast their votes chiefly on a partisan basis, nearly three-quarters of all voters cast their ballots along party lines.[28] Such high levels of party-line voting are common in contemporary American politics, and partisanship is among the best predictors of voting in congressional elections, ranking second only to incumbency. The fact that roughly 85 percent of the voting population perceives, retains, and responds to political information in a partisan manner means that congressional elections, and elections more generally, are not entirely candidate-centered.[29] Yet the degree of partisanship that exists in the contemporary United States is not strong enough to encourage a return to party-line voting or to foster the development of a party-focused election system.

Campaign Technology

Political campaigns are designed to communicate ideas and images that will motivate voters to cast their ballots for particular candidates. Some voters are well-informed, have strong opinions about candidates, issues, and parties, and will vote without ever coming into contact with a political campaign. Others will never bother to vote, regardless of the efforts that politicians undertake. Many voters need to be introduced to the candidates and made aware of the issues in order to become excited enough to vote in a congressional election. The communication of information is central to democratic elections, and those who are able to control the flow of information have tremendous power. Candidates, campaign organizations, parties, and other groups employ a variety of technologies to affect the flow of campaign information and win votes.

Person-to-person contact is one of the oldest and most effective approaches to winning votes. Nothing was or is more effective than having a candidate, or one of the candidate's supporters, directly ask an individual for his or her support. During the heyday of the political machines, local party committees employed armies of volunteers to learn first-hand the needs and aspirations of voters residing in their neighborhoods and to deliver the message that, if elected, the party's candidates would help them solve their problems and achieve their goals.[30] Once these organizations lost their control over the flow of political information they became less important, and candidate-assembled campaign organizations became more relevant players in elections.

The dawning of the television age and the development of modern campaign technology helped solidify the system of candidate-centered congressional elections.[31] Television and radio studios, printing presses, public opinion polls, high-speed computers, and sophisticated targeting techniques are well suited to candidate-centered campaign organizations because they, and the services of the political consultants who know how to use them, can easily be purchased. Congressional candidates can assemble organizations that meet their specific needs without having to turn to party organizations for help, though many candidates request assistance from their parties' congressional, senatorial, state, or local campaign committees.

New technology also has encouraged a major change in the focus of most congressional election campaigns. It has enabled campaigns to communicate more information about candidates' personalities, issue positions, and qualifications for office. As a result, less campaign activity is now devoted to party-based appeals. Radio and television were especially important in bringing about this change because they are well suited to conveying and evoking images and less useful in providing information about abstract concepts, such as partisan ideologies.[32] The overall impact of the electronic mass media is to direct attention away from parties and party-sponsored activities and toward candidates and the events they organize in their own behalf.

The increased focus on candidate imagery that is associated with the "new-style" politics encourages congressional candidates to hire professional technicians to help them convey their political personas to voters. Press secretaries, "spin doctors," pollsters, issue researchers, fund-raising specialists, and targeting experts are commonplace in most congressional campaigns. As the importance of professional political consultants grew and the contributions of semiskilled and unskilled volunteers diminished, local party activists became less important in congressional elections. The introduction of direct-mail fund-raising and the emergence of PACs further increased the candidate-centered character of election campaigns because they provide candidates with the means for raising the contributions needed to purchase the services of campaign consultants.

The overall effect of technological change was to transform most congressional campaigns from labor-intensive grass-roots undertakings, at which local party committees excelled, to money-driven, merchandised activities requiring the services of skilled experts. Most local party committees were unable to adapt to the new style of campaign politics.[33] Initially, party committees in Washington, D.C., and in many states were also unprepared to play a significant role in congressional elections. However, the parties' national, congressional, and senatorial campaign committees and several state party organizations proved more adept at making the transition to the new-style politics. They began to play a meaningful role in congressional election campaigns during the late 1970s and early 1980s.[34]

The Political Climate

Candidates, campaign managers, party officials, PAC managers, and others who are active in congressional elections consider more than the institutional framework, available technology, and the culturally and historically conditioned expectations of voters when planning and executing their electoral strategies. They also assess the political climate, including the circumstances in their district, state, or the nation as a whole. At the local level, important considerations include the party affiliation, tenure, and intentions of the incumbent and the partisan history of the seat. Relevant national-level factors include whether it is a presidential or midterm election year, the state of the economy, presidential popularity, and international affairs. In 1992 the populist anti-Washington sentiments that crystallized in the independent presidential candidacy of Ross Perot were also significant.

Potential candidates survey the local political scene to determine whether conditions are ripe for a competitive election. Often they are not, and the result is that most congressional incumbents face weak challengers and many win by large margins. Between 1950 and 1990, House incumbents enjoyed reelection rates of better than 90 percent; the 1988 and 1990 elections returned to Congress 98.3 percent and 96 percent, respectively, of those who sought to keep their jobs.[35] Most potential challengers find these success rates discouraging and choose to wait until a seat becomes vacant rather than run against an incumbent. Consequently, many House seats go uncontested, and a substantial portion fail to attract meaningful two-party competition.[36]

Senate elections have been more competitive. Senate reelection rates ranged from 55.2 percent to 96.9 percent between 1946 and 1992. Between 1986 and 1990 only 5 percent of all Senate incumbents had no major-party opponent, and 58 percent of those involved in contested races won by 60 percent or more of the two-party vote. Fourteen percent of all senators seeking reelection during this six-year span were defeated.[37]

There are a number of explanations for the lack of competition in House elections. Some districts or states are so dominated by one party that few individuals of the opposite party are willing to commit their time, energy, or money to running for office. In many cases, the tradition of one-party dominance is so strong that virtually all of the talented, politically ambitious individuals living in the area join the dominant party. When an incumbent in these districts faces a close challenge it usually takes place in the primary, and the winner is all but guaranteed success in the general election.[38]

Uncompetitive House districts are sometimes the product of the redistricting process. In states where one party controls both the governorship and the state legislature, partisan gerrymandering is often used to maximize the number of House seats the dominant party can win. In states where each party controls at least some portion of the state government, compromises are frequently made to design districts that protect congressional incumbents. Party officials and political consultants armed with computers, election returns, and demographic statistics can "pack" and "crack" voting blocs in order to promote either of these goals.[39] The result is that large numbers of congressional districts are designed to be uncompetitive.

The desire of incumbents to retain their seats has changed Congress in ways that help discourage electoral competition. Most who are elected to Congress quickly come to terms with the fact that they will probably never hold a higher office because there are too few of these to go around. Like most people, they do everything in their power to hold on to their jobs. Congress has adapted to the career aspirations of its members by providing them with resources that can be used to increase their odds of reelection. Members use free mailings, WATS lines, district offices, and subsidized travel to gain visibility among their constituents. Federal "pork-barrel" projects also help incumbents gain popularity and visibility among voters.[40] Congressional staffs help members write speeches, respond to constituent mail, resolve problems that constituents have with executive branch agencies, and follow the comings and goings in their bosses' districts.[41] These "perks" of office give incumbents tremendous advantages over challengers. They also work to discourage those experienced politicians who could put forth a competitive challenge from taking on an entrenched incumbent.

The dynamics of campaign finance have similar effects. Incumbents have tremendous fund-raising advantages over challengers, especially among PACs. Many incumbents build up large war chests to discourage potential challengers from running against them. Those challengers who decide to contest a race against a member of the House or Senate typically find they are unable to raise the funds needed to mount a viable campaign.

Given that the cards tend to be so heavily stacked in favor of congressional incumbents, most electoral competition takes place in open seats, especially those that are not dominated by one party. Open-seat contests draw a larger than usual number of primary contestants. They also attract significantly more money and election assistance from party committees, PACs, and individuals than do challenger campaigns.[42] Special elections are a form of open-seat contest that tend to be particularly competitive and unpredictable. They bring out even larger numbers of primary contenders than normal open-seat elections, especially when the seat that has become vacant was formerly held by a long-time incumbent.

The concentration of competition in open-seat elections and the decennial reapportionment and redistricting of House seats have combined to produce a ten-year, five-election cycle of political competition.[43] Redistricting leads to the creation of many new House seats and the redrawing of the boundaries of numerous others. It encourages an increase in congressional retirements, leads more nonincumbents than usual to run for the House, and thereby increases competition in many House elections.[44] Competition in the four election cycles that follow redistricting generally decreases as incumbents shore up their electoral support and work to discourage challenges by potentially strong opponents.[45]

Another cyclical element of the national political climate that can influence congressional elections is the presence or absence of a presidential election. Presidential elections have higher levels of voter turnout than midterm elections, and they have the potential for coattail effects. A presidential candidate's popularity can become infectious and lead to some increase in support for the party's congressional contestants. A party that enjoyed much success in electing congressional candidates during a presidential election year is, of course, likely to lose some of these seats in the midterm election that follows.[46] An unpopular president can further drag down a party's congressional contestants.[47] Presidential election politics had a strong impact on the election of 1932, in which the Democrats gained ninety seats in the House and thirteen seats in the Senate. The Democratic congressional landslide was a sign of widespread support for Democratic presidential candidate Franklin Roosevelt as well as a repudiation of incumbent president Herbert Hoover and his policies for dealing with the Great Depression.[48] Although coattail effects appear to be declining in importance, Ronald Reagan's 1980 presidential campaign is credited with helping the Republicans gain thirty-three seats in the House and twelve seats in the Senate.[49] Bill Clinton's ascendance to the Oval Office was conspicuous for its lack of coattails. Democrats suffered a net loss of ten House seats and broke even in the Senate. Coattail effects are rarely visible when a presidential candidate wins by a margin as small as Clinton's 43 percent of the popular vote.

Congressional candidates who belong to the same party as an unpopular president also run the risk during midterm elections of being blamed for the failures of their party's chief executive.[50] The Republicans' forty-nine-seat House and four-seat Senate losses in 1974, for example, are widely attributed to a sense of disgust that grew from revelations about the Nixon administration's role in the Watergate break-in and President Ford's decision to pardon Nixon.[51] The Democrats' loss of fifteen seats in the House and three seats in the Senate in 1978 have been attributed to dissatisfaction with President Jimmy Carter's job performance.

The economy, foreign affairs, and other national issues have some effect on congressional elections. The president's party often loses congressional seats in midterm elections when economic trends are unfavorable, though the relationship between economic performance and congressional turnover has been declining in recent years.[52] Foreign affairs can also be influential. They may have contributed to the Democrats' congressional losses in 1972 during the Vietnam War.[53] Americans, however, tend to be less concerned with "guns" than with "butter," and so international events generally have less of an impact on elections than domestic conditions.

Other national issues that can affect congressional elections are civil rights, social issues, and the attitudes of voters toward political institutions. The civil rights revolution, the women's movement, urban decay, the emergence of the hippie counterculture, and the protests that these issues spawned—by both liberals and conservatives—are believed to have influenced voting behavior during the 1960s and 1970s.[54] Political scandal, and the widespread distrust of government that usually follows, can lead to the defeat of politicians accused of committing ethical transgressions, but as the post-Watergate election of 1974 demonstrates, individual members of Congress who are not directly implicated in scandal can also suffer because of it.

National issues are likely to have the greatest impact on congressional elections when candidates take unambiguous stands on them.[55] Presidential politics are also likely to have the greatest influence on congressional elections when voters closely identify congressional candidates with a party's presidential nominee or an incumbent president. House and Senate candidates generally respond strategically to national politics in order to improve their electoral fortunes. When their party selects a popular presidential candidate or has a popular incumbent in the White House, congressional candidates ally themselves with that individual in order to take advantage of the party cue. When their party selects an unpopular nominee or is saddled with an unpopular president, congressional candidates seek to protect themselves from the effects of partisanship by distancing themselves from the comings and goings of the executive branch. The party-focused campaigns that Democratic congressional candidates ran during the New Deal era and many Republicans mounted during the height of Ronald Reagan's presidency exemplify the former strategy. The independent, nonpartisan campaigns that many congressional Republicans carried out in 1990 and 1992 are representative of the latter.

The 1992 Elections

Many aspects of the political climate surrounding the 1992 congressional elections were typical of recent election cycles. The Democrats had majorities in both chambers of Congress and a Republican occupied the White House; that is a familiar pattern in contemporary American politics. The nation was suffering from a weak economy, and Americans were taking pride in their country's most recent display of military force in the Middle East. Following the completion of the census and the reapportionment of House seats, state governments began redrawing their district lines.

Civil rights continued to occupy a place on the political agenda. Racial and gender discrimination were issues in many campaigns due to the highly publicized studies of the unequal salaries and advancement prospects for women and African Americans and due to the beating of African American motorist Rodney King by four white police officers and the riots that ensued in Los Angeles. The Senate Judiciary Committee's treatment of Anita Hill and her allegations of sexual harassment against Supreme Court nominee Clarence Thomas during his confirmation hearings called further attention to racial and gender issues. Gay rights found its place on the agenda after the military's longstanding policy against homosexuals serving in the military became an issue.

A final arena in which civil rights issues were fought was redistricting. In 1986 the Supreme Court ruled that any gerrymandering of a congressional district that purposely diluted minority strength was illegal under the 1982 Voting Rights Act.[56] Most states interpreted the ruling cautiously, redrawing many districts with the explicit purpose of electing a minority group member to the House.

Perennial issues, such as the economy, are usually important to voters and occupied a place on the political agenda in 1992. As has been the case in most recent elections, voter dissatisfaction with the political establishment in Washington was also high. The savings and loan crisis and congressional scandal left many voters frustrated with their government. Much of this hostility was directed toward Congress, and many incumbents were preparing to respond using a strategy that had served them well in the past—running for reelection by campaigning against Congress itself.[57] Nevertheless, all of these issues took a back seat to the nation's declining economy, which was on almost everyone's mind.[58]

Although none of the events or conditions that preceded the 1992 election was particularly unusual, collectively they created some unique possibilities for politicians, parties, PACs, and other politically active groups. The redrawing of House seats, scandal, declining job satisfaction, the pursuit of some other office, and a myriad of personal considerations led an unprecedented 66 House members to retire.[59] Many of these factors encouraged a record 1,666 Democratic and Republican nonincumbents to declare their candidacies for the House, an increase of nearly 700 from 1990. They also led record numbers of women and minorities to declare their candidacies.

Other opportunities were created by the primary defeats of nineteen members of the House and the death of another incumbent, Democratic representative Ted Weiss of New York, shortly after he won his primary. The retirement of eight senators and the defeat of another, Sen. Alan Dixon, in the Illinois Democratic primary, also ensured turnover in the upper chamber.[60] The sheer number of open-seat contests—ninety-one for the House and nine for the Senate—meant that many contests would be run on a level playing field.[61] It also gave parties and interest groups the opportunity to try to replace some of their old foes in Congress with more sympathetic members.

Political scandal and the anti-Washington mood gave open-seat and challenger candidates for Congress a number of powerful issues to use in their election campaigns. Anti-Congress sentiments were ignited in 1990 by the Keating Five scandal, which implicated five senators in improperly lobbying federal bank regulators in behalf of Charles Keating, who was a major campaign supporter. Also in 1990, House Speaker Jim Wright (D-Texas) and House Democratic Whip Tony Coelho (D-Calif.) were forced to retire amid scandal, and Congress raised its own pay. In 1992 anti-Congress sentiment was further fanned by the House banking scandal, which revealed that 325 current or former House members had made 8,331 overdrafts at the House bank; by the House Post Office scandal, which implicated some high-ranking House members and staff in exchanging stamps for money; and by the savings and loan crisis, which left American taxpayers footing a bill for failed banking institutions that is estimated to reach $180 billion.[62] Political scandal, congressional perquisites, the federal deficit, and government gridlock were easily identifiable issues that could be used effectively against long-term incumbents. In combination, these issues led to calls for political change, creating new possibilities for congressional nonincumbents and their supporters.

The political climate affected many aspects of the 1992 congressional elections. It affected who ran for office, the strategies they used, the resources at their disposal, and the decisions made by 104,426,659 citizens who voted on election day.[63] It also influenced the funding decisions of political parties, PACs, and wealthy campaign contributors.

The record number of open seats and the huge number of highly qualified politicians who decided to run for the House and the Senate made the allocation of campaign money and services monumental tasks

Table 1-1 Number of Unchallenged and Defeated House Incumbents, 1982-1992

	1982	1984	1986	1988	1990	1992
Incumbent unchallenged by major-party opposition in general election	49	63	71	81	76	25
Incumbent defeated						
In primary	10	3	3	1	1	19
In general election	29	16	6	6	15	24

Sources: Compiled by the author from various editions of *Congressional Quarterly Weekly Report.* The primary and general election results are from Norman J. Ornstein, Thomas E. Mann, and Michael J. Malbin, *Vital Statistics on Congress, 1993-1994* (Washington, D.C.: Congressional Quarterly, 1994), 58.

Note: The 1982 and 1992 figures include incumbent-versus-incumbent races.

for party officials and PAC managers. Although many had anticipated the effects of redistricting on the number of candidates, even the most astute political insiders could not have foreseen the avalanche of quality candidates that would be created by the political context in which the 1992 congressional elections would be fought. The heightened competitiveness and uncertainties associated with the 1992 election posed tremendous challenges to the party committee and PAC leaders who distribute campaign resources to congressional candidates. That year an unusually large number of political elites voiced the sentiment that there were just too many good candidates and not enough campaign money and services to go around. Many congressional candidates and campaign managers held similar views, lamenting that another one or two media buys or an additional $20,000 to $30,000 would have turned their loss into a win.

The political conditions that were the setting for the election produced heightened competition, particularly in House contests. Nineteen House incumbents lost their primaries—a post-World War II record (see Table 1-1). Twenty-five (7 percent) of the incumbents who won their party's nomination were unopposed by a major-party candidate in the general election. A combination of primary and general election defeats resulted in the ouster of forty-three (12 percent) of all incumbents who sought to remain in the House.

The competitiveness of the 1992 elections becomes even more apparent once the candidates are divided into categories based on the "marginality" or "safeness" of their seats. Fourteen percent of all 1992 House candidates involved in contested races were incumbents "in jeopardy," who either lost the election or won by a margin of 20 percent or less of the

Table 1-2 Competition in House Elections, 1982-1992

	1982	1984	1986	1988	1990	1992
Incumbents						
In jeopardy	15%	13%	9%	8%	15%	14%
Shoo-ins	27	34	35	39	32	25
Challengers						
Hopefuls	15	13	9	8	15	14
Likely losers	27	34	35	39	32	25
Open-seat candidates						
Prospects	8	5	7	5	5	13
In one-party districts	7	1	4	3	1	9
(N)	(750)	(736)	(720)	(712)	(696)	(794)

Source: Compiled by the author from Federal Election Commission data.

Notes: Figures are for general election candidates in major-party contested races, excluding those in incumbent-versus-incumbent races. Incumbents in jeopardy are defined as those who lost or who won by 20 percent or less of the two-party vote. Shoo-ins are defined as incumbents who won by more than 20 percent of the two-party vote. Hopeful challengers are defined as those who won or who lost by 20 percent or less of the two-party vote. Likely loser challengers are defined as those who lost by more than 20 percent of the two-party vote. Open-seat prospects are defined as those whose election was decided by 20 percent or less of the two-party vote. Open-seat candidates in one-party districts are defined as those whose election was decided by more than 20 percent of the two-party vote. Some columns do not add to 100 percent because of rounding.

two-party vote (see Table 1-2). Twenty-five percent of all candidates, labeled incumbent "shoo-ins," won reelection by margins of greater than 20 percent. The figures for "hopeful" and "likely loser" challengers mirror those for the incumbents because the former category includes all victorious challengers and challengers who lost by 20 percent or less of the two-party vote, and the latter category includes all challengers who lost by 20 percent or more of the two-party vote. Thirteen percent of all House candidates, classified as open seat "prospects," ran in contests that were decided by 20 percent or less of the two-party vote. The remaining candidates—open-seat candidates who ran in "one-party districts"—were involved in contests that were decided by more than 20 percent of the two party vote.[64]

The figures indicate that the election of 1992 was more competitive than the five elections that preceded it, but it was not completely out of line with most of them and was only slightly more competitive than 1982—the previous post-redistricting election. The most important difference among the elections is that more open-seat elections were held in 1992 than previously. The presence of so many open-seat contests makes

Table 1-3   Number of Unchallenged and Defeated Senate Incumbents, 1982-1992

	1982	1984	1986	1988	1990	1992
Incumbent unchallenged by major-party opposition in general election	0	1	0	0	5	1
Incumbent defeated						
In primary	0	0	0	0	0	1
In general election	2	3	7	4	1	4

Sources: Compiled by the author from various issues of *Congressional Quarterly Weekly Report.* The primary and general election results are from Norman J. Ornstein, Thomas E. Mann, and Michael J. Malbin, *Vital Statistics on Congress, 1993-1994* (Washington, D.C.: Congressional Quarterly, 1994), 59.

1992 an excellent year for studying congressional elections because it allows for the development of reliable generalizations about these contests as well as incumbent-challenger races.

The 1992 Senate elections were not nearly as unusual as the House contests. While 1992 is the first election in more than a decade marked by an incumbent's primary defeat, the swearing in of five new senators is far from record-breaking (see Table 1-3). Dividing Senate candidates using a classification scheme similar to that used for the House (the only difference is that all open-seat races are classified as "prospects," reflecting the greater competitiveness and unpredictability of these contests) further shows that the 1992 Senate elections were not significantly more competitive than those that preceded them (see Table 1-4).

The competitiveness of the 1992 House elections and the large number of open seats in both chambers ensured the appearance of many new faces in the 103rd Congress. When the mist had cleared, 110 new House members and 12 new senators (plus one appointed to take the seat previously occupied by Vice President Al Gore) were preparing to be sworn in as members of Congress.[65] The election gave the GOP a net gain of 10 seats in the House, marking the first time in 100 years that an incumbent president was thrown out of the White House at the same time that his party increased its presence in the lower chamber.[66] The partisan balance of power in the Senate remained unchanged. The 103rd Congress opened with 258 Democrats, 176 Republicans, and one independent in the House and 57 Democrats and 43 Republicans in the Senate.

As a group, those who were sworn in as members of Congress in 1992 were more diverse than previous classes. The number of women in the

Table 1-4   Competition in Senate Elections, 1982-1992

	1982	1984	1986	1988	1990	1992
Incumbents						
In jeopardy	26%	17%	21%	21%	20%	22%
Shoo-ins	20	27	22	24	25	16
Challengers						
Hopefuls	26	17	21	21	20	22
Likely losers	20	27	22	24	25	16
Open-seat candidates	10	13	15	12	10	24
(N)	(66)	(64)	(68)	(68)	(60)	(68)

Source: Compiled by the author from Federal Election Commission data.

Notes: Figures are for general election candidates in major-party contested races. Incumbents in jeopardy are those who lost or who won by 20 percent or less of the two-party vote. Shoo-ins are incumbents who won by more than 20 percent of the two-party vote. Hopeful challengers include those who won or who lost by 20 percent or less of the two-party vote. Likely loser challengers are those who lost by more than 20 percent of the two-party vote. Some columns do not add to 100 percent because of rounding.

House grew by nineteen, the number of African Americans by thirteen, and the number of Hispanics by six. Women senators grew in number by four, and the elections of Carol Moseley-Braun (D-Ill.) and Ben Nighthorse Campbell (D-Colo.) meant that African Americans and Native Americans would enjoy demographic representation in the upper chamber. Despite this diversity, the vast majority of newcomers had at least one thing in common with one another and with their more senior colleagues: they came to Congress with significant political experience under their belts. Seventy-three percent of the new House members had held another public office, served as a party official, worked as a political aide or consultant, or ran for Congress prior to being elected in 1992. All but one of the new members of the Senate—Republican Robert Bennett of Utah—had similar levels of political experience, and Bennett, whose father had been a senator for twenty-four years, was no political neophyte.[67]

Notes

1. These themes are well developed in Leon D. Epstein, *Political Parties in the American Mold* (Madison: University of Wisconsin Press, 1986); and Epstein, *Political Parties in Western Democracies* (New York: Praeger, 1967).

2. Epstein, *Political Parties in Western Democracies,* chapter 8.
3. The specific districts, dates, times, and places for electing House members were originally left to the states to determine. Many states used multiple-member districts or at-large districts (or the general ticket) for choosing their House members until the passage of the Apportionment Act of 1842. See Kenneth Martis, *The Historical Atlas of US Congressional Districts, 1789-1983* (New York: Free Press, 1982), 4-7.
4. See, for example, George Thayer, *Who Shakes the Money Tree? American Campaign Financing Practices from 1789 to Present* (New York: Simon and Schuster, 1973), 63.
5. Single-member districts were mandated at several points in American history. The Apportionment Act made it difficult for states to create multimember or at-large districts but allowed them in the event that a state legislature could not agree on a redistricting plan. A 1967 amendment to the general apportionment law completely banned the use of at-large representation. See Martis, *The Historical Atlas of US Congressional Districts,* 5-6.
6 In Great Britain, for example, an election must be held at least once every five years.
7. See, for example, Frank J. Sorauf, "Political Parties and Political Action Committees: Two Life Cycles," *Arizona Law Review* 22 (1980): 445-464.
8. Jerrold B. Rusk, "The Effect of the Australian Ballot Reform on Split Ticket Voting: 1876-1908," *American Political Science Review* 64 (December 1970): 1220-1283; Austin Ranney, *Curing the Mischiefs of Faction* (Berkeley: University of California Press, 1975), 78-80; Walter Dean Burnham, *The Current Crisis in American Politics* (Oxford: Oxford University Press, 1982), 76; Epstein, *Political Parties in the American Mold,* 159-167.
9. See, for example, V. O. Key, *Politics, Parties, and Pressure Groups* (New York: Thomas Y. Crowell, 1964), 371; Ranney, *Curing the Mischiefs of Faction,* 25-30, 115-134; and David E. Price, *Bringing Back the Parties* (Washington, D.C.: CQ Press, 1984), 32-33.
10. Key, *Politics, Parties, and Pressure Groups,* 389-391; Eugene H. Roseboom, *A History of Presidential Elections* (New York: Macmillan, 1970), 263.
11. Committee on Political Parties, American Political Science Association, "Toward a More Responsible Two-Party System," *American Political Science Association* supplement 44 (1950): 21.
12. The Federal Election Campaign Act of 1974 had a predecessor that was enacted in 1971, but it had little effect on congressional elections.
13. The only subsidy the FECA gives to the parties comes in the form of a grant that helps to pay for their presidential nominating conventions. As nonprofit organizations, the parties also receive a discount for bulk postage.
14. Karl-Heinz Nassmacher, "Comparing Party and Campaign Finance in Western Democracies," in *Campaign and Party Finance in North America and Western Europe,* ed. Arthur B. Gunlicks (Boulder, Colo.: Westview Press, 1993), 233-263.
15. Arthur B. Gunlicks, "Introduction," in *Campaign and Party Finance,* 6.
16. Sorauf, "Political Parties and Political Action Committees," 445-464.
17. Paul S. Herrnson, *Party Campaigning in the 1980s* (Cambridge, Mass.: Harvard University Press, 1988), 82.
18. Louis Hartz, *The Liberal Tradition in America* (New York: Harcourt, Brace, and World, 1955), passim.
19. See, for example, Robert A. Dahl, *Democracy in the United States: Promise and Performance* (Chicago: Rand McNally, 1967), 252; Herbert McClosky

and John Zaller, *The American Ethos: Public Attitudes Toward Democracy* (Cambridge, Mass.: Harvard University Press, 1984), 62-100.

20. See Rusk, "The Effect of the Australian Ballot Reform on Split Ticket Voting."

21. Key, *Politics, Parties, and Pressure Groups*, 342, 386; Ranney, *Curing the Mischiefs of Faction*, 128-130; Nelson W. Polsby, *The Consequences of Party Reform* (Oxford: Oxford University Press, 1983), 72-74; William J. Crotty, *American Parties in Decline* (Boston: Little, Brown, 1984), 277-278.

22. Lee Ann Elliot, "Political Action Committees—Precincts of the '80s," *Arizona Law Review* 22 (1980): 539-554; Kay Lehman Schlozman and John T. Tierney, *Organized Interests and American Democracy* (New York: Harper and Row, 1986), 75-78; Sorauf, "Political Parties and Political Action Committees."

23. John R. Petrocik, *Party Coalitions: Realignments and the Decline of the New Deal Party System* (Chicago: University of Chicago Press, 1981), especially chapters 8 and 9; James L. Sundquist, *Dynamics of the Party System: Alignment and Realignment of Political Parties in the United States* (Washington, D.C.: Brookings Institution, 1983), especially chapter 17; Paul Allen Beck, "A Socialization Theory of Partisan Realignment," in *Controversies in American Voting Behavior,* ed. Richard G. Niemi and Herbert F. Weisberg (Washington, D.C.: CQ Press, 1984), 396-411; Martin P. Wattenberg, *The Decline of American Political Parties, 1952-1988* (Cambridge, Mass.: Harvard University Press, 1990), chapter 4.

24. See Austin Ranney, *Channels of Power: The Impact of Television on American Politics* (New York: Basic Books, 1983), 110; Doris Graber, *Mass Media and American Politics,* 4th ed. (Washington, D.C.: CQ Press, 1993), 250-252; Xandra Kayden and Eddie Mahe, Jr., *The Party Goes On: The Persistence of the Two-Party System in the United States* (New York: Basic Books, 1985), 95; Wilson Carey McWilliams, "Parties as Civic Associations," in *Party Renewal in America,* ed. Gerald M. Pomper (New York: Praeger Publishers, 1981), 51-68; and Sorauf, "Political Parties and Political Action Committees."

25. Jack Dennis, "Support for the Party System by the Mass Public," *American Political Science Review* 60 (September 1966): 605.

26. CBS News/*New York Times* poll, October 1986, cited in Bruce E. Keith, David B. Magleby, Candice J. Nelson, Elizabeth Orr, Mark C. Westlye, and Raymond E. Wolfinger, *The Myth of the Independent Voter* (Berkeley: University of California Press, 1992), 8. See Keith et al. chapter 1 for an excellent review of the literature on partisanship, independence, and citizen attitudes on parties.

27. See Keith et al., table 1.1 and chapters 4 and 5.

28. See Keith et al., fn. 8, p. 19.

29. This group includes independents who lean toward one of the two parties. See Keith et al., passim.

30. Sorauf, "Political Parties and Political Action Committees," 447.

31. Robert Agranoff, "Introduction/The New Style of Campaigning: The Decline of Party and the Rise of Candidate Centered Technology," in *The New Style in Election Campaigns,* ed. Robert Agranoff (Boston: Holbrook Press, 1972), 3-50; Larry J. Sabato, *The Rise of the Political Consultants: New Ways of Winning Elections* (New York: Basic Books, 1981), passim.

32. See Ranney, *Channels of Power,* 110; and Graber, *Mass Media and American Politics,* 250.

33. Sorauf, "Political Parties and Political Action Committees."
34. Cornelius P. Cotter and John F. Bibby, "Institutional Development and the Thesis of Party Decline," *Political Science Quarterly* 95 (Spring 1980): 1-27; John F. Bibby, "Party Renewal in the National Republican Party," in *Party Renewal in America: Theory and Practice,* ed. Gerald M. Pomper (New York: Praeger Publishers, 1981), 102-115; F. Christopher Arterton, "Political Money and Party Strength," in *The Future of American Political Parties: The Challenge of Governance,* ed. Joel L. Fleishman (Englewood Cliffs, N.J.: Prentice-Hall, 1982), 101-139; M. Margaret Conway, "Republican Political Party Nationalization, Campaign Activities, and their Implications for the Political System," *Publius* 13 (Winter 1983): 1-17; David Adamany, "Political Parties in the 1980s," in *Money and Politics in the United States: Financing Elections in the 1980s,* ed. Michael J. Malbin (Washington, D.C.: American Enterprise Institute, 1984), 70-121; Epstein, *Political Parties in the American Mold,* 216-225; Herrnson, *Party Campaigning in the 1980s,* chapters 3 and 4; Larry J. Sabato, *The Party's Just Begun: Shaping Political Parties for America's Future* (Glenview, Ill.: Scott, Foresman, 1988), 90-102; Stephen E. Frantzich, *Political Parties in the Technological Age* (New York: Longman, 1989), 81-90, 182-186.
35. These figures are from Norman J. Ornstein, Thomas E. Mann, and Michael J. Malbin, *Vital Statistics on Congress, 1993-94* (Washington, D.C.: Congressional Quarterly, 1994), table 2-7. For an excellent discussion of the effects of incumbency see Thomas E. Mann, *Unsafe at any Margin: Interpreting Congressional Elections* (Washington, D.C.: American Enterprise Institute, 1978).
36. The figure for noncontested races is calculated from Federal Election Reports. The other figures are from Ornstein, Mann, and Malbin, *Vital Statistics on Congress,* tables 2-7 and 2-10.
37. The figures are from Ornstein, Mann, and Malbin, *Vital Statistics on Congress,* tables 2-8 and 2-11.
38. See, for example, Key, *Politics, Parties, and Pressure Groups,* 421.
39. See, for example, David R. Butler and Bruce Cain, *Congressional Redistricting: Comparative and Theoretical Perspectives* (New York: Macmillan, 1992), 10, 87.
40. David R. Mayhew, *Congress: The Electoral Connection* (New Haven: Yale University Press, 1974), passim; Morris P. Fiorina, *Congress: Keystone of the Washington Establishment* (New Haven: Yale University Press, 1978), 19-21, 41-49, 56-62; Diane E. Yiannakis, "The Grateful Electorate: Casework and Congressional Elections," *American Journal of Political Science* 25 (1981): 568-580; Laurily L. Epstein and Kathleen A. Frankovic, "Casework and Electoral Margins: Insurance is Prudent Policy," *Polity* 14 (1982): 691-700; Bruce Cain, John Ferejohn, and Morris Fiorina, *The Personal Vote* (Cambridge, Mass.: Harvard University Press, 1987), 103-106; Barbara G. Salmore and Stephen A. Salmore, *Candidates, Parties, and Campaigns,* 2d ed. (Washington, D.C.: CQ Press, 1989), 65-70; and Gary C. Jacobson, *The Politics of Congressional Elections,* 3d ed. (New York: HarperCollins, 1992), 38-44.
41. Harrison W. Fox and Susan Webb Hammond, *Congressional Staffs: The Invisible Force in American Lawmaking* (New York: The Free Press, 1977), 88-99, 154-155; Kenneth Kofmehl, *Professional Staffs of Congress* (West Lafayette, Ind.: Purdue University Press, 1977), 171-173; Michael J. Malbin, *Unelected Representatives: Congressional Staff and the Future of Representative Government* (New York: Basic Books, 1980), 14.

42. Herrnson, *Party Campaigning in the 1980s,* chapter 4; Frank J. Sorauf, *Inside Campaign Finance* (New Haven: Yale University Press, 1992), 80-84.

43. Reapportionment and redistricting usually take place during the second election cycle in each decade. Sometimes, however, House districts must be redrawn a second time. Following the postredistricting election of 1982, for example, the courts ruled that the House districts that the state of California had created were illegal and forced it to redraw a number of them a second time.

44. On the patterns for congressional retirements, see Ornstein, Mann, and Malbin, *Vital Statistics on Congress,* table 2-7. On the patterns for the number of nonincumbent candidacies, see Federal Election Commission, "1992 Congressional Election Spending Jumps 52% to $678 Million," press release, March 4, 1993.

45. On the patterns for electoral competition, see Ornstein, Mann, and Malbin, *Vital Statistics on Congress,* table 2-10.

46. Bruce I. Oppenheimer, James A. Stimson, and Richard W. Waterman, "Interpreting U.S. Congressional Elections: The Exposure Thesis," *Legislative Studies Quarterly* 11 (1986): 227-247.

47. For a review of the literature and recent findings on forecasting congressional elections see Michael S. Lewis-Beck and Tom W. Rice, *Forecasting Elections* (Washington, D.C.: CQ Press, 1992), chapters 4, 5, 6.

48. Jerome M. Clubb, William H. Flanigan, and Nancy H. Zingale, *Partisan Realignment: Voters, Parties, and Government in American History* (Beverly Hills: Sage Publications, 1980), 258-260.

49. On coattail effects see especially Walter Dean Burnham, "Insulation and Responsiveness in Congressional Elections," *Political Science Quarterly* 90 (1975): 411-435; Randall L. Calvert and John A. Ferejohn, "Coattail Voting in Recent Presidential Elections," *American Political Science Review* 77 (1983): 407-419; George C. Edwards III, *Presidential Influence in Congress* (San Francisco: W. H. Freeman, 1980), 74-75; Richard Born, "Reassessing the Decline of Presidential Coattails: U.S. House Elections, 1952-1980," *Journal of Politics* 46 (1980): 60-79; James E. Campbell, "Predicting Seat Gains from Presidential Coattails," *American Journal of Political Science* 30 (1986): 397-418; Gary C. Jacobson, *Electoral Origins of Divided Government, 1946-1988* (Boulder, Colo.: Westview Press, 1990), 80-81.

50. See especially Edward R. Tufte, "Determinants of the Outcomes of Midterm Congressional Elections," *American Political Science Review* 69 (1975): 812-826; Gary C. Jacobson and Samuel Kernell, *Strategy and Choice in Congressional Elections* (New Haven: Yale University Press, 1983), chapter 6; Lewis-Beck and Rice, *Forecasting Elections,* 60-75.

51. Morris P. Fiorina, *Retrospective Voting in American National Elections* (New Haven: Yale University Press, 1981), 165; Eric M. Uslaner and M. Margaret Conway, "The Responsible Electorate: Watergate, the Economy, and Vote Choice in 1974," *American Political Science Review* 79 (1985): 788-803.

52. Gerald Kramer, "Short-Term Fluctuations in U.S. Voting Behavior," *American Political Science Review* 65 (1971): 131-143; Howard S. Bloom and H. Douglas Price, "Voter Response to Short-Run Economic Conditions: The Asymmetric Effect of Prosperity and Recession," *American Political Science Review* 69 (1975): 1240-1254; Jacobson and Kernell, *Strategy and Choice in Congressional Elections,* chapter 6; Benjamin Radcliff, *Journal of Politics* 50 (1988): 440-455; Gary C. Jacobson, "Does the Economy Matter in Midterm Elections?" *American Journal of Political Science* 34 (1990): 400-404. For an

alternative interpretation see Robert S. Erikson, "Economic Conditions and the Vote: A Review of the Macro Level Evidence," *American Journal of Political Science* 34 (1990): 373-399.

53. During the period from World War II through 1972, Republicans tended to do better in elections when foreign policy issues were salient. They were particularly likely to do well in 1972 because Democratic presidential candidate George McGovern's dovish positions caused deep divisions among Democrats. See John F. Bibby, *Parties, Politics, and Elections in America* (Chicago: Nelson Hall, 1987), 239-240.

54. Norman Nie and Kristi Andersen, "Mass Belief Systems Revisited: Political Change and Attitude Structure," *Journal of Politics* 36 (1974): 540-591; Crotty, *American Parties in Decline*, 49-50.

55. Richard A. Brody and Benjamin I. Page, "The Assessment of Policy Voting," *American Political Science Review* 66 (1972): 450-458; Norman H. Nie, Sidney Verba, John R. Petrocik, *The Changing American Voter* (New York: Twentieth Century Fund, 1979), especially chapter 18.

56. *Thornburg v. Gingles,* 478 U.S. 30 (1986).

57. Richard F. Fenno, Jr., *Home Style: House Members in Their Districts* (Boston: Little, Brown, 1978), 164-168.

58. See, for example, Gerald M. Pomper, "The Presidential Election," in *The Elections of 1992*, ed. Pomper, table 5.3.

59. The previous "modern" record for House retirements was forty-nine, set in 1978. Ornstein, Mann, and Malbin, *Vital Statistics on Congress*, table 2-7.

60. The number of Senate retirements in 1992 has only been exceeded twice since 1950. Ornstein, Mann, and Malbin, *Vital Statistics on Congress*, table 2-8.

61. The previous postwar record for open seats was sixty-five, and the average between 1946 and 1990 was roughly forty-four. Newly drawn House seats account for the open-seat contests that did not result from incumbent resignations, primary defeats, or deaths.

62. The estimate for the savings and loan cleanup is from Barbara Miles and Thomas Woodward, "The Savings and Loan Cleanup: Background and Progress," CRS Issue Brief, Washington, D.C.: Library of Congress, updated March 10, 1994.

63. This number includes all votes cast for president. Only 98,756,123 individuals cast votes in House elections, and 71,828,239 voted in Senate contests. Federal Election Commission, *Federal Elections 92* (Washington, D.C.: Federal Election Commission, 1993), 5.

64. These classifications are discussed further in the appendix.

65. The number for the Senate does not include Sen. Kent Conrad (D-N.D.), who retired from one Senate seat and was elected to another.

66. The last president to lose reelection while his party picked up House seats was Benjamin Harrison, in 1882.

67. Bennett's father, Wallace F. Bennett, represented Utah in the Senate from 1951 to 1974.

Chapter 2

Candidates and Nominations

Can I win? Is this the right time for me to run? Who is my competition likely to be? These are the kinds of questions that go through the minds of prospective candidates. This chapter examines who decides to run for Congress, how potential candidates reach their decisions, and the influence that different individuals and groups have on these decisions. It also examines the impact of political experience on a candidate's prospects of winning the nomination and the influence of the nomination process on the representativeness of the national legislature.

Strategic Ambition

The Constitution, state laws, and the political parties pose few formal barriers to running for Congress, enabling virtually anyone to declare him- or herself a candidate. Members of the House are required to be at least twenty-five years of age, to have been U.S. citizens for at least seven years, and to reside in the state they represent. The requirements for the Senate are only slightly more stringent. In addition to residing in the state they represent, senators must be at least thirty years old and have been U.S. citizens for at least nine years. Some states bar prison inmates or individuals who have been declared insane from running for Congress or voting in an election, and most states require candidates to pay a small filing fee or to collect anywhere from a few hundred to several thousand signatures prior to having their names placed on the ballot. As is typical for election to public offices in many democracies, a dearth of formal requirements allows almost anyone to run for Congress. And more than a thousand people run in an average two-year election cycle.

Although the formal requirements are minimal, other factors, related to the candidate-centered nature of the electoral system, favor individuals with certain personal characteristics. Strategic ambition, which is the combination of a desire to get elected, a realistic understanding of what it takes to win, and an ability to assess the opportunities presented by a given political context, is one such characteristic that distinguishes most successful candidates for Congress from the general public.[1] Most successful candidates must also be self-starters, since the electoral system lacks a tightly controlled party-recruitment process or a well-defined career path to the national legislature. And, because the electoral system is candidate-centered, the desire, skills, and attitudes that candidates bring to the electoral arena are the most important criteria separating serious candidates from those who have little chance of getting elected. Ambitious candidates, sometimes referred to as *strategic, rational,* or *quality* candidates, are political entrepreneurs who make rational calculations about when to run. Rather than plunge right in, they assess the political context in which they would have to wage their campaigns, consider the effects that a bid for office could have on their professional careers and families, and carefully weigh their prospects for success.[2]

Strategic politicians examine a number of institutional, structural, and subjective factors when considering a bid for Congress.[3] The institutional factors include filing deadlines, campaign finance laws, prohibitions for or against preprimary endorsements, and other election statutes or party rules. The structural factors include the social, economic, and partisan composition of the district, its geographic compactness, the media markets that serve it, the degree of overlap between the district and lower-level electoral constituencies, and the possibilities that exist for election to some alternative office. One structural factor that greatly affects the strategic calculations of nonincumbents and is prone to fluctuate more often than others is whether an incumbent plans to run for re-election.

Potential candidates also assess the political climate in deciding whether to run. Strategic politicians focus mainly on local circumstances, particularly whether a seat will be vacant or an incumbent appears to be vulnerable.[4] National forces, such as a public mood that favors Democrats or Republicans or challengers or incumbents, are usually of secondary importance. The convergence of local and national forces can have a strong impact on the decisions of potential candidates. The bounced checks and other ethical transgressions that cast a shadow over many House incumbents and the widespread hostility that was directed against Congress as an institution played a major role in shaping the pool of candidates that competed in the 1992 primaries and general election. These forces motivated many House incumbents to retire.[5] They also encouraged many would-be House members to believe that a seat in Congress was not beyond their reach. Favorable circumstances and the candidates' positive assessments of their own abilities encouraged the candidates to think they could win the support of local, state, and national political elites, raise the money, build the name recognition, and generate the momentum needed to propel them into office.[6]

Incumbents

For House incumbents the decision to run for reelection is usually an easy one. Congress offers its members many reasons to want to stay, including the ability to affect issues they care about, a challenging environment in which to work, political power, and public recognition. Moreover, incumbents are usually confident of their ability to get reelected. Name recognition and the advantages inherent in incumbency—such as paid staff and the franking privilege (which have an estimated worth of more than $1.5 million over a two-year House term)—are two factors that discourage strong opposition from arising.[7] Furthermore, most House members recognize that the "home styles" they use to present themselves to constituents create bonds of trust that have important electoral implications.[8]

Incumbents undertake a number of additional preelection activities to build support and ward off opposition. Many raise large war chests early in the election cycle in order to intimidate potential opponents.[9] Many also keep a skeletal campaign organization intact between elections and send to their supporters campaign newsletters and other political communications. Some even shower their constituents with greeting cards, flowers, and other gifts.[10] Their congressional activities, preelection efforts, and the fact that they have been elected to Congress at least once before make most incumbents fairly secure in the knowledge that they will be reelected.

Under certain situations, however, incumbents recognize that it may be more difficult than usual for them to hold on to their seats. Redistricting, for example, can change the partisan composition of a House member's district or it can force two incumbents to compete for one seat. Ethical transgressions, such as involvement in a highly publicized scandal, can also weaken an incumbent's reelection prospects. A poor economy, an unpopular president or presidential candidate, or a wave of antigovernment hostility also has the potential to bring down legislators who represent marginal districts. These factors can influence incumbents' expectations about the quality of the opposition they are likely to face, the kinds of reelection campaigns they will need to wage, the toll those campaigns could take on themselves and their families, and their desire to stay in Congress.

When the demands of campaigning outweigh the benefits of getting reelected, strategic incumbents retire. Elections that immediately follow

Figure 2-1 Number of Retirements by House Incumbents, 1950–1992

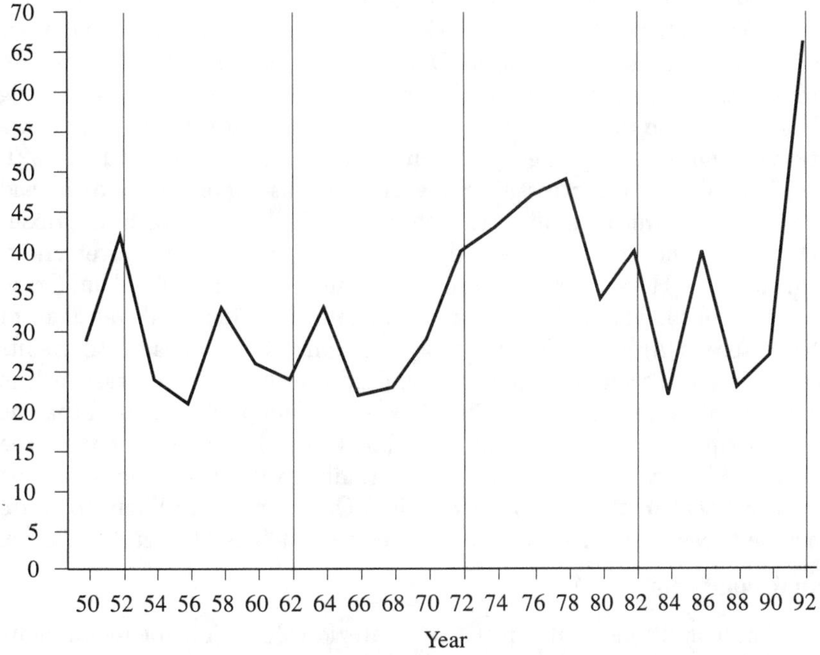

Source: Compiled by the author from Norman J. Ornstein, Thomas E. Mann, and Michael J. Malbin, *Vital Statistics on Congress, 1993–1994* (Washington, D.C.: Congressional Quarterly, 1994), 58.

redistricting are often preceded by a jump in the number of incumbents who retire, as was the case in 1952, 1972, 1982, and 1992 (see Figure 2-1). Elections held during periods of voter frustration or congressional scandal are also preceded by high numbers of retirements.[11] A combination of redistricting and anti-incumbent sentiments led 15 percent of all House members to retire in 1992—a post-World War II record.

Elections that occur following upheaval within Congress itself are also marked by large numbers of congressional retirements. The political reforms passed during the mid-1970s, which redistributed power from conservative senior House members to more liberal junior ones, encouraged many senior members to retire from the House between 1974 and 1978.[12] Included among these were Reps. F. Edward Hébert of Louisiana and W. Robert Poage of Texas, who retired less than two years after being stripped of their committee chairmanships by the House Democratic Caucus in 1975.

Among the individuals who are most likely to retire from Congress are senior members who decide they would rather enjoy the fruits of old age than face a tough opponent, members who find their districts largely obliterated, and those who are implicated in some kind of scandal.[13] The pre-1992 election period was marked by several retirements that were motivated by these reasons. Rep. Dante Fascell, a senior House Democrat from Florida and chair of the Armed Services Committee, was among those who chose to retire rather than wage a difficult campaign against a strong opponent. Rep. George Allen (R-Va.), who was elected in 1991, decided to leave Congress after his district was carved up and instead pursued the governor's office (which he won in 1993). Rep. Bob Traxler (D-Mich.), who had only recently assumed a much sought after chairmanship of a House Appropriations subcommittee, and Sen. Alan Cranston (D-Calif.), who had served in the Senate since 1968 and was chair of the Veterans Affairs Committee, were among those whose retirements were related to scandal. Traxler recognized that his 201 overdrafts at the House bank were a major liability. Cranston, who publicly stated that he was retiring for health reasons, also knew that his involvement in the Keating Five scandal would make it virtually impossible for him to hang on to his seat in the upcoming election. Others who are likely to retire include those shorn from positions of power, such as Hébert and Poage.

Nonincumbents

The conditions that affect the strategic calculations of incumbents also influence the decision making of nonincumbents who plan their political careers strategically.[14] Redistricting has a tremendous impact on these individuals. More state and local officeholders run for the House in election cycles that follow redistricting than in other years (see Figure 2-2). Many of these candidates anticipate the opportunities that arise from the creation of new seats, the redrawing of old ones, or the retirements that often accompany post-redistricting elections. The effects of redistricting and the anti-incumbent mood that gripped the nation encouraged roughly 350 candidates who had officeholding experience to run in 1992.

Candidates who have significant campaign and political experience but who have never held elective office also respond to the opportunities that emerge in specific election years. These "unelected politicians" include legislative and executive branch aides, political appointees, state and local party officials, political consultants, and individuals who have previously lost a bid for Congress. Most of these politicians think strategically. Prior to deciding to run, they monitor voter sentiment, assess the willingness of political activists and contributors to support their campaigns, and keep close tabs on who is likely to oppose them for the nomination or in the general election.

Unelected politicians differ from elected officials in their perceptions

Figure 2-2 Number of House Primary Candidates by Political Experience, 1978–1992

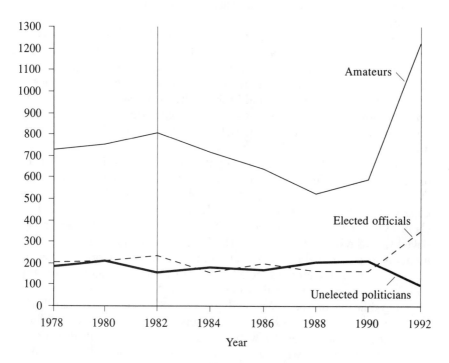

Source: Compiled by the author from various issues of *Congressional Quarterly Weekly Report* and other sources discussed in the appendix.

of what constitutes a good time to run. Elected officials are more likely than unelected politicians to view post-redistricting elections favorably. The major reason for this difference is that the candidacies of elected officials weigh heavily in the strategic calculations of unelected politicians. Unelected politicians are well aware that most elected officials possess name recognition and fund-raising advantages over them. Unelected politicians typically balk at the opportunity to contest a primary against an elected official, even when other circumstances appear favorable. Indeed, the two most recent post-redistricting elections witnessed large numbers of candidates who had previously held elective office and correspondingly few unelected politicians.

Political amateurs are an extremely diverse group, and it is difficult to generalize about their political decision making. Only a small subgroup of amateurs, referred to as *ambitious amateurs,* behave strategically, responding to the same opportunities and incentives that influence the decisions of more experienced politicians. The majority of amateurs do not spend much time assessing these factors. *Policy amateurs,* comprising another subgroup, are driven by issues, while *experience-seeking* or *hopeless amateurs* run out of a sense of civic duty or for the thrill of running itself.[15]

Record numbers of amateurs ran in the 1982 and 1992 elections. A few of these amateurs were ambitious challengers, who after weighing the costs of campaigning and the probability of winning declared their candidacies. Many policy and experience-seeking amateurs were also compelled to run in 1992. They found in the political landscape an ideal backdrop for running advocacy-oriented or anti-incumbency campaigns. Calls for change, pervasive incumbent-bashing, and the predictions of tremendous turnover attracted all types of amateurs.

What appears to be a year of opportunity for strategic politicians of one party is often viewed as a bad year by their counterparts in the other. Democrats with experience in lower office considered 1978 and 1982 to be good years to run for the House, while Republicans with comparable levels of experience did not (see Figure 2-3). In 1978, many Democrats believed that the lingering effects of the Watergate scandal and the retirements of forty-nine House members improved their electoral prospects. In 1982, many Democrats expected to benefit from the sluggish economy and declining popularity of President Reagan.[16]

Republicans, on the other hand, judged 1980 to be a good year. Double-digit inflation and the failures of Jimmy Carter's presidency encouraged many experienced Republicans to run for Congress, while discouraging qualified Democratic candidates.[17] The 1990 election cycle also attracted many highly qualified Republican candidates, while discouraging the candidacies of similarly qualified Democrats. Many of these GOP members apparently thought that the Keating Five scandal (which implicated four Democrats and only one Republican), the congressional pay raise, the forced retirements of House Speaker Jim Wright (D-Texas) and House Majority Whip Tony Coelho (D-Calif.), and the diffuse hostility that voters were directing at Congress could be used to whip up sentiment against Democratic incumbents.

The 1992 election was somewhat unusual in that strategic politicians of both parties judged it to hold tremendous possibilities. The effects of redistricting, a weak economy, congressional scandal, and voter antipathy encouraged record numbers of Democratic and Republican officeholders to run for Congress. Nearly 190 state and local officials ran in Democratic congressional nominating contests, while GOP contests attracted more than 160 Republican elected officials.

Because it is so difficult to defeat an incumbent, most of the best-qualified office seekers usually wait until a seat opens, either through retirement or death of the incumbent, before throwing their hats into the ring. Once a seat becomes vacant, it acts like a magnet, drawing the atten-

Figure 2-3 House Primary Candidacies of Politicians by Party and Experience, 1978–1992

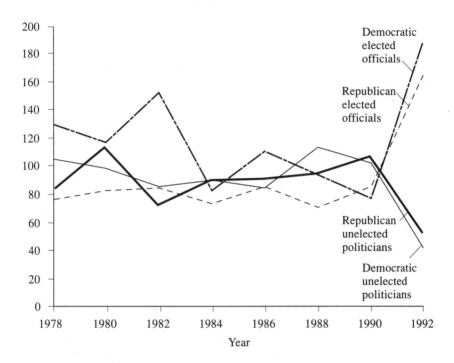

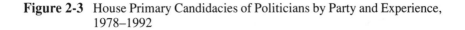

Source: Compiled by the author from various issues of *Congressional Quarterly Weekly Report* and other sources discussed in the appendix.

tion and candidacies of many individuals. Several strategic politicians will usually express their interest in an open seat. Sixty-three percent of the Democratic state and local officials who ran for the House in 1992 ran in the 18 percent of the races in which there was no incumbent at the beginning of the 1992 election (see Table 2-1).[18] Open seats also drew the greatest number of Republicans with officeholding experience and disproportionate numbers of unelected politicians from both parties.

Incumbency discourages strategic competition, especially within one party. Only 15 percent of the Democratic candidates who had officeholding experience and 17 percent of the Democratic unelected politicians who ran for the House in 1992 were willing to challenge one of their party's incumbents for the nomination.[19] Republican officeholders and unelected politicians were even more "gun shy" about attempting to commit political fratricide: only 9 percent of the former and 4 percent of the latter were willing to challenge a GOP House member in the primary.

However, because Democrats control the majority of House seats,

Table 2-1   The Impact of Seat Status on Nonincumbent Candidates for House Nominations, 1992

	Democrats			Republicans		
	Elected officials	Unelected politicians	Political amateurs	Elected officials	Unelected politicians	Political amateurs
Open seat	63%	55%	29%	46%	40%	28%
Democratic incumbent seeking reelection	15	17	32	45	56	60
Republican incumbent seeking reelection	21	29	40	9	4	1
(N)	(188)	(42)	(598)	(164)	(52)	(622)

Sources: Compiled by the author from various issues of *Congressional Quarterly Weekly Report* and other sources discussed in the appendix.

the odds are greater that a candidate of either party will run against a Democratic incumbent. The Democratic majority therefore explains why experienced GOP candidates were somewhat more willing than their Democratic counterparts to run for the right to challenge an incumbent of the opposing party in the general election. The Democratic majority also increases the likelihood that Democratic strategic politicians will challenge one of their party's incumbents for the nomination. These individuals recognize that they may have no choice but to challenge an incumbent of their own party if they wish to serve on Capitol Hill.

The differences between Democrats and Republicans pale next to the differences between experienced and amateur candidates. Political amateurs are the more willing to engage in internecine warfare with one of their party's House incumbents or to run in a primary for a seat that is controlled by an incumbent from the opposing party. Thirty-two percent of the Democratic political amateurs who ran for the House in 1992 challenged Democratic incumbents. Another 40 percent ran in primaries for seats that were held by the GOP. Republican amateurs were even more likely to run for a seat being defended by an incumbent. The relatively small numbers of political amateurs of both parties who ran in primaries for open seats further demonstrate that these candidates are less strategic in their decision making than are those who have a history of political involvement.

Others Involved in the Decision to Run

The drive to hold elective office may be rooted in an individual's personality and tempered by the larger political environment, but potential candidates rarely reach a decision about running for Congress without touching base with a variety of people.[20] Nearly all candidates single out their family and friends as having a decisive impact on their decision to enter or forgo the race.[21] In Virginia's 8th district, for example, Kerry Donley, a young, ambitious, and highly regarded Democrat from a politically active family remarked that his family "would probably shoot him" if he decided to run in 1992. Donley's sentiments echo those of multitudes of politicians who decide not to set their sights on a seat in Congress because of family pressures or for career reasons.[22]

Political parties, labor unions and other organized groups, and political consultants can also affect a prospective candidate's decision, but they have far less impact than the people who are directly involved in an individual's daily life. Potential candidates usually discuss their plans with these groups only after mulling for a long time the idea of running. Sometimes, would-be candidates approach local party leaders, fellow party members in the House or the Senate, or officials from their party's state, national, congressional, or senatorial campaign committee to learn about the kinds of assistance that would be available should they decide to run. On other occasions the party initiates the contact, seeking to nurture the interest of good prospects.

Barred from simply handing out the nomination, party leaders can influence a prospective candidate's decision to run in a variety of ways. State and local party leaders can help size up the potential competition and try to discourage others from contesting the nomination.[23] In some states party leaders can help a candidate secure a preprimary endorsement, but this does not guarantee nomination.

Members of Congress and the staffs of the Democratic and Republican congressional and senatorial campaign committees often encourage prospective candidates to run. Armed with favorable polling figures and the promise of party assistance in the general election, they search out local talent. Promising individuals are invited to meet with members of Congress and party leaders in Washington and to attend campaign seminars. They are also given lists of PACs and political consultants who possess some of the resources and skills needed to conduct a congressional campaign.[24]

During the early and mid-1980s, national party committees also attempted to winnow the field of primary contestants by discouraging some individuals from filing candidacies. The goal of this activity, dubbed "negative recruitment," was to prevent candidates from damaging one another in a divisive primary and to enable party members to unify quickly behind a nominee. National party activity in candidate recruitment can be risky, however. If the national party backs a candidate who is not the favorite of state or local party activists, it can demoralize local party members and damage the chances of the eventual nominee.[25] As a result of the conflicts that occasionally emerged and a belief that negative recruitment caused more harm than good, party organizations in Washington reduced their intervention in congressional primaries in the late 1980s. Since that time, when more than one candidate has signed up to run for a nomination, the national parties usually have remained neutral, waiting until the primary was over before becoming involved. The major exception to this rule has been when a primary challenger seriously threatens an incumbent.

Party recruitment is especially important and difficult when local or national forces favor the opposing party. Just as a strong economy or popular president can encourage members of the president's party to run, it can discourage members of the opposition party from declaring their candidacies, especially when an incumbent of the opposing party is seeking to remain in the seat. Sometimes the promise of party support can encourage a wavering politician to run under what at the outset appear to be less than optimal conditions.

Recruiting candidates to run for traditionally uncompetitive seats is not a major priority, but party committees work to prevent those seats from going uncontested. According to staffers from both parties' congressional and senatorial campaign committees, getting candidates to run for these seats is an important part of building for the future. These candidacies can strengthen state and especially local party committees by giving them a campaign on which to focus and deepening the farm team from which candidates emerge. These candidacies help prepare a party for opportunities that might arise when an incumbent retires, House districts are redrawn, or a scandal or some other event changes the partisan dynamics in the district.

Labor unions, PACs, and other organized groups typically play more limited roles in candidate recruitment than parties. A few labor PACs and some trade association committees, such as the AFL-CIO's Committee on Political Education (COPE) and the American Medical Association's AMPAC, take polls to encourage experienced politicians to run.[26] Others, such as the Women's Campaign Fund, EMILY's List, and WISH List, which are pro-women PACs, search out members of specific demographic groups and offer them financial support.[27] Labor unions focus most of their candidate-recruitment efforts, and campaign activities in general, on Democrats. Ideological PACs are among the most aggressive in searching out candidates, and many offer primary assistance to those who share their views. Few corporate PACs become involved in recruiting candidates because they fear offending incumbents.

Finally, political consultants can become involved in a potential candidate's decision making. In addition to taking polls and participating in candidate-training seminars, consultants can use their knowledge of a state or district to assist a would-be candidate in assessing political conditions and sizing up the potential competition.

Passing the Primary Test

There are two ways to win a major-party nomination for Congress: in an uncontested nominating race or by defeating an opponent. Victory in an uncontested primary or caucus is common in situations where a congressional seat is held by an incumbent. Even in the 1992 elections, which were marked by a record number of nonincumbent candidacies, 52 percent of all representatives and 42 percent of all senators who sought reelection were awarded their party's nomination without having to defeat an opponent.

Incumbent Victories in Uncontested Primaries

Victories by default occur mainly when an incumbent is perceived to be invulnerable. The same advantages of incumbency and preelection activities that make incumbents confident of reelection make them seem invincible to those contemplating a primary challenge. Good constituent relations, policy representation, and other job-related activities are sources of incumbent strength. A hefty campaign account is another.

The loyalties of political activists and organized groups also discourage party members from challenging their representatives for the nomination. While in office, members of Congress work to advance the interests of those who supported their previous election, and in return they routinely receive the support of these individuals and groups. With this support comes the promise of endorsements, campaign contributions, volunteer campaign workers, and votes. Would-be primary challengers often recognize that the groups whose support they would need to win the nomination are often among the incumbent's staunchest supporters.

Senior incumbents also benefit from the clout—real and perceived—that comes with moving up the ranks of the congressional leadership. Rep. Vic Fazio (D-Calif.), who completed his seventh term in Congress in 1992, is typical of most senior incumbents who are awarded their party's nomination without a fight. Fazio could have been vulnerable to a primary challenge in 1992 because redistricting forced him to run for a seat that contained only 65 percent of his previous constituents. Also, as chair of the Democratic Congressional Campaign Committee (DCCC) he was extremely vulnerable to the anti-Washington sentiments that gripped the nation. Nevertheless, no Democrats in California's 3rd district chose to oppose Fazio in the primary. The major reason Fazio was given a free ride is that he had performed his job as a representative well: he returned to California often, he maintained three district offices to provide constituent services, and he voted in accordance with his constituents' views on most issues. As a member of the "College of Cardinals" (one of thirteen Appropriations subcommittee chairs), he had brought many federal grants and projects to his constituents and state.[28]

Fazio was and continues to be an excellent fund-raiser. By the close of the 1991 calendar year, a full six months before the date of the primary election, he had already raised nearly $420,000. His campaign spending in the 1990 election—over $1 million—and his record fund-raising at the DCCC easily intimidated most primary challengers.[29]

Fazio has also enjoyed the support of many national and local interest groups. In 1992, as in previous years, he received the support of the California chapter of the National Abortion and Reproductive Rights Action League, the United Auto Workers, and the American Federation of Labor-Congress of Industrial Organizations (AFL-CIO). He also had won awards from these groups' local affiliates and other organizations.[30] The backing that Fazio received from these groups deprived would-be primary challengers of much of the organizational support that they would need to win. Finally, most of the Democrats who would normally be included on a list of Fazio's rivals or potential successors could be counted among his political allies.[31]

Junior incumbents rarely have the same kind of clout in Washington or as broad a base of support as senior legislators, but because they tend to devote a great deal of time to expanding their bases of support they too typically discourage inside challenges.[32] Junior members also may receive special attention from national, state, and local party organizations. Both the DCCC and the NRCC hold seminars immediately after the election to instruct junior members on how to use franked mail, town meetings, and the local press to build voter support. Prior to the start of the campaign season these party committees advise junior members on how to defend their congressional roll-call votes, raise money, and discourage opposition.[33]

State party leaders also give junior members of Congress advice and assistance. In 1992 Rep. James Moran (D-Va.) received what is perhaps the most important form of help state party leaders can bestow upon a candidate: a supportive district. Democrats in Virginia's capital redrew the state's congressional map with an eye toward improving Moran's re-election prospects. They added heavily Democratic areas to the district, let it be known that they considered this Moran's seat, and even invited one of his potential rivals to run for another House seat.

Local party activists, who form the pool of potential candidates from which inside opposition usually emerges, are generally more inclined to help junior legislators than challenge them because these activists often worked to elect that individual in the first place. Their loyalties tend to be especially strong when the seat is competitive or was held by the opposition party for a long period of time. As several Democrats in Moran's district explained, teamwork was essential in winning the seat and the same team that helped elect Moran would discourage other Democrats from running against him.[34]

Considerations of teamwork rarely protect House members who are vulnerable because of scandal. Incumbents who are implicated in some highly publicized ethical transgression face more challenges from within their own party than others. The 1992 elections were unique for the number of House members who were under the cloud of scandal. Yet some of these legislators, including several who were implicated in the House banking scandal, faced no primary opposition. Most often, opposition failed to materialize because the member's ethical difficulties did not become public until after the state's primary filing deadline had already passed or it was too late for a challenger to mount a campaign. Republican incumbent Bill Goodling of Pennsylvania's 19th district was able to avoid a primary opponent because his state's filing deadline fell on March 19th, just days after news of his overdrafts at the House bank became public. When outraged Republicans failed to get the state to extend the filing deadline, Tom Humbert, a conservative Republican and former top aide to secretary of Housing Urban and Development Jack Kemp, filed as an independent and sought unsuccessfully to defeat Goodling in the general election.[35]

Contested Primaries with an Incumbent

When incumbents do face challenges for their party's nomination, they almost always win. Of the 174 House members who had to compete for their party's nomination in 1992, only 19 were defeated, including 4 who were defeated in incumbent-versus-incumbent primaries that were brought about by redistricting. Only those members of Congress who have been accused of an ethical transgression, lost touch with their district, or suffer from failing health run a significant risk of falling to a primary challenger.

What kinds of challengers succeed in knocking off an incumbent for the nomination? The answer is candidates who have either held lower-level office or had some other significant political experience. Only 14 percent of the 1992 challengers who sought to defeat an incumbent in the primary had been elected to lower office, and fewer than 3 percent had significant nonelective political experience (see Table 2-2). Yet, these candidates accounted for 60 percent of the Democrats and 40 percent of the Republicans who defeated an incumbent in the primary.

Individuals who have held elective office or have some significant unelective political experience are generally more successful than political

Table 2-2   Political Experience and Primary Challenges to House
Incumbents, 1992

	Democrats		Republicans	
	Percent	Number	Percent	Number
Level of experience				
Elected officials	13	30	15	14
Unelected politicians	3	8	2	2
Political amateurs	83	187	83	79
Primary winners				
Elected officials	40	4	20	1
Unelected politicians	20	2	20	1
Political amateurs	40	4	60	3
Primary success rates				
Elected officials	14	29	7	14
Unelected politicians	30	7	50	2
Political amateurs	2	189	4	79

Sources: Compiled by the author from various issues of *Congressional Quarterly Weekly Report* and other sources discussed in the appendix.

Note: Figures are for nonincumbents only.

amateurs. Experienced candidates are able to take advantage of previous contacts to gain the support of the political and financial elites who contribute to or volunteer in political campaigns. Candidates who have officeholding experience are usually in a very strong position in this regard because they often enjoyed these elites' backing in previous campaigns and can make the case that they know what it takes to get elected. Some of these candidates have consciously used a lower-level office as a stepping-stone to Congress.[36] The success rates that these candidates enjoy demonstrate that political experience can improve one's odds of wresting a party nomination from an incumbent.

Ernest Jim Istook's victory over Rep. Mickey Edwards in Oklahoma's 5th district GOP primary in 1992 is typical of a nomination contest in which a challenger edges out an incumbent. Edwards, who had been in Congress for eight terms and was serving as chair of the House Republican Policy Committee, was counting on an easy reelection in 1992. His 386 overdrafts at the House bank radically changed that outlook. Istook, a state legislator, and former U.S. attorney Bill Price stepped forward to challenge Edwards. Both sought to capitalize on public demand for change and Edwards's check-bouncing problems. Price spent lavishly on television advertisements and attacked Edwards for his overdrafts and lengthy tenure in Washington. Edwards counterattacked with an equally media-intensive campaign. Istook, who had spent much of his seven years in the state legislature championing government ethics reform, took the high road, refraining from attacking Edwards in his campaign ads. Rather than run a negative media-oriented campaign, Istook ran a finely targeted grass-roots effort that used direct mail and phone banks to contact likely Republican voters. When the dust settled from the August 25th primary, Price had finished first with 37 percent of the vote, Istook came in second with 32 percent, Edwards came in third with 26 percent, and two lesser candidates split the remainder. The outcome left Istook well positioned in the runoff to attract the votes of Edwards supporters, many of whom were angered by Price's negative ads. Istook won the September 15th runoff with 56 percent of the vote and went on to win the general election.[37]

Open Primaries

Opposing-incumbent primaries are those primaries in which an incumbent of the opposing party has decided to seek reelection. A second type of open nomination, called open-seat primaries, occurs in districts in which there is no incumbent seeking reelection. Both types of primaries attract more candidates than contests in which a nonincumbent must defeat an incumbent in the primary in order to win the nomination, but opposing-incumbent primaries are usually the less hotly contested of the two.

Political experience was a determining factor in many opposing-incumbent primaries in 1992. Elected officials comprised about 14 percent of the candidates but 22 percent of the winners in these contests (see Table 2-3). They enjoyed a success rate of about 65 percent. Unelected politicians accounted for a smaller portion of the candidates and winners, but they had very high success rates. Political amateurs overwhelmed the other two groups both in numbers of candidates and in numbers of victorious candidates. Nevertheless, their success rates were far lower than those of more experienced primary contestants.

The Republican primary in Virginia's 8th district is typical of most opposing-incumbent primaries in that the local heavyweights sat out the race in order to pursue safer options. U.S. District Attorney Henry Hudson and former House member Stan Parris, arguably two of the best potential Republican candidates, opted not to seek the nomination to challenge Democratic incumbent James Moran. Hudson instead chose to become head of the U.S. Marshal's Office, while Parris accepted an appointment to the St. Lawrence Seaway Commission.[38] Three less-qualified candidates were left to fill the void: Bill Cleveland, a Capitol Hill police officer; Joe Vasipoli, a member of Alexandria Virginia's city council; and Kyle McSlarrow, an environmental lawyer and GOP activist with strong ties to the conservative wing of the district's Republican Party.

Table 2-3   Political Experience and Primary Contestants in Opposing-
Incumbent House Primaries, 1992

	Democrats		Republicans	
	Percent	Number	Percent	Number
Level of experience				
Elected officials	14	42	15	73
Unelected politicians	4	12	6	30
Political amateurs	81	238	78	369
Primary winners				
Elected officials	22	26	23	47
Unelected politicians	7	8	10	20
Political amateurs	72	85	67	136
Primary success rates				
Elected officials	65	40	63	74
Unelected politicians	67	12	72	29
Political amateurs	36	240	28	370

Sources: Compiled by the author from various issues of *Congressional Quarterly Weekly
Report* and other sources discussed in the appendix.

Note: Figures are for nonincumbents only.

After a hard-fought contest, McSlarrow was able to rally enough GOP
conservatives to win 54 percent of the primary vote. However, the ideological position that helped him win the nomination contributed to his
fifteen-point general election defeat.

Open-seat primaries are the most competitive of all nominating contests. They typically attract many highly qualified candidates, often pit-
ting one elected official against another. Large numbers of experienced
candidates ran for open seats in 1992, and they enjoyed very high success
rates (see Table 2-4). Large numbers of political amateurs also ran, but
they enjoyed less success than their better-qualified opponents.

The Democratic and Republican primaries in Florida's 3rd congressional district, like most open-seat primaries, were hard-fought contests
that featured a number of qualified candidates.[39] The district was designed to promote the representation of African Americans, and the
Democratic primary drew three African American candidates, two of
whom had considerable political experience: Corrine Brown had been a
Florida state representative since 1982, and Arnett Girardeau had
served in both chambers of Florida's statehouse. A third African American candidate, Glennie Mills, had no prior political experience. Andrew
Johnson, a white real estate developer and radio talk show host who had
been a state representative between 1978 and 1982, also ran. The pri-

Table 2-4 Political Experience and Primary Contestants in House
Primaries for Open Seats, 1992

	Democrats		Republicans	
	Percent	Number	Percent	Number
Level of experience				
Elected officials	37	116	28	77
Unelected politicians	7	22	7	20
Political amateurs	56	173	65	174
Primary winners				
Elected officials	62	51	47	35
Unelected politicians	7	6	15	11
Political amateurs	31	25	38	28
Primary success rates				
Elected officials	43	119	46	76
Unelected politicians	26	73	52	21
Political amateurs	15	169	16	173

Sources: Compiled by the author from various issues of *Congressional Quarterly Weekly Report* and other sources discussed in the appendix.

Notes: Figures are for nonincumbents only. They include nomination contests for seats that were open at the beginning of the election cycle and exclude contests for seats that became open as a result of incumbent defeats, retirements, or deaths.

mary contest was highly spirited and expensive, but the September 1 election was inconclusive: Brown won 43 percent, Johnson 31 percent, Girardeau 18 percent, and Mills 7 percent. Because none of the candidates won a majority of the vote, a run-off election was required. Brown defeated Johnson in the October 3 runoff 64 percent to 36 percent of the vote.

The Republican primary did not feature as many experienced politicians as the Democratic contest, nor were they mostly African American. Yet it, too, was extremely competitive. Three of the candidates were white: Ron Weidner, a lawyer who was general council to the Florida Physicians Association and a former executive of the Republican State Committee; Stephen Kelley, who owned a termite and pest control company; and Robert Harms, who owned a mortgage brokering company. The final candidate was George Grimsley, an African American who owned a fence company. When the primary ballots were counted, Weidner had received 35 percent of the vote, Kelley 34 percent, Grimsley 17 percent, and Harms 13 percent. The GOP contest was declared a stalemate, and Weidner defeated Kelly by an eighteen-point vote margin in the runoff.

Nominations, Elections, and Representation

The electoral process—which transforms private citizen to candidate to major-party nominee to House member—greatly influences the makeup of the first branch of the national government. Those parts of the process leading up to the general election, especially the decision to run, play a major role in producing a Congress that is not demographically representative of the U.S. population. The willingness of women and minorities to run for Congress during the last few decades and of voters to support them have helped make the national legislature somewhat more representative in terms of gender and race. Still, in many respects Congress does not mirror American society.[40]

Occupation

Occupation has a tremendous impact on the pool of House candidates and on the candidates' prospects for success. Individuals who claim law, politics, or public service (many of whom have legal training) as their profession are a minuscule portion of the general population but comprise 35 percent of all nomination candidates, 46 percent of all successful primary candidates, and 57 percent of all House members (see Table 2-5). The analytical, verbal, and organizational skills that it takes to succeed in the legal profession or in public service help these individuals undertake a successful bid for Congress.[41] The high salaries that members of these professions earn give them the wherewithal to take a leave of absence from work so they can campaign full time. These highly paid professionals can also afford to make the initial investment that is needed to get a campaign off the ground. Moreover, their professions place many attorneys and public servants in a position to rub elbows with political activists and contributors whose support can be crucial to winning a House primary or general election.

Business professionals and bankers are not as overrepresented among nomination candidates, major-party nominees, or House members as are public servants and lawyers, but persons in business tend to be very successful in congressional elections. Many possess money, skills, and contacts that are useful in politics. Educators (particularly college professors), entertainers, and other white-collar professionals also enjoy a modicum of success in congressional elections. Of these, educators comprise the largest group of candidates. They rarely possess the wealth of lawyers and business professionals, but educators frequently have the verbal, analytical, and organizational skills that are needed to get elected.

Just as some professions are overrepresented in Congress, others are underrepresented. Disproportionately few persons employed in agriculture or blue-collar professions either run for Congress or are elected. Even

Table 2-5   Occupational Representativeness of House Candidates and
Members, 1992

Occupation	General population	Nomination candidates	General election candidates	House members
Agricultural or blue-collar workers	26%	7%	6%	4%
Business or banking	12	18	18	17
Clergy or social work	0.4	1	1	1
Education	2	7	9	10
Entertainer, actor, writer, or artist	1	1	2	3
Law	0.3	16	23	34
Medicine	1	3	2	1
Military or veteran	1	0.5	1	0.2
Politics or public service	—	19	23	23
Other white-collar professionals	17	6	5	6
Outside work force	35	2	1	1
Unemployed	4	—	—	—
Unidentified, nonpolitical occupation	—	20	8	0
(N)	(248,718,000)	(2,015)	(843)	(435)

Sources: General population figures are from U.S. Department of Commerce, Bureau of the Census, *Statistical Abstract of the United States* (Washington, D.C.: U.S. Government Printing Office, 1992), xii, 18, 392-394; candidate occupation data are from various issues of *Congressional Quarterly Weekly Report* and other sources discussed in the appendix.

Notes: Figures include all 1992 major-party House candidates and all members of the 103rd Congress, including Rep. Bernard Sanders (I-Vt.). The figures for the general population are from 1990. Some columns do not add to 100 percent because of rounding.

Figure 2-4   Gender Representativeness of House Candidates and Members

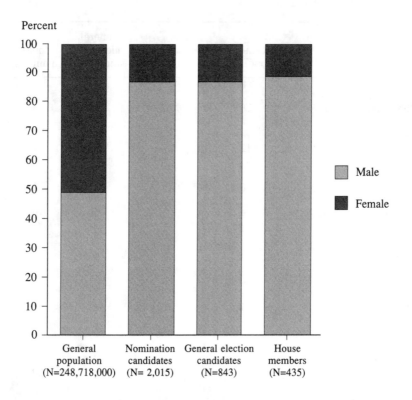

Percent

Sources: General population figures are from U.S. Department of Commerce, Bureau of the Census, Statistical Abstract of the United States (Washington, D.C.: U.S. Government Printing Office, 1992), xii, 18, 392–394; candidate gender data are from various issues of *Congressional Quarterly Weekly Report* and other sources discussed in the appendix.

Notes: Figures include all 1992 major-party House candidates and all members of the 103rd Congress, including Rep. Bernard Sanders (I-Vt.). The figures for the general population are from 1990.

fewer students, homemakers, and others who are considered outside the work force attempt to win a congressional seat.

Closely related to the issue of occupation is wealth. There were seventy-two millionaires in the House—17 percent of its members—following the 1992 election, far outstripping the less than one-half of one percent of the population who enjoy similar wealth.[42]

Gender

Far fewer women than men run for Congress (see Figure 2-4). Even in 1992, which was widely proclaimed the "Year of the Woman," only 13 percent of all contestants for major-party nominations were female.

Women are underrepresented among congressional candidates for a number of reasons. Active campaigning demands greater time and flexibility than most people—but in particular, women—can afford. Women continue to assume primary parenting responsibilities in most families, a role that is difficult to combine with long hours of campaigning. It is only since the 1980s that significant numbers of women have entered the legal and business professions, which often serve as training grounds for elected officials and political activists.[43] Women also continue to be underrepresented in state legislatures and other elective offices, which commonly serve as stepping-stones to Congress.[44]

Once women decide to run, gender does not affect their election prospects.[45] Women are just as likely to advance from primary candidate to nominee to House member as are men. As more women come to occupy lower-level offices or to hold positions in the professions from which congressional candidates usually emerge, the proportion of women candidates and members of Congress can be expected to increase.

Age

Congressional candidates are also somewhat older than the general population, and this is only partly due to the age requirements imposed by the Constitution. The average candidate for the nomination is almost twice as likely to be 40-to-54 years of age as to be 25-to-39 years of age (see Figure 2-5). Moreover, successful nomination candidates tend to be older than than those whom they defeat. The selection bias in favor of 40-to-74-year-olds continues into the general election; as a result, Congress is made up largely of persons who are middle-aged or older.

The underrepresentation of young people is due to an electoral process that allows older individuals to benefit from their greater life experiences. People who have reached middle age typically have greater financial resources, more political experience, and a wider network of political and professional associates to help them with their campaigns. Moreover, a formidable group of 40-to-74-year-olds—current representatives—also benefit from considerable incumbency advantages.

Race and Ethnicity

Race and ethnicity, like gender, have a greater impact on candidate emergence than on electoral success.[46] Whites are heavily overrepresented in the pool of nomination candidates, while persons of other races are underrepresented (see Figure 2-6). This reflects the disproportionately small numbers of minorities who have entered the legal or business professions or who occupy state or local offices.

Once minority persons declare their candidacies, they have fairly good odds of winning. The recent successes of minority House candidates

Figure 2-5   Age Representativeness of House Candidates and Members, 1992

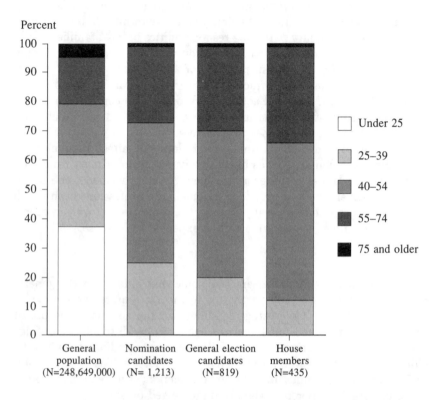

Percent

	Under 25
	25–39
	40–54
	55–74
	75 and older

General population (N=248,649,000)   Nomination candidates (N= 1,213)   General election candidates (N=819)   House members (N=435)

Sources: General population figures are from U.S. Department of Commerce, Bureau of the Census, *Statistical Abstract of the United States* (Washington, D.C.: U.S. Government Printing Office, 1992), xii, 18, 392–394; candidate age data are from various issues of *Congressional Quarterly Weekly Report* and other sources discussed in the appendix.

Notes: Figures include 1992 major-party House candidates and all members of the 103rd Congress, including Rep. Bernard Sanders (I-Vt.). The figures for the general population are from 1990. The N's differ from those in Figures 2-4 and 2-6 because of missing data.

are largely due to redistricting processes that were intended to promote minority representation. A few House members, such as Gary Franks, an African American Republican who represents the 5th district of Connecticut, Jay Kim, an Asian American GOP-member who was recently elected in California's 41st district, and Ron Dellums, a twelve-term African American Democrat from California's 9th district, were elected in districts that were not specifically carved to promote minority representation in Congress. However, most minority candidates are elected in districts that have large numbers of voters belonging to their racial or ethnic group.

Figure 2-6 Racial and Ethnic Representativeness of House Candidates and Members, 1992

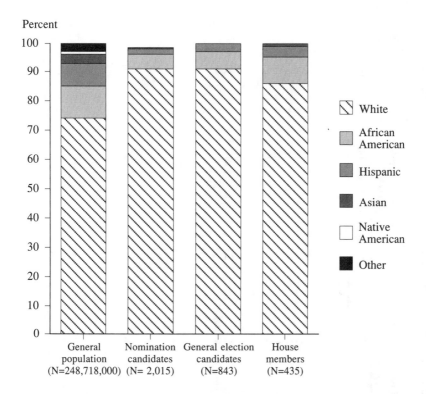

Percent

Legend:
- White
- African American
- Hispanic
- Asian
- Native American
- Other

X-axis labels:
- General population (N=248,718,000)
- Nomination candidates (N= 2,015)
- General election candidates (N=843)
- House members (N=435)

Sources: General population figures are from U.S. Department of Commerce, Bureau of the Census, Statistical Abstract of the United States (Washington, D.C.: U.S. Government Printing Office, 1992), xii, 18, 392–394; candidate race data are from various issues of *Congressional Quarterly Weekly Report* and other sources discussed in the appendix.

Notes: Figures include all 1992 major-party House candidates and all members of the 103rd Congress, including Rep. Bernard Sanders (I-Vt.). The figures for the general population are from 1990.

Party Differences

Public servants and members of the legal profession comprise a large portion of each party's candidate pool, but many Republican candidates come from the business world, and many Democratic candidates are educators (see Table 2-6). These differences reflect patterns of support that exist for the parties among voters. The GOP's overrepresentation of business professionals continues through each stage of the election, but the differences for teachers disappear after the nomination stage. Educators comprised 10 percent of both the House Democratic Caucus

Table 2-6 Major-Party Nomination Candidates, General Election Candidates, and House Members, 1992

	Nomination candidates		General election candidates		House members	
	Democrats	Republicans	Democrats	Republicans	Democrats	Republicans
Occupation						
Agricultural or blue-collar workers	6%	7%	5%	8%	3%	6%
Business or banking	13	23	13	23	12	25
Clergy or social work	1	1	2	1	2	1
Education	8	5	11	7	10	10
Entertainer, actor, writer, or artist	1	2	1	3	1	5
Law	16	14	27	19	37	27
Medicine	3	3	2	2	1	1
Military or veteran	0.3	1	0.2	2	0.4	1
Politics or public service	20	18	24	23	24	23
Other white-collar professionals	7	6	6	4	8	3
Outside work force	2	2	1	1	1	1
Unidentified, not politics	22	18	8	9	0	0
(N)	(1,039)	(976)	(424)	(419)	(258)	(176)
Gender						
Male	85%	91%	83%	91%	86%	94%
Female	15	9	17	9	14	6
(N)	(1,039)	(976)	(424)	(419)	(258)	(176)

Age						
Under 25	0%	0.2%	0%	0%	0%	0%
25-39	21	28	15	26	10	16
40-54	53	43	57	44	59	47
55-74	24	28	27	30	30	38
75 and older	1	1	2	0.3	2	1
(N)	(878)	(835)	(413)	(406)	(258)	(176)
Race and Ethnicity						
White	87%	98%	84%	96%	79%	97%
African American	9	0.4	9	3	14	0.6
Other	4	2	6	2	6	3
(N)	(1,039)	(976)	(424)	(419)	(258)	(176)

Sources: Compiled by the author from various issues of *Congressional Quarterly Weekly Report* and other sources discussed in the appendix.

Notes: Figures are for all major-party nomination candidates, all major-party general election candidates, and all major-party members of the 103rd Congress (which excludes Rep. Bernard Sanders (I-Vt.)). Some data are missing for the age representation of nomination and general election candidates. Some columns do not add to 100 percent because of rounding.

and the House Republican Conference after the 1992 election.

Candidates from the legal and entertainment professions are the sources of the largest occupational differences between the parties. Attorneys from both parties do well in House elections, but lawyers are more heavily overrepresented in the Democratic than the Republican Party. Entertainers, on the other hand, have a bigger presence in the ranks of Republican legislators. Even though Republicans have historically been viewed as the defenders of the rich, slightly more House Democrats than Republicans are among Congress's wealthiest members.[47]

More women run for Democratic than Republican nominations for Congress. This gender gap reflects the greater number of women who identify with the Democratic Party and that party's greater acceptance of female candidates. Democratic and Republican women enjoy similar success rates in congressional primaries, but Democratic women have greater success in the general election than their GOP counterparts.

More Democratic than Republican primary candidates are 40-to-54 years of age, reflecting the different orientation of the two parties' activists toward politics. Democratic activists are more likely to consider politics a profession and to view a congressional election as an opportunity for midcareer advancement. Their Republican counterparts are more apt to pursue careers in the private sector. Many Republican activists run for Congress before they have taken major strides in their profession or after they have reached 55, an age at which many individuals' careers have peaked.[48] The initial age difference between Democratic and Republican candidates lays the foundation for an uneven trend toward a middle-aged Congress that continues through the primary and the general election.

The parties also draw candidates from different racial and ethnic groups. Republican primary contestants are overwhelmingly white, as are the GOP's nominees and House members. The Democratic Party attracts candidates from a wider array of groups. African Americans comprise 9 percent of all Democratic primary winners and 14 percent of all Democratic members of the House. Candidates of other races and Hispanics also do well, comprising 6 percent of all victorious Democratic primary contestants and House members.

The Senate

The Senate historically has been less demographically representative than the House, but it, too, has been moving toward more accurately mirroring the U.S. population in some important ways. Prior to the 1992 elections, the Senate had only two women. It also had two Asian American members (both from Hawaii), but no Native Americans or African Americans. Over 60 percent of its members were at least 55 years of age. Senate members came from a variety of occupations, but most—roughly

47 percent—were lawyers. Another 25 percent were drawn from the business and banking communities, and 8 percent were journalists. An additional 8 percent were educators, and 6 percent were from the agricultural sector.[49] The remainder held a variety positions, with 4 percent claiming politics or public service as their profession. In short, descriptions of the Senate as a bastion for white, middle-aged, professional men were very close to the mark.

Part of the reason that the Senate has been slower to change than the House is that Senate terms are six years, and only one-third of the upper chamber is up for election at a time. Other reasons have to do with the heightened demands of Senate campaigns. As statewide races, Senate primary and general election campaigns require larger amounts of money, more extensive organizations, and more complex strategies than do House campaigns. Successful Senate candidates generally possess more skill, political connections, and campaign experience than do their House counterparts. The fact that so many members of the Senate had extensive political experience prior to their election suggests that the dearth of minorities in lower-level offices may help to explain why the upper chamber is changing more slowly than the lower. In order to gain seats in the Senate, members of traditionally underrepresented groups have had first to place citizens in the offices that serve as stepping-stones to that body. As more women, African Americans, and members of other underrepresented groups are elected or appointed to local, state, and federal offices, their numbers in the Senate will probably increase.

Nevertheless, a single election can have a tremendous impact on the Senate's makeup. After the polls closed in 1992, twelve new members had been elected to the upper chamber. Among these were five women, including the Senate's first African American woman, Carol Moseley-Braun (D-Ill.), as well as its first Native American, Ben Nighthorse Campbell (D-Colo.). The election also lowered the age distribution of senators but not enough to bring the members' average age below fifty-eight years. Some noteworthy changes took place in the professional backgrounds of members: the number of business executives and bankers fell from thirty-two to twenty-four, the number of lawyers fell by three, and the number of members claiming politics or public service as a career rose by five.[50] The number of millionaires in the Senate remained unchanged at twenty-eight.[51]

The addition of so many new senators who claim public service as a profession is particularly telling, as it alludes to the fact that few of the individuals who are nominated to run for the Senate or eventually win a seat in the upper chamber lack political experience. Even 1992, which was considered one of the most promising years for outsider candidates in decades, resulted in the election of only one individual who had not previously worked in politics or run for office—Robert Bennett (R-Utah).

Even Bennett was no newcomer to politics, having grown up the son of a senator. Despite the rhetoric of some of the candidates or the insurgent nature of their campaigns, all of those who were elected had some form of political experience. Senator Moseley-Braun had been Cook County recorder of deeds from 1988 through 1992 and assistant majority leader in the Illinois house prior to that. Patty Murray (D-Wash.), the self-styled "mom in tennis shoes," had served four years in the state senate. And Russ Feingold (D-Wis.), a "liberal-populist" who went so far as to paint a contract with the voters on the garage doors of his middle-class home, had been a state senator for ten years.

A total of thirty-two of the senators in the 103rd Congress had previously served in the U.S. House of Representatives, sixteen had been governors of their states, thirteen previously held some other statewide office, twelve had been state legislators, and fifteen had served in a local office. Another eight had served as party officials, political aides, or presidential appointees or had previously run for the Senate. Besides Bennett, only three senators—Bill Bradley (D-N.J.), Frank Lautenberg (D-N.J.), and Orrin Hatch (R-Utah)—were elected to the Senate without having previously held public office or some other important political position.

Although senators are more likely than representatives to have to defend their nominations, Senate primaries tend to be less competitive than those for the House. Not a single senator who sought to be renominated was defeated between 1982 and 1990. This helps to explain why Moseley-Braun's 1992 defeat of Sen. Alan Dixon in the Illinois primary sent such shock waves through Congress. The relative ease with which members of the Senate secure renomination can be attributed to a number of factors besides the tremendous demands that Senate primary contests make on challengers and their supporters. For one thing, senators and Senate candidates are highly strategic. Like their counterparts in the House, members of the Senate use their office to help their state receive its share of federal projects, to garner positive coverage in the press, and to build support among voters. Senators, like representatives, also build huge campaign treasuries to discourage potential opponents. Finally, as the retirements of Sens. Alan Cranston (D-Calif.), Dennis DeConcini (D-Ariz.), and Don Riegle (D-Mich.)—who were each implicated in the Keating Five scandal—and Dave Durenberger (R-Minn.) (who had been the subject of a federal indictment alleging that he billed the Senate for renting a condominium that he actually owned and who went through a highly publicized, messy divorce) attest, members of the Senate are shrewd enough to recognize when it is time to retire. The impact that scandal has on Senate turnover tends to be felt more through strategic retirements than primary defeats.

On the other side of the ledger, the most qualified opponent that a senator is likely to face in a primary is a current House member or some other elected official. Because these individuals are also highly strategic, only a few are willing to risk their current positions by picking a primary fight. Most prefer to wait until a seat becomes open.

When an incumbent does announce his or her retirement, or a member of the opposite party appears vulnerable, political parties, interest groups, and even some campaign consultants help to shape the field of Senate candidates by encouraging potential candidates to declare their candidacies. These organizations promise the same types of support and under the same kinds of circumstances to potential Senate candidates as they offer to House candidates.

Party organizations rarely become involved in contested Senate primaries even though they may promise a candidate hundreds of thousands of dollars in campaign support upon winning the nomination. The parties' senatorial campaign committees are singled out by candidates as the most influential organizations in the candidate-recruitment process. Nevertheless, the decision to run for the Senate, like the decision to run for the House, is a highly personal one. Political organizations are not nearly as important as are the candidate's family and friends, nor are they as important as issues or ideology, a desire to improve government, or the goal of becoming a national leader.[52] In other words, the decisions made by potential Senate candidates may be influenced by a variety of political organizations, but these candidates, like most potential officeholders, tend to be self-starters.

Notes

1. On strategic ambition, see James David Barber, *The Lawmakers: Recruitment and Adaptation to Legislative Life* (New Haven: Yale University Press, 1965), 165-169, 191-197; Joseph A. Schlesinger, *Ambition and Politics: Political Careers in the United States* (Chicago: Rand McNally, 1966), 11-12, 16-19, 198-199; Gary C. Jacobson and Samuel Kernell, *Strategy and Choice in Congressional Elections* (New Haven: Yale University Press, 1983), chapter 3; William T. Bianco, "Strategic Decisions on Candidacy in U.S. Congressional Districts," *Legislative Studies Quarterly* 9 (1984): 360-362; Jon R. Bond, Cary Covington, and Richard Fleisher, "Explaining Challenger Quality in Congressional Elections," *Journal of Politics* 47 (1985): 510-529; Thomas A. Kazee, "The Emergence of Congressional Candidates," in *Who Runs for Congress? Ambition, Context, and Candidate Emergence,* ed. Kazee (Washington, D.C.: Congressional Quarterly, 1994); David T. Canon, *Actors, Athletes, and Astronauts: Political Amateurs in the United States* (Chicago: University of Chicago Press, 1990), 76-79; Gary C. Jacobson, *The Politics of Congressional Elections* (New York: HarperCollins, 1992), 47-48.
2. See note 1, especially Kazee, "The Emergence of Congressional Candidates."
3. See especially L. Sandy Maisel, Linda L. Fowler, Ruth S. Jones, and Walter J. Stone, "The Naming of Candidates: Recruitment or Emergence?" in *The*

Parties Respond: Changes in the American Party System, ed. L. Sandy Maisel (Boulder, Colo.: Westview Press, 1990), chapter 7; Linda L. Fowler and Robert D. McClure, *Political Ambition: Who Decides to Run for Congress* (New Haven: Yale University Press, 1989), 231.

4. Gary C. Jacobson and Samuel Kernell, "National Forces in the 1986 U.S. House Elections," *Legislative Studies Quarterly* 15 (1990): 65-87; Canon, *Actors, Athletes, and Astronauts,* 106-108.

5. Timothy Groseclose and Keith Krehbiel, "Golden Parachutes, Rubber Checks, and Strategic Retirements from the 102nd House," *American Journal of Political Science* 38 (1994): 75-99; Gary C. Jacobson and Michael Dimock, "Checking Out: The Effects of Bank Overdrafts on the 1992 House Election," *American Journal of Political Science* 38 (forthcoming 1994).

6. See note 3.

7. See David R. Mayhew, *Congress: The Electoral Connection* (New Haven: Yale University Press, 1974); Morris P. Fiorina, *Congress: The Keystone of the Washington Establishment* (New Haven: Yale University Press, 1980). The estimated value of congressional perquisites is from Jacobson, *The Politics of Congressional Elections,* 38.

8. Richard F. Fenno, Jr., *Home Style: House Members in their Districts* (Boston: Little Brown, 1973).

9. Preemptive incumbent fund-raising does not always discourage quality challengers from running. See Jonathan S. Krasno and Donald Philip Green, "Preempting Quality Challengers in House Elections," *Journal of Politics* 50 (1988): 920-936; Peverill Squire, "Preemptive Fundraising and Challenger Profile in Senate Elections," *Journal of Politics* 53 (1991): 1150-1164.

10. Sara Fritz and Dwight Morris, *Gold-Plated Politics: Running for Congress in the 1990s* (Washington, D.C.: Congressional Quarterly, 1992), especially chapter 2.

11. Stephen E. Frantzich, "De-Recruitment: The Other Side of the Congressional Equation," *Western Political Quarterly* 31 (1978): 105-126; Frantzich, "Opting Out: Retirement from the House of Representatives," *American Politics Quarterly* 6 (1978): 251-273; Michael K. Moore and John R. Hibbing, "Is Serving in Congress Fun Again? Voluntary Retirements from the House Since the 1970s," *American Journal of Political Science* 36 (1992): 824-828.

12. Stephen E. Frantzich, "De-Recruitment," 105-126; Joseph Cooper and William West, "The Congressional Career in the 1970s," in *Congress Reconsidered,* ed. Lawrence Dodd and Bruce Oppenheimer (Washington, D.C.: CQ Press, 1981); and John R. Hibbing, "Voluntary Retirement from the U.S. House: The Costs of Legislative Service," *Legislative Studies Quarterly* 8 (1982): 57-74.

13. Steven G. Livingston and Sally Friedman, "Reexamining Theories of Congressional Retirement: Evidence from the 1980s," *Legislative Studies Quarterly* 18 (1993): 231-254.

14. For a comprehensive assessment of these factors see Canon, *Actors, Athletes, and Astronauts,* 103-110.

15. On ambitious, policy and experience-seeking (or hopeless) amateurs see Canon, *Actors, Astronauts, and Athletes,* xv, 26-32; and Canon, "Sacrificial Lambs or Strategic Politicians? Political Amateurs in U.S. House Elections," *American Journal of Political Science* 37 (1993): 1119-1141. Canon also suggests a fourth category, *mixed amateurs,* which consists of those who do not fall into one of the previous groups.

16. Jacobson and Kernell, *Strategy and Choice in Congressional Elections,* 94-96, 102.
17. Ibid., 77-78.
18. The percentage of open seats increased from 18 (N=78) to 20 (N=91) as the result of incumbents' defeats, retirements, and deaths. Throughout this chapter seats are categorized according to their status (open or incumbent-occupied) at the beginning of the election cycle. Seats that began the election cycle as incumbent-occupied but featured two nonincumbents in the general election are classified as open from chapter 3 forward.
19. The analysis in this section excludes the four Democratic incumbents who ran against one another.
20. On political personality, see Harold D. Lasswell, *Psychopathology and Politics* (Chicago: University of Chicago Press, 1930), especially chapter 5; and Lasswell, *Power and Personality* (Boston: W. W. Norton, 1948), 39-41.
21. The generalizations that follow are drawn from question 18 of the 1992 Congressional Campaign Study (see the appendix) and from Louis Sandy Maisel, *From Obscurity to Oblivion: Running in the Congressional Primary* (Knoxville: University of Tennessee Press, 1982), 31-32; Paul S. Herrnson, *Party Campaigning in the 1980s* (Cambridge, Mass.: Harvard University Press, 1988), 86; and Kazee, "The Emergence of Congressional Candidates."
22. On Donley, see Paul S. Herrnson and Robert M. Tennant, "Running for Congress Under the Shadow of the Capitol Dome: The Race for Virginia's Eighth District," in *Who Runs for Congress?* ed. Kazee, 67-81. See also the other case studies in *Who Runs for Congress?* ed. Kazee.
23. Thomas A. Kazee and Mary C. Thornberry, "Where's the Party? Congressional Candidate Recruitment and American Party Organizations," *Western Political Quarterly* 43 (1990): 61-80; Steven H. Haeberle, "Closed Primaries and Party Support in Congress," *American Politics Quarterly* 13 (1985): 341-352.
24. See Herrnson, *Party Campaigning in the 1980s,* 51-56.
25. Ibid., 48-56, 85-88.
26. See, for example, Fowler and McClure, *Political Ambition,* 205-207.
27. On WISH List, see Craig A. Rimmerman, "New Kids on the Block: WishList and the Gay and Lesbian Victory Fund," in *Risky Business? PAC Decisionmaking in Congressional Elections,* ed. Robert Biersack, Paul S. Herrnson, and Clyde Wilcox (Armonk, N.Y.: M. E. Sharpe, 1994), 214-223.
28. Caryn R. Sagal, "1992: The Year of the Challenger or the Year of the Incumbent? The Showdown in California's 3rd Congressional District," independent honors thesis, University of Maryland, 1994; Phil Duncan, ed., *Politics in America, 1994: The 103rd Congress* (Washington, D.C.: Congressional Quarterly, 1993), 111-114.
29. See, for example, Tom Kenworthy, "Collaring Colleagues for Cash," *Washington Post,* May 14, 1991.
30. Sagal, "1992: The Year of the Challenger or the Year of the Incumbent?"
31. Adam Steinhauer, "Fazio in Woodland to Start Campaign," *The Daily Democrat,* February 15, 1992.
32. Fenno, *Home Style,* 176-189.
33. See Paul S. Herrnson, "National Party Organizations and the Postreform Congress," in *The Post Reform Congress,* ed. Roger H. Davidson (New York: St. Martin's Press, 1992), 48-70.
34. Herrnson and Tennant, "Running for Congress Under the Shadow of the Capitol Dome," 73.

35. Margaret Talev, "Bill Goodling Bounces Back: The 1992 Congressional Race in Pennsylvania's 19th District," unpublished paper, University of Maryland, 1992.
36. See, for example, Joseph A. Schlesinger, *Ambition and Politics*, 99; and Canon, *Actors, Athletes, and Astronauts*, 50-53, 56-58.
37. Much of this information is drawn from Duncan, *Politics in America, 1994*, 1249.
38. See Herrnson and Tennant, "Running for Congress Under the Shadow of the Capitol Dome," 76.
39. Much of the material on the primaries in Florida's 3rd congressional district is drawn from Katina Rae Stapleton, "The Wild Race to Washington: The Making of Florida 3," unpublished paper, University of Maryland, 1992.
40. On demographic (or descriptive) representation, see Hannah Pitkin, *The Concept of Representation* (Berkeley: University of California Press, 1967), especially 60-61. On changes in the composition of Congress, see Norman J. Ornstein, Thomas E. Mann, and Michael J. Malbin, *Vital Statistics on Congress, 1993-1994* (Washington, D.C.: Congressional Quarterly, 1994), tables 1-8 and 1-17.
41. Donald R. Matthews, "Legislative Recruitment and Legislative Careers," *Legislative Studies Quarterly* 9 (1984): 551.
42. Glenn R. Simpson, "One-Fifth of Congress Now Millionaires as Number in House Climbs to 13 Percent," *Roll Call*, June 30, 1984, 1, 12.
43. R. Darcy, Susan Welch, and Janet Clark, *Women, Elections, and Representation* (New York: Longman, 1987), 93-108.
44. Prior to the 1992 election, women accounted for roughly 18 percent of all state legislators. See for example, Robert Biersack and Paul S. Herrnson, "Political Parties and the Year of the Woman," in *The Year of the Woman: Myth or Reality*, ed. Elizabeth Adell Cook, Sue Thomas, and Clyde Wilcox (Boulder, Colo.: Westview Press, 1994), 164.
45. Darcy, Welch, and Clark, *Women, Elections, and Representation*, 138-140; Robert A. Bernstein, "Why Are There So Few Women in the House?" *Western Political Quarterly* 29 (1986): 155-164; Linda L. Fowler, *Candidates, Congress, and the American Democracy* (Ann Arbor: University of Michigan Press, 1993), 127-136.
46. On the impact of race on candidate selection, see Fowler, *Candidates, Congress, and the American Democracy*, 136-142.
47. Craig Winneker, "The Roll Call Fifty," *Roll Call*, January 24, 1994, 17.
48. Alan Ehrenhalt, *The United States of Ambition: Politicians, Power, and the Pursuit of Office* (New York: Random House, 1991), 225-226.
49. It should be noted that some members of Congress list more than one occupation. Percentages are compiled from Ornstein, Mann, and Malbin, *Vital Statistics on Congress, 1993-1994*, table 1-11.
50. Ornstein, Mann, and Malbin, *Vital Statistics on Congress, 1993-1994*, table 1-11.
51. Simpson, "One-Fifth of Congress Now Millionaires."
52. This generalization is drawn from question 18 of the 1992 Congressional Campaign Study.

Chapter 3

The Anatomy of a Campaign

Highly specialized, professional organizations dominate campaigns for Congress. This chapter describes these organizations, focusing on the personnel who work in them and how they spend their money. Comparisons between Democratic and Republican campaigns and among the campaigns of incumbents, challengers, and candidates for open seats give insights into the different types of campaigns. Additional comparisons are drawn between campaigns for the House and Senate.

Campaign Organizations

Candidates need to accomplish several interrelated objectives to compete successfully in an election. Specialized skills and training are required to meet many of these objectives. This was not always the case. House campaigns were largely amateur operations until the 1970s, when they became significantly more professional.[1] Senate campaigns, which had become more professional somewhat earlier, continue to employ more paid staff and consultants than do their House counterparts.

The biggest factor in House campaigns is incumbency. Assembling a campaign organization is an easy task for incumbents. Most merely reassemble the personnel who worked on their previous campaign. A substantial number of incumbents keep elements of their organizations intact between election cycles. Some of these organizations consist only of a part-time political aide or fund-raiser. Others are quite substantial, possessing the characteristics of a permanent business. They own a building and have a large professional staff, a fund-raising apparatus, an investment portfolio, a campaign car, an entertainment budget, and a team of lawyers, accountants, and consultants on retainer. The average House incumbent spent roughly $117,000 on organizational maintenance during the two years leading up to the 1992 election.[2] Majority Leader Richard Gephardt (D-Mo.) put together the "Cadillac" of campaigns, spending more than $904,000 on overhead between 1991 and 1992, including $413,000 on staff, $80,000 on rent, and $170,000 on computers, furniture, other office equipment, and supplies.[3]

Few House challengers or open-seat candidates possess a permanent or even temporary organization capable of contesting a congressional election until just before their declaration of candidacy. Nonincumbents who have held an elective post usually possess advantages over those who have not in assembling a campaign organization. Some have steering committees, "Friends of 'Candidate X' " clubs, or working relationships with political consultants from previous campaigns. Candidates who have never held an elective office or run for Congress but have been active in politics usually have advantages over political amateurs in building an organization. Previous nonelective political involvement gives such people as party committee chairs, political aides, and individuals who have previously run for office some knowledge of how to wage a campaign and ties to others who can help them. The organizational advantages that incumbents possess over challengers are usually greater than those advantages that experienced nonincumbents have over political amateurs.[4]

Virtually every House member's campaign organization is managed by a paid staffer, or some combination of paid staffer, outside consultant, and volunteer. Very often the campaign manager is the administrative assistant (AA) in the House member's congressional office. AAs and other congressional staffers routinely take leaves of absence from their jobs to work for their boss's reelection. Challengers' campaigns are less likely to be professionally managed. Only 68 percent are managed by a paid staffer or political consultant, and 35 percent are managed by a volunteer (see Table 3-1). Open-seat campaigns fall between campaigns waged by incumbents and challengers: 65 percent of them are managed by a paid staffer, and over 90 percent are managed by some combination of staffer, consultant, and volunteer. More Democratic than Republican campaigns are managed professionally, but this is largely due to the fact that there are more Democratic than Republican House incumbents. Candidates in competitive contests (those won or lost by margins of 20 percent or less) are more likely to wage professionally managed campaigns than others. Very few campaigns are managed by personnel provided by a political party or interest group.

Press relations is a second area of campaigning that is commonly handled by professional staff. Nearly 80 percent of all incumbents have a paid staffer, frequently a congressional press secretary who is on a leave of absence, handling their relations with the media. Some incumbents hire political consultants to issue press releases and handle calls from journalists. In 11 percent of all incumbent races, a salaried press secretary or consultant is assisted by one or more volunteers. Challenger and open-seat campaigns are less likely than incumbent campaigns to depend on paid staff and are more likely to rely on volunteers to handle their press relations. Open-seat candidates, however, are more likely than challengers to hire a professional consultant for this purpose. Democratic and Republican campaigns staff their press relations almost identically. Contestants in close races rely more than do those in one-sided races on paid staff and consultants.

Issue and opposition research is often carried out by a combination of professional staff, outside consultants, and volunteers. Challengers and open-seat candidates, who generally have less money than incumbents, depend more heavily on volunteers to conduct research. Many nonincumbents also depend on party organizations, particularly the Democratic and Republican congressional campaign committees, for research. In 1992 the National Republican Congressional Committee (NRCC), which was the wealthier and more heavily staffed of the two campaign committees, furnished 27 percent of all Republican challengers and 17 percent of all GOP open-seat contestants with opposition and issue research.[5] The Democratic Congressional Campaign Committee (DCCC) provided research for 18 percent of its House and 13 percent of its open-seat candidates.

Fewer incumbents than nonincumbents depend on their party's congressional campaign committee for research materials because their congressional staffs routinely provide much of the information they need. One of the perquisites of office is having a staff that can write memos on the major issues facing the nation and the district. These are normally drafted to help House members represent their districts, but the political payoffs from them are significant. In fact, both congressional campaign committees offer training seminars for House members to inform them of how legally to utilize their congressional staff for political purposes.

Fund-raising is a campaign activity that requires skill and connections with individuals and groups who are able and willing to make political contributions. Most campaigns use a mix of a paid campaign staffer, a private consultant, and volunteers to raise money. Incumbent campaigns are especially likely to use paid staff. Some incumbents hire experts in direct mail and PAC fund-raising specialists to collect contributions continuously between elections. Fewer nonincumbent campaigns have a salaried employee or professional consultant in charge of raising funds. They instead rely heavily on volunteers. One of the ironies of congressional elections is that challengers, who have the greatest need to raise and spend money, are often unable to obtain the services of an experienced fund-raiser.

Polling and advertising are two very specialized aspects of campaign-

Table 3-1 Staffing Activities in House Elections, 1992

	All	Party		Status			Competitiveness	
		Demo-crats	Repub-licans	Incum-bents	Challen-gers	Open-seat candidates	Competitive contests	Uncompetitive contests
Campaign management								
Paid staff	65%	70%	60%	82%	53%	65%	75%	57%
Consultant	19	17	21	18	15	27	23	13
Political party	1	1	1	0	2	1	1	1
Interest groups	2	3	1	2	3	1	3	1
Volunteer	24	20	28	11	35	26	14	31
Not used	4	5	3	3	7	3	1	7
Press relations								
Paid staff	61%	64%	59%	78%	48%	56%	72%	52%
Consultant	14	17	11	14	8	21	18	10
Political party	1	1	1	0	1	4	1	1
Interest groups	1	1	1	1	1	1	1	1
Volunteer	24	24	24	11	34	32	17	32
Not used	4	3	4	3	5	3	3	5
Issue and opposition research								
Paid staff	42%	42%	42%	54%	29%	47%	47%	39%
Consultant	22	26	16	28	12	28	29	14
Political party	15	12	18	5	24	15	16	15
Interest groups	7	6	8	6	8	7	7	8
Volunteer	31	28	33	15	40	40	33	31
Not used	7	8	6	10	6	3	3	11

Fund-raising								
Paid staff	53%	53%	52%	70%	33%	59%	63%	45%
Consultant	24	34	14	34	15	25	32	18
Political party	4	2	5	3	3	7	5	2
Interest groups	5	7	4	4	5	7	8	3
Volunteer	41	37	44	25	53	43	34	46
Not used	4	4	5	1	7	5	4	5
Accounting/FEC reporting								
Paid staff	64%	69%	59%	81%	49%	63%	76%	60%
Consultant	13	16	10	19	6	15	15	11
Political party	1	1	2	0	1	4	2	1
Interest groups	1	1	1	2	1 ,	0	1	1
Volunteer	42	36	48	17	60	53	40	44
Not used	2	2	3	1	4	1	1	3
Polling								
Paid staff	8%	8%	7%	10%	6%	7%	8%	8%
Consultant	60	68	52	77	41	65	82	44
Political party	7	4	11	5	8	9	5	10
Interest groups	4	4	3	4	4	4	5	4
Volunteer	8	7	10	3	15	7	5	11
Not used	14	14	15	9	22	9	4	24
Media advertising								
Paid staff	24%	22%	26%	26%	22%	21%	26%	22%
Consultant	61	66	55	76	39	71	76	48
Political party	2	2	1	1	2	3	1	2
Interest groups	1	1	1	0	2	0	1	1
Volunteer	15	13	18	3	29	11	9	20
Not used	5	4	6	4	8	4	3	7

(continues)

Table 3-1 *(continued)*

	All	Party		Status			Competitiveness	
		Demo-crats	Repub-licans	Incum-bents	Challen-gers	Open-seat candidates	Competitive contests	Uncompetitive contests
Get-out-the-vote drives								
Paid staff	39%	43%	35%	55%	25%	36%	47%	33%
Consultant	5	3	6	7	1	8	7	3
Political party	29	34	23	35	24	25	30	29
Interest groups	20	32	9	21	18	24	25	19
Volunteer	50	50	51	37	55	67	60	47
Not used	6	5	7	4	9	3	4	8
Legal advice								
Paid staff	11%	12%	10%	15%	7%	11%	11%	11%
Consultant	13	14	12	18	8	12	14	12
Political party	10	8	13	10	13	8	12	10
Interest groups	3	2	4	2	4	3	4	2
Volunteer	39	40	38	25	44	55	42	40
Not used	24	24	23	28	24	15	22	25
Average number of activities performed by paid staff or consultants	5.5	5.8	5.2	6.9	4.0	5.8	6.4	4.7
(N)	(331)	(167)	(164)	(120)	(137)	(74)	(151)	(180)

Source: Question 19 of the 1992 Congressional Campaign Study (see appendix).

Notes: Figures are for general election candidates in major-party contested races, excluding those in incumbent-versus-incumbent races. Figures for interest groups include labor unions. Some columns do not add to 100 percent because some activities were performed by more than one person or because of rounding.

ing that are handled primarily by political consultants who are hired on a contractual basis. Virtually every candidate for a competitive seat hires an outside consultant to conduct polls or receives a professionally taken poll from a party or some other group. Most incumbents also obtain surveys from professional pollsters. Incumbents in one-sided races make great use of paid campaign aides to conduct their polling. In 1992 only 9 percent of them forwent the opportunity to have a poll done.[6]

Open-seat campaigns are almost as reliant on professionally conducted polls as are incumbent campaigns. The major difference between them is that more open-seat campaigns have polls contributed or conducted by a party committee or a PAC. Challenger campaigns, which are just as much in need of accurate public opinion information as are others, are substantially less likely to purchase the services of a professional pollster. Only 41 percent of all challengers commission a professional poll, while 21 percent relied on campaign staff or volunteers. Moreover, almost a quarter of all challengers did not conduct a survey, reserving their money for some other campaign activity.

One of the noteworthy partisan differences between campaigns is that more Democrats than Republicans hire outside polling firms. This does not merely reflect the fact that more incumbents are Democrats; nearly half of all Democratic challengers and 77 percent of all Democratic open-seat campaigns contracted the services of a professional pollster, whereas corresponding Republican campaigns hired polling consultants at rates of 36 percent and 52 percent.[7] GOP candidates were also somewhat more likely to use volunteers to conduct their campaign surveys.

Perhaps the most interesting difference between Democratic and Republican House campaigns is the degree to which they rely on their parties for survey research. The NRCC furnished 11 percent of Republican House campaigns, mostly those waged by open-seat candidates and challengers, with survey research, while the DCCC provided only 4 percent of Democratic candidates with polls, and these were distributed fairly evenly among incumbents and nonincumbents.[8] These differences reflect the NRCC's greater emphasis on polls.

Incumbents are the most likely to have professionally produced campaign communications. Virtually every incumbent hires a media consultant or uses some combination of media consultant and campaign aide to design literature, radio ads, or television commercials. Slightly fewer open-seat candidates hire professional media consultants. Challengers, who usually face the biggest hurdles in conveying a message and developing name recognition among voters, are by the far the least likely to employ the services of a media consultant.

Parties, PACs, and other groups figure prominently in the field activities of virtually all campaigns. Incumbents depend as much, if not more, on these groups as do challenger and open-seat candidates, even though the majority of incumbent campaigns also assign paid staffers to work on their voter registration and get-out-the-vote drives. More Democrats than Republicans depend on outside groups, but organized groups are a significant force in the campaigns of both parties' candidates. The fact that nearly half of all Democratic incumbents rely on local party activists for voter mobilization attests to the contributions that local party organizations make to preserving Democratic control of the House.[9] The Democratic party's historical ties with the labor movement account for the greater level of support it receives from interest groups.

All campaign organizations make heavy use of volunteers for their voter mobilization activities. Registering voters, reminding them to vote, and driving them to the polling place are activities that traditionally have been, and continue to be, carried out mainly by volunteers. Challenger and open-seat campaigns, which tend to be dependent on free help, rely more than do incumbent campaigns on volunteer efforts.

Most House campaigns depend on volunteers for legal counseling. More incumbent than nonincumbent campaigns keep an election-law expert on the payroll or on retainer, but incumbents also draw heavily on the services of volunteers. The fact that only 24 percent of all 1992 House campaigns were waged without the assistance of an attorney reflects the complexity of modern elections and the legal codes that govern them.

The overall professionalism of contemporary House campaigns is reflected in the fact that the average campaign uses paid staff or political consultants to carry out between five and six of the preceding nine activities (see Table 3-1). The typical incumbent campaign uses skilled professionals to carry out roughly seven of these activities, while the typical challenger uses only four. Open-seat campaigns are nearly as professional as incumbent contests, relying on skilled personnel to carry out roughly six of these activities. Candidates involved in competitive contests assemble more professional staffs than those in uncompetitive races.

The organization that Rep. David Price assembled to conduct his 1992 reelection campaign in North Carolina's 4th district is typical of those assembled by most shoo-in incumbents (those who won by more than 20 percent of the vote). Price, a former congressional aide, Duke University political science professor, and North Carolina Democratic State Committee chair, represents a diverse district which includes Raleigh (the state capital), Chapel Hill, several smaller cities, and several suburban and rural areas. The 4th district seat was one of the most competitive House seats during the 1980s.[10] Price wrested it from one-term incumbent Bill Cobey by a twelve-point margin in 1986 and had to defend it against experienced and well-funded opponents in both 1988 and 1990.[11] Price began the 1992 election with the same core campaign team that he had used in 1990, but he did not expand on it as much as he had previously because the campaign of his opponent, LaVinia "Vicky"

Goudie, never got off the ground. Gene Conti, the AA in Price's Washington office, took a leave of absence from his congressional duties in September to work full-time on the campaign.[12] He was joined by Scott Forrester, a caseworker on leave of absence from Price's district office in Raleigh, and Dot Turner, a Democratic activist from the district. These three full-time workers were assisted by about a dozen volunteers for most of the three-month campaign season. An additional full-time employee, four part-time employees, and another twenty-five volunteers joined the Price effort during the final two weeks of the election.

The campaign also used the services of a number of nationally known political consultants who had worked in previous Price campaigns. Mellman and Lazarus of Washington, D.C., did the candidate's polling. Linda Davis, of Creative Campaign Consultants Inc., also of Washington, raised money from PACs and solicited large contributions from individuals. Saul Shorr, of Shorr and Associates of Philadelphia, produced the television commercials. Donald Draper and Craig Adams, the only North Carolina-based consultants, handled the campaign's direct-mail solicitations and accounting. Because of the lack of competitiveness of the election, Conti handled press relations instead of hiring a full-time press aide.

The DCCC furnished Price with some policy research. The North Carolina Democratic State Committee provided some opposition research, which Conti supplemented with interviews he held with Goudie's professional colleagues. The National Committee for an Effective Congress (NCEC), a leading liberal PAC, provided the precinct-level demographic and vote analysis that guided the campaign's targeting. The campaign's voter mobilization and other field activities were run cooperatively with the Democratic "coordinated campaign" in Raleigh. The coordinated campaign conducted literature drops and registration and get-out-the-vote drives on behalf of the party's presidential, congressional, state, and local candidates. The Price campaign was based in the same building as the Clinton-Gore campaign and the statewide Democratic coordinated campaign committee.

The campaign team that Vicky Goudie put together to challenge David Price was severely underfunded and understaffed, as is typical of the campaigns waged by likely loser challengers (those who lost by more than 20 percent of the vote). Goudie, who is executive director of the North Carolina Board of Cosmetic Art Examiners, depended entirely on volunteers to run her campaign. Her son, Richard Goudie, a 25-year-old employee in the asbestos program of the North Carolina Department of Environmental Health, managed the campaign. Her husband, Richard Blaine Goudie, was its treasurer. A core of twenty volunteers, each of whom contributed two-to-three hours a day, comprised the rest of the Goudie for Congress Committee. The Goudie campaign did not hire any professional consultants and commissioned no polls. Mark Hilpert, a

Wake Forest University student, conducted its issue research. The Goudie campaign did not rent a visible downtown office, instead operating out of a spare bedroom in the candidate's home.[13]

The 1992 campaign of Rep. Vic Fazio, a Democratic House leader from California, is typical of those run by House incumbents in jeopardy (those who lost or won by less than 20 percent of the vote). Well before the 1992 campaign season began, Fazio recognized that redistricting could encourage a strong challenger. Although registered Democrats slightly outnumber Republicans in California's 3rd district, the district is a competitive mix of Democrats, Republicans, and nonpartisans.[14]

Fazio assembled a highly professional team to mount his reelection effort. He hired veteran campaigner Richard Harris as his campaign manager and the Washington-based firm of Squier/Eskew/Knapp/Ochs Communications to produce his television and radio ads. Springer Associates and Garin-Hart, both of Washington, D.C., carried out his fundraising and polling. The Campaign Performance Group of San Francisco designed that portion of his direct mail devoted to communicating with voters. The Fazio campaign also recruited scores of volunteers, and Eric Wilson, the deputy political director of the DCCC, helped with the campaign. Like Price and many other Democrats, Fazio relied on the combined efforts of Democratic national, state, and local party organizations for much of his field activity. The California coordinated campaign set up telephone banks, established a field organization, and provided some of the volunteers who mobilized Democratic voters.[15] By integrating his field activities with those carried out by the Democrats' coordinated campaign, Fazio was able to reserve most of his resources to pay for television, radio, direct-mail advertising, and other candidate-focused activities.

The organization put together by Fazio's opponent, H. L. "Bill" Richardson, is typical of those assembled by hopeful challengers (those who won or lost by 20 percent of the vote or less), most of whom have held elective office or had some other significant political experience. Richardson had served in the California state senate from 1969 to 1988 and had run for the U.S. Senate in 1974. He founded and serves as president of the 220,000-member Gun Owners of America and created two PACs which spent a combined $7 million on political campaigns between 1975 and 1991.[16] Richardson assembled a very professional campaign team which was managed by John Stoos and had former California state senator Brian Lungren as its general consultant. Wayne Johnson and Associates of Sacramento designed the campaign's direct mail, and META Information Services, also of Sacramento, conducted the candidate's polls. Republican national, state, and local committees assisted the campaign with voter registration, get-out-the-vote drives, and other field work. The NRCC also contributed a poll and a variety of other campaign services to Richardson.[17] Because the NRCC designated the California

3rd district contest as an "opportunity" (or competitive) race, its California field representative, Joe Weber, regularly advised Richardson and his staff.

The campaigns waged by Democrat Corrine Brown and Republican Ron Weidner in Florida's 3rd district resemble those waged by most open-seat prospects (those in races decided by margins of 20 percent or less). Both campaigns hired experienced staff and consultants to carry out specialized election activities. Brown hired Joy Rogers as her manager, commissioned Ron Lester and Associates to take her polls, and used David Heller of Austin-Scheinkopf Limited of Washington, D.C., as her media consultant. Rogers also designed the Brown campaign's direct mail. Weidner hired Dick Morris of Connecticut, who has run campaigns for Massachusetts governor William Weld and Sens. Trent Lott (R-Miss.) and Jesse Helms (R-N.C.), for general consulting and polling. The campaign was managed by Rusty Huseman. Both the Brown and Weidner campaigns relied on party committees to help them with their field work.[18]

Campaign Budgets

The professionalism of contemporary congressional campaigns is reflected in how they budget their money. House candidates spend roughly 76 percent of their campaign funds communicating with voters and 18 percent on overhead (see Figure 3-1).[19] Polling and other research account for the final 6 percent. The amounts budgeted for electronic media show the importance that modern communication techniques play in most House campaigns. The typical campaign spends 11 percent of its budget on radio and 18 percent on television. Next comes direct mail, which accounts for roughly 18 percent. Newspapers account for an additional 4 percent. The remaining 25 percent is spent largely on travel, registration and get-out-the-vote drives, billboards, yard signs, the distribution of campaign literature, and other field activities.

One of the most interesting things about congressional elections is how few differences there are among campaigns waged by different kinds of candidates. Democrats spent 9 percent more than Republicans on television ads in 1992, whereas Republicans spent 5 percent more on campaign literature and 4 percent more on yard signs. Other than those differences, the budgets of Democratic and Republican candidates were virtually identical. Challengers budgeted 10 percent more funds than incumbents for voter contact and compensated by scrimping on overhead and polling. Challengers also allocated the least for television advertising and the most for campaign literature. Incumbents, by contrast, allocated the most for television ads and the least for literature. Candidates in contests decided by 20 percent or less of the two-party vote allocated a larger portion of their funds to television than candidates in one-sided races.

Figure 3-1 The Budget of a Typical House Campaign, 1992

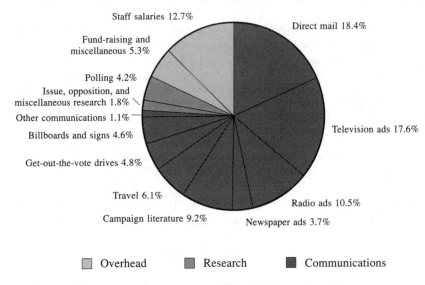

Staff salaries 12.7%

Fund-raising and miscellaneous 5.3%

Polling 4.2%

Issue, opposition, and miscellaneous research 1.8%

Other communications 1.1%

Billboards and signs 4.6%

Get-out-the-vote drives 4.8%

Travel 6.1%

Campaign literature 9.2%

Newspaper ads 3.7%

Direct mail 18.4%

Television ads 17.6%

Radio ads 10.5%

▨ Overhead   ▨ Research   ▨ Communications

Source: Questions 20 and 21 of the 1992 Congressional Campaign Study. See Figure A-1 in the appendix.

Note: Figure is for general election candidates in major-party contested races, excluding those in incumbent-versus-incumbent races. N=319.

Of course, candidates tailor their campaign budgets to suit the nature of their districts. The Price campaign spent nothing on radio, choosing instead to commit the largest portion of its expenditures to television advertising to take advantage of the fact that the entire district is located within one relatively inexpensive media market.[20] Brown and Weidner, whose districts spanned several media markets, spent slightly less than average on electronic advertising and devoted roughly one-quarter of their budgets to direct mail.[21]

The overall similarity in campaign budgets is remarkable given the different sums that incumbent, open-seat, and challenger campaigns spend. The widespread availability of campaign technology, the tremendous growth of the political consulting industry, and the increase in the numbers of campaign seminars sponsored by universities, parties, and interest groups have fostered a set of shared expectations about how a campaign should spend its funds. These expectations are reinforced when campaign personnel negotiate their salaries and draw up budgets, when political consulting firms set their rates, and when party officials and PAC managers scrutinize campaign budgets prior to giving a contribution.

Senate Campaigns

Senate campaigns are usually more expensive, run by more professional organizations, and attract more party assistance than House campaigns. Senate candidates rely primarily on paid staffs and nationally known political consultants to develop their strategies and carry out their campaigns. Most Senate incumbents keep a substantial organization intact between elections. The average senator spent in excess of $830,000 in overhead to maintain a campaign organization over the six-year period prior to the 1992 election.[22] Sen. Alfonse D'Amato (D-N.Y.) set the record for keeping the most elaborate organization between 1987 and 1992, spending almost $2.4 million on overhead, including $1.3 million on staff salaries and $218,000 for rent.[23]

Senate campaigns often have combinations of individuals sharing responsibilities for various aspects of the campaign. In 1992 virtually every campaign assigned a paid aide to work with a mass media advertising firm to develop the candidate's communications. Opposition research is typically conducted by a campaign aide in conjunction with a private consultant or party official. Campaign staff, consultants, volunteers, party committees, and interest group representatives make substantial contributions to Senate candidates' fund-raising efforts. Most Senate campaigns also hire one or more field managers to participate in coordinated voter mobilization efforts that draw on the resources of national, state, and local party committees. Democratic Senate candidates also coordinate their field work with labor unions, and most Senate candidates of both parties rely on volunteers to help with their voter registration and get-out-the-vote efforts.

The major difference in spending between Senate and House contests is in the allocation of media expenditures. The average Senate campaign spends almost 30 percent of its money on television advertising, whereas the typical House campaign spends only a quarter of its money on television. Senate campaigns also allocate far smaller portions of their budgets to radio advertising, campaign literature, newspaper ads, billboards, and yard signs than do House contestants. The differences in communications expenditures reflect both the greater practicality and the necessity of using television advertising in statewide races.

Notes

1. See, for example, Edie N. Goldenberg and Michael W. Traugott, *Campaigning for Congress* (Washington, D.C.: CQ Press, 1984), 19-24.
2. The figure includes office furniture, supplies, rent, salaries, taxes, bank fees, lawyers, accountants, telephone, automobile, computers, other office equip-

ment, restaurants, and food but excludes campaign travel. See Dwight Morris and Murielle E. Gamache, *Handbook of Campaign Spending* (Washington, D.C.: Congressional Quarterly, 1994), table 1-5.

3. Ibid., 18-19.

4. There have been some important exceptions to this generalization in recent years. See David Canon, *Actors, Athletes, and Astronauts: Political Amateurs in the United States Congress* (Chicago: University of Chicago Press, 1990), 3, 36.

5. These percentages are based on further breakdowns of question 19 of the 1992 Congressional Campaign Study (see the appendix).

6. See note 5.

7. See note 5.

8. The NRCC provided survey research to 6 percent of its incumbents, 12 percent of its challengers, and 14 percent of its open-seat candidates. The DCCC provided survey research to 5 percent of its incumbents, 2 percent of its challengers, and 5 percent of its open-seat candidates.

9. On local party organizations and voter mobilization see Cornelius P. Cotter, James L. Gibson, John F. Bibby, and Robert J. Huckshorn, *Party Organizations in American Politics* (Pittsburgh: University of Pittsburgh Press, 1989), especially 53-54; Robert Huckfeldt and John Sprague, "Political Parties and Electoral Mobilization: Political Structure, Social Structure, and the Party Canvass," *American Political Science Review* 86 (1992): 70-86; Gregory A. Caldeira, Samuel C. Patterson, and Gregory A. Markko, "The Mobilization of Voters in Congressional Elections," *Journal of Politics* 47 (1985): 490-509; Michael A. Krassa, "Context and the Canvass: The Mechanisms of Interactions," *Political Behavior* 10 (1988): 233-246; and Peter W. Wielhower and Brad Lockerbie, "Party Contacting and Political Participation, 1952-90," *American Journal of Political Science* 38 (1994): 211-229.

10. David E. Price, *The Congressional Experience* (Boulder, Colo.: Westview Press, 1992), 1-3.

11. In 1988 Price faced Tom Fetzer, a former operative in Jesse Helms's National Congressional Club. Price and Fetzer spent $1,006,000 and $759,000, respectively, in a race that ended in a 58 percent to 42 percent Price victory. In 1990 Price was pitted against John Carrington, a millionaire businessman who had previously come close to winning two statewide elections. Carrington outspent Price $891,000 to $793,000, only to go down to defeat 58 percent to 42 percent. See Phil Duncan, ed., *Politics in America, 1992: The 102nd Congress* (Washington, D.C.: Congressional Quarterly, 1991), 1100-1101.

12. Eugene Conti, Price's campaign manager and administrative assistant, personal interview, July 8, 1993.

13. Richard Goudie, campaign manager, Vicky Goudie for Congress Committee, telephone interview, April 8, 1994.

14. Phil Duncan, ed., *Politics in America, 1994: The 103rd Congress* (Washington, D.C.: Congressional Quarterly, 1993), 112-113.

15. Caryn R. Sagal, "1992: The Year of the Challenger or the Year of the Incumbent? The Showdown in California's 3rd Congressional District," independent honors thesis, University of Maryland, 1994.

16. Phil Duncan, ed., *Politics in America, 1994*, 113; Sagal, "1992: The Year of the Challenger or the Year of the Incumbent?"

17. Sagal, "1992: The Year of the Challenger or the Year of the Incumbent?"

18. Katina Rae Stapleton, "The Wild Race to Washington: The Making of Florida 3," unpublished paper, University of Maryland, 1992.

19. These are estimates for budgetary allocations made during the campaign season by candidates and campaign aides who responded to the mail questionnaire. Studies that examine the money collected and spent over the course of an entire two-year House or six-year Senate election cycle report lower expenditures for voter contact and higher expenditures on overhead, research, and other activities that take place before the campaign season. For these figures see Sara Fritz and Dwight Morris, *Gold Plated Politics: Running for Congress in the 1990s* (Washington, D.C.: Congressional Quarterly, 1992); and Morris and Gamache, *Handbook of Campaign Spending*. For additional information on campaign budgets see Goldenberg and Traugott, *Campaigning for Congress*, 85-92.

20. It cost only $2,000 to air a thirty-second television ad during prime-time viewing hours in North Carolina's 4th district. Conti, personal interview; Saul Shorr, president of Shorr and Associates, telephone interview, July 8, 1993.

21. Stapleton, "The Wild Race to Washington"; Morris and Gamache, *Handbook of Campaign Spending.*

22. This includes office furniture, supplies, rent, salaries, taxes, bank fees, lawyers, accountants, telephone, automobile, computers, other office equipment, restaurants, and food and excludes campaign travel. Morris and Gamache, *Handbook of Campaign Spending,* table 1-3.

23. Ibid., 127.

Chapter 4

Party Campaigning

Party committees in Washington, D.C., have a tremendous interest in maximizing the number of members they have in the House and Senate. They are motivated by both policy and pragmatic concerns. Like PACs and other organized interests, party committees have core policies and legislative goals that they try to promote by influencing the outcomes of House and Senate elections nationwide. Toward that end, the parties spend huge sums of money and provide extensive campaign services in order to maintain or try to win procedural control of Congress.

The roles played by political parties in congressional election campaigns have been shaped by the same forces that fostered the development of the modern, candidate-centered election system.[1] This system emphasizes campaign activities requiring technical expertise and in-depth research. Many candidates, especially nonincumbents running for the House, lack the money or professional know-how needed to run a modern congressional campaign. Candidates' needs created the opportunity for party organizations to assume a more important role in congressional elections.[2] The national parties have responded to these needs not by doing away with the candidate-centered election system but by assuming a more important role in it.[3] This chapter discusses the reasons that parties assist candidates for Congress, the kinds of assistance they give, the strategies that inform their giving, how they select candidates for support, and the effects of their assistance on candidates' campaigns.

The National, Congressional, and
Senatorial Campaign Committees

Party organizations in the nation's capital have developed into major sources of campaign money, services, and advice for congressional candidates. The Democratic National Committee (DNC) and Republican National Committee (RNC) focus most of their efforts on presidential elections but also pay some attention to gubernatorial, statehouse, and a small number of mayoral elections. They also work to strengthen state and local party organizations. The national committees' involvement in House and Senate elections is relatively limited. It usually involves conducting a few candidate training seminars, furnishing candidates with party platforms, campaign manifestos, and "talking points," and coordinating with congressional, senatorial, state, and local party campaign committees to mobilize partisan voters. Congressional candidates in search of money, election services, or assistance in running their campaigns rarely turn to their national committee for help.

The parties' congressional and senatorial campaign committees, sometimes referred to as the "Hill committees," conversely, have developed into major support centers for House and Senate candidates.[4] The congressional campaign committees focus their efforts on House races, and the two senatorial campaign committees focus on Senate contests. In 1992 the Democratic Congressional Campaign Committee (DCCC) amassed a budget in excess of $12.8 million, and its rival, the National Republican Congressional Committee (NRCC), raised just under $34.4 million. The two senatorial committees—the Democratic Senatorial Campaign Committee (DSCC) and the National Republican Senatorial Committee (NRSC)—raised $25.4 million and $72.3 million, respectively.[5]

The chairs, vice chairs, and members of the Hill committees are all members of Congress who are selected by their colleagues in the House or Senate. In addition, the Hill committees employ many highly skilled political professionals. The DCCC and DSCC employed 64 and 35 full-time staff, and their Republican counterparts had 89 and 130 full-time employees during the 1992 election cycle.[6] For the most part, the members of each committee function like a board of directors, setting priorities and giving staff the support they need to raise money, recruit candidates, and participate in campaigns. The staffs oversee the committees' daily operations, are influential in formulating campaign strategies, and play a major role in the implementation of those strategies. The campaign committee staffs are divided along functional lines; different divisions are responsible for administration, fund-raising, research, communications, and campaign activities. In 1992 both the DCCC and the NRCC added redistricting divisions to focus on the decennial redrawing of House districts. The NRCC also added an in-house polling operation to its political division.

As major centers of political expertise and campaign support, the Hill committees are very expensive to operate. Roughly 60 percent of the DCCC's funds and 53 percent of the DSCC's money were used to pay for voter lists, computers, media studios, financial transfers to state parties, staff salaries, fund-raising, loan repayments, and other overhead between 1991 and 1992. The NRCC and NRSC spent even more on these activities, committing 82 percent and 76 percent of their funds to them.

Strategy, Decision Making, and Targeting

The Hill committees have a common overriding goal of maximizing the number of seats their party holds in Congress.[7] They become heavily involved in some elections, giving selected candidates large contributions and making substantial expenditures on their behalf. Many of these candidates are also given assistance in the form of technical expertise, in-depth research, or connections with PACs, campaign consultants, and other groups that possess some of the resources needed to conduct a congressional campaign. Finally, the Hill committees participate with the national committees and state and local party organizations in generic, party-focused election activities that are designed to help candidates for Congress and other offices get elected.

The campaign committees try to focus most of their efforts on competitive House and Senate contests. Protecting incumbents in jeopardy is a major priority. Pressures from nervous incumbents can skew the distribution of committee resources from competitive challenger and open-seat candidates toward members of Congress who hold safe seats. The funds available to a committee and the aspirations of its chair and other members can also affect the way it distributes its resources. In 1984, for example, the NRCC had sufficient funds to give all of its incumbents the maximum legal contribution, regardless of the competitiveness of their contests.[8] Both the NRCC's former chair, Guy Vander Jagt (R-Mich.), and the DCCC's former chair, Tony Coelho (D-Calif.), used their chairmanships to help them advance in the ranks of the House leadership.[9]

National political and economic conditions are additional factors that influence which candidates get campaign resources. When the president is popular and the economy is strong, the campaign committees of the president's party usually invest more resources in competitive challenger and open-seat races. Conversely, the out-party committees use more of their resources to support incumbents. When national conditions do not favor the president's party, the patterns are reversed: the in-party committees take a "protectionist" posture that favors incumbents and the out-party committees go on the offensive, using more of their resources to help nonincumbents.[10] The unpredictable nature of national political conditions and economic trends and of events that take place in states and congressional districts means that committee decision making and targeting are necessarily imperfect. As a result, some safe incumbents and uncompetitive nonincumbents inevitably receive committee assistance, while a number of competitive nonincumbents get little or no help.

The conditions surrounding the 1992 election made strategic decision making and targeting very difficult, especially for the two House campaign committees.[11] Redistricting, a process that is always fraught with ambiguities, was further complicated by a Supreme Court decision handed down in 1986. In *Thornburg v. Gingles,* the Court ruled that redistricting practices that dilute minority influence in congressional elections are unconstitutional.[12] That caused many states to run behind schedule in redrawing the boundaries of their congressional districts, resulted in many redistricting plans being challenged in court, and delayed primary elections in several states.

The huge number of redrawn or newly created seats was only one of several factors complicating the committees' tasks. President Bush's popularity seesawed up and down, making it difficult for the committees to decide whether to pursue offensive or defensive strategies.[13] The House banking and Post Office scandals and the hostility that voters directed toward Congress had similar effects. Bounced checks and unrelated ethical lapses resulted in many incumbents unexpectedly finding themselves in jeopardy and gave numerous challengers a correspondingly unexpected boost. The late retirements of some House members and the primary defeats of others further complicated the committees' efforts.

Because of the uncertainty surrounding the 1992 elections, the NRCC and DCCC delayed drawing up their "watch" lists of "opportunity" (or competitive) races and had difficulty paring those lists. The lists that the committees initially compiled were huge. Each included roughly 300 elections, more than three times the number in a normal election. The lists were shortened over the course of the campaign season, but going into the last week of the election each committee listed more than 150 races as top priorities—more than three times the number they had included at that point in the 1990 election.[14]

Individual candidates are selected for placement on the committees' watch lists on the basis of several criteria. The competitiveness of the district and incumbency are the first two considerations. Candidates running in districts that were decided by close margins in the last election or who are competing for open seats are likely to be placed on a committee's watch list. In 1992 House members running in incumbent-versus-incumbent contests or who were in danger for other reasons were considered top priorities by both House campaign committees.

The strength of the candidate is another consideration in the case of nonincumbents. Those who have had political experience or have celebrity status are also likely to be targeted for assistance. Challengers and open-seat contestants who have assembled professional campaign organizations are also likely to receive party support.[15] Having a professional organization assures the committee that the resources it contributes will be properly utilized; this is especially true if campaign committee officials are familiar with the consultants who have been hired.[16]

A variety of idiosyncratic factors can also come into play when the committees select the candidates who will be given the most support initially. An incumbent who is accused of committing an ethical transgression, is perceived to be out of touch with people in the district, or is in trouble for some other reason is a likely candidate for extra committee help. These difficulties often provoke a response by the other party's campaign committee, resulting in the incumbent's opponent also benefiting from extra party money and campaign services.

Although 1992 was proclaimed the "Year of the Woman" and party leaders worked aggressively to recruit women to run for Congress, campaign committee staff maintain that gender was not a criterion in deciding who would be given assistance.[17] Women were targeted only to the degree their races were expected to be competitive.[18]

Ideology is not a criterion for selecting candidates for support. Campaign committee staff explain that ideology is irrelevant in all of their decisions except to the degree that it influences a particular candidate's competitiveness. An extreme right-wing Republican challenger running in a very liberal Democratic district, for example, would be evaluated as uncompetitive not because of the candidate's political leanings per se but because those leanings were out of step with the district. As Deborah Flavin, director of political education at the NRCC, explains,

> At the NRCC, our only ideology is that you have a "big R" by your name. There is no litmus test on any issue. We ask candidates how they feel on "issue X" and "issue Y." Then, we help them articulate what they feel. We are here to help Republicans win.[19]

The staffs of the Democratic committees voiced similar sentiments.

The committees' lists of competitive elections are revised throughout the election cycle. Field coordinators who are assigned by the campaign committees to monitor congressional races within designated regions advise their colleagues in Washington, D.C., about the latest developments in individual elections. As a result, some candidates drop in priority and are cut off from party help, while others gain more committee attention and support. Because of the tremendous uncertainty surrounding the 1992 elections, both the Democratic and Republican House campaign committees decided early in the election cycle to distribute their resources broadly. As Tom Cole, executive director of the NRCC, stated in

December 1991, "We are going hunting with a shotgun instead of a rifle this year." DCCC national political director Rob Engel confirmed that his committee would also use the "shotgun" approach.

Rather than drop a large quantity of money or extensive election services in a candidate's lap early in the cycle, the Hill committees distribute them piecemeal in response to the candidate's ability to meet a series of discrete fund-raising and organizational goals. Incumbents usually meet these quickly, but the goals pose more formidable hurdles for challengers and open-seat candidates. Nonincumbents who meet their goals in a timely fashion are usually within reach of victory at the end of the election season and receive substantial party contributions, services, and help with fund-raising. Of course, the distribution of campaign resources is also affected by the Hill committees' own fund-raising success.

Campaign Contributions and Expenditures

Party contributions to candidates in congressional elections are severely restricted by the Federal Election Campaign Act of 1974 (FECA). National, congressional, and state party campaign committees can each give $5,000 to a House candidate at each stage of the election process: primary, runoff, and general election.[20] The parties' national and senatorial campaign committees can give a combined total of $17,500 in an election cycle to a Senate candidate.[21] State committees can contribute an additional $5,000 to Senate candidates.

Parties can also spend larger sums of money on behalf of individual candidates. These outlays, referred to as "coordinated expenditures" because they can be made in direct coordination with a candidate's campaign, typically are for campaign services that a Hill committee or some other party organization gives to an individual candidate or purchases from a political consultant on the candidate's behalf.[22] Coordinated expenditures often take the form of polls, radio ads, television commercials, fund-raising events, direct-mail solicitations, or issue research. They differ from campaign contributions in that both the party and the candidate share control over them, giving the party the ability to influence some aspects of how the campaign is run. Originally set in 1974 at $10,000 for all national party organizations, the limits for coordinated expenditures on behalf of House candidates are adjusted for inflation and reached $27,620 in 1992.[23] The limits for national party coordinated expenditures in Senate elections vary by state population and are also indexed to inflation. In 1992 they ranged from $55,240 per committee in the smallest states to $1,227,322 in California. State party committees are authorized to spend the same amounts in coordinated expenditures in House and Senate races as the parties' national organizations, but state party committees often do not have the funds to do so. In races where a state party

Table 4-1 Party Spending in the 1992 Congressional Elections

	House		Senate	
	Contributions	Coordinated expenditures	Contributions	Coordinated expenditures
Democratic				
DNC	$0	$913,935	$0	$195,351
DCCC	818,846	4,132,292	18,682	2,606
DSCC	10,000	2,600	618,450	11,233,120
State and local	366,477	750,451	72,699	487,415
Total Democratic	$1,195,323	$5,799,278	$709,831	$11,918,492
Republican				
RNC	$778,503	$832,347	$9,000	$0
NRCC	686,916	5,166,647	3,500	0
NRSC	78,500	0	614,814	16,485,039
State and local	626,057	868,908	127,960	3,617,303
Total Republican	$2,169,976	$6,867,902	$755,274	$20,102,342

Source: Compiled by the author from Federal Election Commission data.

lacks resources and a national party organization—usually the parties' congressional or senatorial campaign committee—deems it important for the party to spend as much money as possible, the state and national party organizations form "agency agreements" that transfer the state party's quota for coordinated expenditures to the national party.[24]

Coordinated expenditures are the vehicle of choice for most party activity in congressional elections (see Table 4-1). Their higher limits, the possibility for creating agency agreements, and the control they afford party committees in candidates' campaigns make coordinated expenditures an attractive avenue for party involvement. Coordinated spending also enables the parties to take advantage of economies of scale when purchasing and distributing campaign services. Because the parties purchase the services of political consultants in large quantities, they pay below-market rates, which enables them to provide candidates with services whose true market value exceeds the FECA's coordinated expenditure limits.[25]

The four Hill committees are the parties' key vehicles for campaign spending and they deliver most of the parties' campaign services. In 1992 the NRCC spent over $5.85 million in the campaigns of Republican House candidates, roughly $900,000 more than the DCCC. The RNC and NRSC spent an additional $1.7 million. Total Republican Party spending in House races reached $9.04 million, over $2 million more than that spent by the Democrats. Although the Democrats were outspent by their Republican counterparts in 1992, the spending gap between the two parties has closed considerably over the last six election cycles.[26] This is mainly due to a fall-off in Republican receipts and improved Democratic fund-raising. An NRCC decision to transfer almost $1.9 million to twenty-one state party committees instead of forming agency agreements with those committees is also reflected in the decline in NRCC money contributed to or spent on behalf of Republican House candidates. According to Tom Cole, the NRCC arranged to transfer "soft" money funds that could not be spent directly on federal candidates, with the understanding that the state committees receiving them would spend an equal amount of "hard" money (which can legally be spent in conjunction with federal elections) on their House candidates' campaigns.[27]

Democratic and Republican state and local party committees spent $1.1 million and $1.5 million, respectively, in the 1992 House elections. This accounts for only 16 percent of all party spending made directly in House campaigns. Although House campaigns are waged locally, national parties play a bigger financial role in them than do state and local parties.

National party organizations also outspend state and local parties in Senate elections. The NRSC was the more active of the senatorial campaign committees, outspending its rival by $5.3 million in 1992. The Republican committee also transferred almost $2 million more to state party committees than did the DSCC.[28] The two senatorial committees account for the lion's share of party spending in Senate elections.

National party organizations distribute most of their money to candidates in close elections (see Table 4-2).[29] The Republicans' allocation patterns for House candidates in 1992 are indicative of an aggressive, offensive strategy. The NRCC and other Washington-based Republican committees directed 75 percent of their contributions and coordinated expenditures to challengers and open-seat candidates. The remaining money was committed to incumbents.

GOP money was fairly well targeted. Hopeful challengers and open-seat prospects received 34 percent and 26 percent of the party's funds, respectively. Incumbents in jeopardy got 20 percent. The party gave 5 percent of its funds to "shoo-ins," 10 percent to "likely loser" challengers, and 5 percent to open-seat candidates running in one-party districts.

The Democrats' allocation strategy is more difficult to discern from its spending patterns. This is partially due to imprecision in DCCC targeting. Democratic incumbents, who outnumbered Republican incumbents 267 to 167, received a total of 43 percent of the party's expenditures, with Democratic shoo-ins raking in 21 percent. Democratic challengers received 36 percent, and the party allocated more money to challengers who were likely to lose than to those who had better odds of winning. As has been the case in previous elections, the Democratic Party continues to spend substantial sums of money on incumbents who do not need it and on challengers who are not likely to benefit from it.[30]

Table 4-2   The Allocation of National Party Money in the 1992 Congressional Elections

	House		Senate	
	Democrats	Republicans	Democrats	Republicans
Incumbents				
In jeopardy	22%	20%	18%	39%
	(72)	(41)	(6)	(6)
Shoo-ins	21	5	5	8
	(121)	(79)	(8)	(6)
Challengers				
Hopefuls	16	34	42	19
	(41)	(72)	(6)	(6)
Likely losers	20	10	5	5
	(79)	(121)	(6)	(8)
Open-seat candidates				
Prospects	15	26	29	29
	(50)	(50)	(8)	(8)
In one-party	5	5	—	—
districts	(34)	(34)	—	—
Total ($, thousands)	$5,479	$7,074	$10,907	$16,037
	(397)	(397)	(34)	(34)

Source: Compiled by the author from Federal Election Commission data.

Notes: Incumbents in jeopardy are defined as those who lost or who won by 20 percent or less of the two-party vote. Shoo-ins are defined as incumbents who won by more than 20 percent of the two-party vote. Hopeful challengers are defined as those who won or who lost by 20 percent or less of the two-party vote. Likely loser challengers are defined as those who lost by more than 20 percent of the two-party vote. Open-seat prospects are defined as those whose election was decided by 20 percent or less of the two-party vote. Open-seat candidates in one-party districts are defined as those whose election was decided by more than 20 percent of the two-party vote. All Senate open-seat candidates are in the prospects category. Figures include contributions and coordinated expenditures by the parties' national, congressional, and senatorial campaign committees to general election candidates in major-party contested races, except incumbent-versus-incumbent House races. They do not include soft money expenditures. Some columns do not add to 100 percent because of rounding. The numbers of candidates are in parentheses.

The disparities in party targeting merit some explanation. First, the Republican Party organizations have traditionally taken a more business-like approach to allocating campaign funds. The NRCC's decision-making process is more staff-driven and less politicized than that of its Democratic counterpart.[31] The Democrats' control of the House, greater number of incumbents, and greater diversity as well as the leadership aspirations of DCCC chairs and members occasionally make it difficult for the committee to pursue its stated goal of maximizing House seats. Second, the NRCC has been one step ahead of the DCCC in gathering campaign information. The Republican committee was the first to have staff observing campaigns in the field, and its new polling division may have given it an advantage over the DCCC in targeting. Third, incumbent Democrats' heavy use of the DCCC's media center inflates the figures for party money spent in connection with shoo-in races. Finally, a difference in philosophy might have been at work. In Rob Engel's words, the DCCC has traditionally tried to "keep more races alive, for a longer period, before bailing out." [32] This has led Democratic funds to be less narrowly targeted than Republican money.

It is relatively easy for the parties to target their money in Senate elections. DSCC and NRSC officials have to assess their candidates' prospects in only thirty-three or thirty-four races per election, and those races take place within borders that do not shift every ten years because of redistricting. As a result, virtually all of the parties' funds are spent in close elections. In 1992 the Democrats spent all but 10 percent of their money in competitive contests, favoring hopeful challengers and open-seat candidates the most, followed by incumbents in jeopardy. Shoo-ins and likely losers received considerably less support.[33] The Republicans distributed all but 13 percent of their funds to candidates in close elections but favored incumbents in jeopardy over hopeful challengers and open-seat contestants. Both parties perceived open-seat elections to be where some hard-fought battles would take place. The parties' spending patterns indicate that the Democrats took a highly aggressive posture, and the Republicans took the complementary defensive position.

Campaign Services

The parties' congressional and senatorial campaign committees provide selected candidates with assistance in specialized campaign activities, such as management, gauging public opinion, issue and opposition research, and communications. They also provide transactional assistance, acting as brokers between candidates and PACs, individual contributors, and political consultants. The DCCC and the NRCC typically become closely involved in the campaigns of candidates on their watch lists and have little involvement in others. The DSCC and the NRCC work with virtually all of their Senate candidates.

Campaign Management

Candidates and their campaign organizations can get help from their Hill committees with hiring and training campaign staff, making strategic and tactical decisions, and other management-related activities. The committees maintain directories of campaign managers, fund-raising specialists, media experts, pollsters, vendors of voter lists, and other political consultants that candidates and managers can use to hire staff and purchase campaign services. Committee officials sometimes recommend particular consultants, especially to House challengers and open-seat candidates, some of whom are involved in their first major campaign.[34]

The Hill committees also train candidates and managers in the latest campaign techniques. The DCCC and the NRCC hold training seminars to introduce the latest innovations in targeting, fund-raising, and other election activities. Seminars for incumbents, which are held in the committees' headquarters, cover such topics as staying in touch with constituents, getting the most political mileage out of franked mail, defending unpopular votes, and PAC fund-raising. Seminars for challengers and open-seat candidates focus on more basic subjects, such as the "stump" speech, filing campaign finance reports with the FEC, and building coalitions. Even long-term members of the House and Senate find the seminars beneficial as reminders of what they ought to be doing.[35]

In 1992 both committees introduced a number of innovations in their management-related service programs, including the use of precinct-level results from previous elections, polls, and geodemographic data that describe the political, demographic, and economic composition of a congressional district. These innovations help campaigns target their mailings, electronic media ads, voter mobilization drives, and other activities. Over the course of the election cycle, the NRCC held training schools which were attended by 199 candidates and 76 spouses. The committee also co-sponsored, with the RNC, a series of week-long, intensive programs in campaign management, communications, and fund-raising which was attended by 314 campaign aides.[36] According to Rob Engel, the Democrats traditionally devote fewer resources to training candidates and campaign managers because the party has "a very deep bench [of candidates and consultants], a much deeper bench than the Republicans."

The Hill committees' field representatives and staffs in Washington also serve as important sources of strategic advice. Because they follow House and Senate elections nationwide and can draw on experiences from previous election cycles, the committees are among the few organizations that have the knowledge and institutional memory to advise candidates and their managers on how to deal with some of the dilemmas they encounter.[37] Staffs of the congressional campaign committees are usually most heavily involved in the planning and tactical decision making of open-seat and challenger candidates. In 1992 they also provided a great deal of advice to House members running in incumbent-versus-incumbent showdowns, in heavily redrawn districts, and in other close races.

Gauging Public Opinion

Many candidates receive significant assistance in gauging public opinion from national party committees. The DNC and RNC discuss the findings of nationwide polls in newsletters and memoranda that they distribute to members of Congress, party activists, and congressional candidates. In 1992 the DNC undertook a major polling effort that included statewide polls designed to furnish information to the Clinton-Gore campaign and Democratic candidates for governor, the House, the Senate, and state legislatures. The RNC focused most of its polling activities on the presidential race.

The parties' congressional and senatorial campaign committees conduct or commission hundreds of polls and targeting studies in a given election cycle. In 1992 the NRCC hired a director of survey research to conduct polls for 117 Republican candidates and to assist others in purchasing and interpreting surveys from private polling firms. The committee took recruitment surveys to show potential candidates the possibilities of their waging competitive races, benchmark polls to inform declared candidates of their levels of support and of public opinion on the major issues, and tracking polls to assist a small group of candidates who were running neck-and-neck with their Democratic opponents at the end of the campaign season. Some of these surveys had a market value in excess of $8,000 and were given to candidates as in-kind contributions or as coordinated expenditures that were valued as low as $1,800 using a depreciation option allowed by the FEC.[38] The Republicans also purchased some polls from private consultants, including one national survey that measured the effects of the check-bouncing scandal on public opinion and tested some anti-Congress and Democratic attack themes and another national survey that examined public responses to several defense-related issues.[39] The NRCC distributed $365,000 in polling services to House candidates, and the RNC distributed another $12,000.[40]

The DCCC did not hire a director of survey research or conduct "in-house" polls for its candidates in 1992. It explored these possibilities after the 1990 election cycle but chose instead to continue relying on private polling firms. As it had in the past, the committee gave surveys that were purchased from prominent Democratic consultants to selected candidates as in-kind contributions or coordinated expenditures. The DCCC also cooperated with the Democratic national and senatorial campaign committees in taking statewide and national polls. The DCCC's share of the Democratic Party's polling effort in the 1992 House races came to roughly $405,000; the DNC spent an additional $909,000.[41]

The national party organizations usually spend considerably less on polling in Senate than in House elections because most Senate campaigns hire their own pollsters and because far fewer Senate than House races take place in any given election year. In 1992 the DSCC provided Democratic Senate candidates with $611,000 in polling services, and the DNC distributed an additional $119,000. Republican national party organizations distributed considerably less, providing roughly $54,000 in polling services to GOP Senate candidates.[42]

Selected candidates also receive precinct-level targeting studies from the Hill committees. In 1992 the DSCC and DCCC used geodemographic data and election returns provided by the National Committee for an Effective Congress (NCEC), a leading liberal PAC, to help Democratic candidates design their voter mobilization strategies, guide their media purchases, and carry out other communications and field activities.[43] Republican House candidates received similar assistance from the NRCC's redistricting and campaign divisions, and Republican Senate candidates got targeting help from the NRSC's campaign division.

Issue and Opposition Research

During the 1980s party organizations in Washington, D.C., became major centers for political research. The DNC and RNC extended their research activities in several directions, most of which were and continue to be party-focused rather than candidate-directed. Members of Congress, governors, state legislators, and candidates and activists at all levels are now routinely sent materials on salient national issues.

Candidates for Congress also receive party-focused research materials from the senatorial and congressional campaign committees and from other party organs. During the last few congresses, the Democratic Caucus of the House of Representatives published a series of issue handbooks, such as *Investing in America's Future* and *Taking Charge of America's Future,* to help House candidates prepare their speeches.[44] The handbooks, which were crammed with statistics, charts, and historical examples, discussed the economy, crime and drugs, health care, and other contemporary problems. They attributed the problems to the shortcomings of Reagan and Bush administration policies and offered a Democratic vision for solving the problems. House Republicans published similar information in the form of "talking points," memoranda, and pamphlets. Every Republican House member and 350 GOP nonincumbents were given an issues pamphlet published by the Republican Conference prior to the 1992 election. House Democrats distributed their issues handbook to all general election candidates, many primary contestants, and thousands of Democratic activists.

More important than the issue booklets are the issue packages the Hill committees provide to selected candidates. These include statistics and thematic information drawn from major newspapers, the Associated Press wire service, the Lexis/Nexis computerized political database, and government publications. The packages present a detailed description of the district (or state), hard facts about issues that are important to local voters, and talking points that help candidates discuss these issues in a thematic and interesting manner. Candidates can access additional information by tapping into the committees' electronic bulletin boards. Many candidates make extensive use of this information when developing their campaign themes and policy positions. Open-seat candidates and challengers, who have none of the perquisites enjoyed by incumbents, use party research as a substitute for the studies that House members get from their staffs or other congressional sources.

In 1992 each congressional campaign committee conducted research on every House member of the opposing party. The NRCC put together highly detailed opposition research packages on the 120 most vulnerable Democratic incumbents.[45] The DCCC also carried out highly detailed research on vulnerable House Republicans. Each Hill committee also conducted "vulnerability studies" on many of its own members to help them prepare responses to attacks that might be made by their opponents.

Campaign Communications

The Hill committees assist selected candidates with campaign communications. Both the DCCC and NRCC have state-of-the-art television and radio production facilities on their premises and furnish candidates with technical and editorial assistance in producing television and radio ads. The committees have satellite capabilities that enable candidates to beam television communications back to their districts instantly and to interact "live" with voters. This technology is extremely popular with incumbents from western states who are not able get back to their districts as frequently as those living on the East Coast or in the Midwest.

Each media center produces several "generic" or "doughnut" ads which they customize to incorporate the names and voices of individual candidates. An example of a generic radio ad that was broadcast in connection with Republican House campaigns across the country was based on the television show "Lifestyles of the Rich and Famous" and portrayed incumbent Democrats as jet-setters who vacation around the world at taxpayers' expense. Originally developed during the 1990 election, this NRCC ad was also used by many Republican challengers in 1992.

House candidates and their consultants can also use the congressional campaign committees' recording and editing suites to produce individualized radio and television commercials.[46] Committee production staffs are available to give technical and editorial advice. In a small number of campaigns, the NRCC goes several steps further. A communications division staffer meets with the candidate, his or her pollster and campaign manager, and a party political operative to design a full-blown media campaign. The staffer develops advertising themes, writes television and radio scripts, and produces the ads. The staffer may help design flyers and other printed matter as well.[47]

In 1992 the NRCC distributed roughly $1.7 million in electronic media services to GOP House candidates, with the RNC distributing an additional $613,000.[48] The NRCC produced 188 television advertisements for 45 House candidates: 23 incumbents and 22 challenger or open-seat candidates. According to Peter Pessel, one of the committee's producers, two-thirds of the ads were created specifically for individual candidates. The remainder were generic advertisements customized with visual inserts and voice-overs. The committee also produced radio ads for 45 House members and 44 nonincumbents.

The DCCC provided a much larger number of candidates with less personalized assistance, distributing roughly $3.2 million worth of television and radio services.[49] Just over 170 House members and 70 nonincumbents used the Democrats' Harriman Communications Center to record and edit their television commercials. Fewer than 20 used the committee's facilities to record their radio advertisements; most preferred to tape their radio ads in their campaign headquarters or other sites.

The national party organizations are heavily involved in their Senate candidates' campaign communications. In 1992 the DSCC distributed $9.6 million in electronic media services to Democratic Senate candidates. The NRSC outspent its rival by more than 60 percent, giving out nearly $15 million in television and radio advertisements to GOP candidates for the Senate.[50]

The parties also help their candidates with other types of campaign communications. In 1992 the Democratic and Republican national party organizations provided their respective House candidates with $725,000 and $3.2 million worth of direct-mail advertising.[51] The national parties spent even more in Senate contests: the DSCC gave its candidates $390,000 in direct-mail services; the NRSC distributed more than $1.1 million in direct-mail assistance to Republican Senate candidates.[52]

By providing candidates with issue packages and communications assistance, the congressional and senatorial campaign committees have clearly contributed to the nationalization of American politics. Few congressional candidates needed to be told the economy was the major issue in 1992, but the Hill committees helped them frame this issue in ways that were more meaningful to voters. The committees' opposition research also contributes to campaigns, but in ways that many voters do not look upon favorably. Just as the Hill committees assist candidates in putting a positive spin on their campaigns, they help the candidates put a negative spin on their opponents' campaigns, thereby contributing to the mudslinging that has become commonplace in congressional elections.

Fund-raising

In addition to providing contributions, coordinated expenditures, and campaign services directly to candidates, the Hill committees also help selected candidates raise money from individuals and PACs. To this end, the committees give the candidates strategic advice and fund-raising assistance. They also furnish PACs and other Washington insiders with information that they can use when formulating their contribution strategies and selecting individual candidates for support.

The Hill committees help candidates in a variety of ways to raise money from individuals. They help candidates design direct-mail fund-raising letters and give them tips on how to organize fund-raising committees and events. Sometimes the committees host the events or assist in setting them up. In 1992 the NRCC introduced a new innovation in fund-raising when it employed satellite technology to help candidates raise large contributions from wealthy individuals. The committee arranged for Secretary of Housing and Urban Development Jack Kemp, House Minority Whip Newt Gingrich of Georgia, and other GOP leaders to address contributors at Republican fund-raisers across the country from the party's national convention in Houston. These satellite broadcasts helped bring in large sums of money.

The committees also steer large contributions from wealthy individuals, PACs, or members of Congress to needy candidates. It is illegal for the parties to "earmark" checks they receive from individuals or PACs for specific candidates, but committee members and staff can suggest to contributors that they consider giving to one of the candidates on the committee's watch list. The NRSC has pioneered new ways of brokering money to congressional candidates. During the 1990 election, the committee expanded its role as a financial conduit by creating an independent, elite fund-raising committee called the "Inner Circle" to raise money for Republican Senate candidates. The Inner Circle offered Republicans who contributed $1,000 a year the opportunity to attend briefings that featured addresses by GOP senators and other party leaders. Because the Inner Circle was technically an independent committee, these contributions did not count against the limits for NRSC contributions. The committee raised roughly $2 million, most of which was distributed to candidates in closely contested elections, before being disbanded following a legal challenge.[53]

The Democrats also use innovative approaches to brokering individual contributions to congressional candidates in competitive races. Some of the most successful innovations have been introduced by DCCC chair Vic Fazio. In 1992 Fazio succeeded in getting his House Democratic colleagues to contribute money from their campaign funds to the DCCC and to Democratic candidates in close contests. He raised more than $600,000 from House Democrats to help retire the DCCC's 1990 election debt.[54] Following the death of Republican House member Silvio Conte in February 1990, Fazio was able to convince more than fifty Democratic House members to contribute to Massachusetts state senator John Olver's special election campaign against Republican Steven Pierce. Fazio and the

DCCC also played a critical role in steering in excess of $300,000 in contributions from Washington PACs, lobbyists, and other insiders to Olver's successful effort.[55]

The Hill committees assist candidates in raising PAC money in two ways. First, they give candidates the knowledge and tools needed to raise PAC money. The committees help candidates design "PAC kits" they can use to introduce themselves to members of the PAC community.[56] Candidates can obtain from the Hill committees lists of PACs that include each PAC's address, the name of a contact person, and a mailing label which can be used to send a solicitation. The lists indicate how much cash each PAC has on hand, so candidates will not waste their time soliciting committees that have no money and will not take "no" for an answer when a PAC manager claims poverty but still has funds.

The committees also tutor candidates on how to approach PACs for money. Kristine Wolfe, the NRCC's director of coalitions and PACs, explains that most nonincumbents need to be coached on how to fill out the questionnaires that many PACs use to learn about candidates' issue positions. According to Wolfe, giving an answer that is only marginally different from a PAC's stand on a core issue can cost a candidate a contribution, particularly if an opponent's position appears to be closer to the PAC's. Moreover, answering a question in a misleading way can earn a candidate a reputation as a "chameleon" and can freeze prospects for raising PAC money once the managers of different PACs confer with one another.[57]

The Hill committees also assist candidates in designing the grassroots part of their PAC fund-raising strategies. They instruct candidates on how to win endorsements from state-level branches of federated PACs and how to build coalitions among local PAC donors. As Wolfe's assistant, Matt Niemeyer, explains, "It's difficult for the manager of a national PAC to say no to a request [for a contribution] when it comes from a PAC's state affiliate or local donors." [58]

The second way the parties help candidates raise money from PACs is through manipulating the informational environment in which PACs make their decisions about contributions. This is one of the major activities of the campaign committees' PAC directors. A PAC director's major goals are to channel the flow of PAC money toward their party's most competitive congressional contenders and away from their opponents. This is an especially difficult task to perform for House challengers and open-seat candidates because they are largely unknown to the PAC community and unable to use the powers of incumbency to leverage PAC money. Some junior House members also need to have attention called to their races. The campaign committees often call on party leaders, committee and subcommittee chairs, or ranking members to attend a candidate's fund-raising event or to telephone a PAC manager on the candidate's behalf. Former DCCC chair Tony Coelho was legendary for his ability to "fry the fat" out of PACs.[59] All four Hill committees make meeting rooms and telephones available to facilitate PAC fund-raising, which cannot be conducted legally on Capitol grounds.

The Hill committees use a variety of approaches to circulating information about House and Senate elections to PACs and other potential contributors. The committees' campaign expenditures are one such form of information that can have a tremendous impact on the fund-raising prospects of nonincumbents. Large party expenditures on behalf of a candidate draw the attention of PACs, wealthy individuals, and political journalists who give contributions or write about congressional elections.[60]

Receptions, often referred to as "meet and greets," serve similar purposes. They give candidates, especially nonincumbents, an opportunity to ask PAC managers for contributions. The Hill committees routinely hold meet and greets in their headquarters buildings. In presidential election years, they are also held at the parties' national conventions.

The committees mail watch lists and information packages that evaluate individual candidates' electoral prospects and financial needs to supportive PACs. Other mailings provide details on candidates' races, including poll results, press clippings, endorsements, campaign highlights, and revelations about problems experienced by their opponents. These mailings commonly range from ten-to-twenty pages in length and are sent to approximately one thousand PACs. During the heat of the election season, the committees send out mailings on a weekly or biweekly basis.

In addition to mailings and meet and greets, the committees hold briefings to discuss their opportunity races and to inform PAC managers about their candidates' progress. These briefings provide PAC managers with the opportunity to ask Hill committee staffers questions about specific campaigns and afford PAC managers an opportunity to discuss their contribution strategies with one another. PAC briefings are an important forum for networking among campaign finance elites.

The campaign committees' PAC directors and party leaders spend a tremendous amount of time making telephone calls on behalf of their most competitive and financially needy candidates. Some of these calls are made to PAC managers who are recognized leaders of PAC networks. The DCCC and DSCC, for example, work closely with the NCEC and the AFL-CIO's Committee on Political Education (COPE); their GOP counterparts work closely with the Business-Industry Political Action Committee (BIPAC). The committees encourage these "lead" PACs to endorse the party's top contestants and to communicate their support to other PACs in their networks.

Finally, the Hill committees send streams of communications to the editors of the *Cook Political Report*, the *Rothenberg Political Report*, and other political newsletters that are heavily subscribed to by PACs. These newsletters handicap congressional races and provide information on developments in campaigns across the country. Party officials undertake tremendous efforts to keep the newsletter editors abreast of the latest developments in their candidates' campaigns, speaking with them several times a week. Charlie Cook and Stuart Rothenberg, who edit the newsletters bearing their names, confirm that Hill committee officials are major sources of their political information.

By helping candidates understand how the PAC community works and by furnishing PACs with information about candidates, the congressional and senatorial campaign committees have become important intermediaries in the fund-raising process. They have entered into symbiotic relationships with some PACs, enabling them to become brokers between candidates and PACs.[61] The relationships are based largely on honest and reliable exchanges of information about the prospects of individual candidates.[62] Hill committee officials recognize that any attempt to mislead a PAC manager by providing inaccurate information could harm their committee's credibility and undercut its ability to help its candidates.[63]

Hill committee communications to PACs are somewhat controversial because they can harm as well as help an individual candidate's fund-raising prospects. Candidates who receive their Hill committee's endorsement derive significant advantages in raising PAC money; nonincumbents who do not are usually unable to collect significant funds from PACs. PAC managers have been known to justify refusing a contribution request because a nonincumbent was not included on a Hill committee's watch list.

The Coordinated Campaign

Not all of the campaign assistance that House and Senate candidates get from parties comes from Washington, and not all of it is given by the parties' congressional and senatorial campaign committees. Some state and local party committees give candidates assistance in a few of the aspects of campaigning discussed above, but these committees tend to be less influential than the Hill committees in areas requiring technical expertise, in-depth research, or connections with Washington PACs and consultants.[64] State and local party committees do, however, provide congressional candidates with substantial help in grass-roots campaigning. Most state committees help fund and organize registration and get-out-the-vote drives, set up telephone banks, and send campaign literature to voters.[65] Many local parties conduct these same activities as well as canvass door-to-door, distribute posters and lawn signs, put up billboards, and engage in other types of campaign field work.[66]

Some of this activity is organized and paid for by the state and local party organizations themselves; however, a significant portion of it is funded by party committees in Washington, D.C., under the guise of the "coordinated campaign." The Democratic national, congressional, and senatorial campaign committees spent more than $33.5 million on coordinated campaigning in 1992. This includes hard and soft money used to purchase party-focused television and radio advertisements, targeting studies, and polls as well as $13.6 million that the committees transferred to their state affiliates for election activities and party-building programs. It also includes an additional $19.9 million that Democratic party organizations in the nation's capital spent on campaign activities conducted jointly with Democratic state and local party organizations. The RNC, NRCC, and NRSC spent even more, transferring more than $17.7 million to GOP state party organizations and spending an additional $22.8 million on joint campaign activities.[67] Most national party money is spent in states and localities that are critical to the parties' presidential, senatorial, or congressional efforts. These expenditures enable party organizations in the nation's capital to make financial contributions to locally executed, grass-roots activities designed to benefit the entire party ticket.

The Impact of Party Services

When asked to rate the importance of campaign assistance from local, state, and national party organizations, PACs, unions, and other groups in aspects of campaigning requiring professional expertise or in-depth research, candidates and campaign aides involved in the 1992 House elections ranked their party's Hill committee first. With respect to campaign management, about one-third of all House candidates and campaign aides consider their congressional campaign committee to be at least moderately helpful.[68] Roughly 40 percent gave similar assessments for Hill committee assistance in gauging public opinion. Over half of all House contestants report that committee issue research plays at least a moderately important role in their campaigns, with 20 percent describing it as very important and another 11 percent asserting that it is extremely important. More than 40 percent of the House candidates, mostly challengers, also rely heavily on their congressional campaign committee for opposition research. About 30 percent of all House campaigns receive significant DCCC or NRCC help in developing their communications. Slightly more candidates and campaign aides find that Hill committees are moderately important to their fund-raising efforts; however, campaigners report receiving greater fund-raising assistance from PACs and other interest groups. The DCCC and NRCC are also rated lower than state and local party organizations and interest groups in grass-roots activities, reflecting their lack of direct involvement in these aspects of campaigning.

The evaluations by House candidates and campaign aides indicate that most congressional campaign committee help is given to candidates in close races, reflecting the parties' goal of winning as many seats in Congress as possible. The evaluations also show that Hill committee assistance is generally more important to hopeful challengers and open-seat prospects than to incumbents in jeopardy, reflecting the fact that incumbents' electoral difficulties are rarely the result of an inability to raise money, assemble a campaign organization, or communicate with voters.[69]

Nevertheless, the Hill committees go to great lengths to protect their endangered incumbents. The DCCC, for example, played an important role in helping Rep. Pat Williams in his incumbent-versus-incumbent match-up with Republican Ron Marlenee in Montana's at-large district in 1992. The committee gave Williams an extensive issue and opposition research package and helped produce his television commercials. Because the committee distributes the costs associated with producing these services among many candidates, the DCCC was able to assign a monetary value of just $48,532 to the campaign contributions and coordinated expenditures it gave to Williams, which was well below their true market value.[70] The NRCC was just as heavily involved in the campaign waged by Marlenee, reporting a total $79,635 in contributions and coordinated expenditures.[71] This figure also underestimates the market value of the services that the committee provided. Moreover, the figures for DCCC and NRCC spending do not include the help they gave the candidates in setting up their campaign organizations, hiring consultants, raising PAC money, and planning and implementing their campaigns. A general consultant would charge tens of thousands of dollars for this help, but the congressional campaign committees' staffs provide it to candidates in close races for free.

Most Senate candidates and campaign aides give evaluations of Hill committee assistance that are as favorable as those given by House candidates even though the DSCC and NRSC staff are typically less involved in formulating or implementing candidates' campaign strategies than are their House counterparts.[72] Instead, senatorial campaign committee staffs give candidates advice, campaign contributions, and election services purchased from political consultants. They also help candidates collect money from PACs and wealthy contributors. The senatorial campaign committees are rated above any other group in every area of campaigning except in providing information about voters, voter mobilization, and volunteer recruitment, where state and local party organizations and interest groups are ranked higher. The NRSC, which is by far the richer of the two senatorial campaign committees, plays a bigger role in Senate campaigns than does its Democratic rival. The gap between the Democrats' and Republicans' senatorial and congressional committees has shrunk in recent years, but a Republican advantage persists.

Notes

1. See Frank J. Sorauf, "Political Parties and Political Action Committees: Two Life Cycles," *Arizona Law Review* 22 (1980): 445-464; Paul S. Herrnson, *Party Campaigning in the 1980s* (Cambridge, Mass.: Harvard University Press, 1988), chapters 2 and 3.
2. Joseph A. Schlesinger, "The New American Political Party," *American Political Science Review* 79 (1985): 1151-1169; Paul S. Herrnson and David Menefee-Libey, "The Dynamics of Party Organizational Development," *Midsouth Political Science Journal* 11 (1990): 3-30.
3. Herrnson, *Party Campaigning,* chapter 2.
4. The term "Hill committees" probably originates from the fact that the congressional and senatorial campaign committees were originally located in congressional office space on Capitol Hill.
5. These figures include only "hard" dollars, which can be spent directly in federal campaigns. Federal Election Commission, "Democrats Narrow Financial Gap in 1991-92," press release, March 11, 1993.
6. These figures do not include staff employed by the candidates' campaign organizations.
7. Gary C. Jacobson, "Party Organization and Campaign Resources in 1982," *Political Science Quarterly* 100 (1985-1986): 604-625.
8. Paul S. Herrnson, "National Party Decision Making, Strategies, and Resource Distribution in Congressional Elections," *Western Political Quarterly* 42 (1989): 301-323.
9. Herrnson and Menefee-Libey, "The Dynamics of Party Organizational Development," 13-16; Brooks Jackson, *Honest Graft: Big Money and the American Political Process* (New York: Alfred A. Knopf, 1988), 286-290.
10. Gary C. Jacobson and Samuel Kernell, *Strategy and Choice in Congressional Elections* (New Haven, Conn.: Yale University Press, 1983), 39-43,76-84.
11. The information on committee strategy, decision making, and targeting in 1992 is drawn from personal interviews conducted before, during, and after the election cycle. Interviews were held with several officials at the congressional and senatorial campaign committees, including Rob Engel, national political director of the DCCC; Eric Wilson, deputy director of the DCCC; Tom Cole, executive director of the NRCC; and Kris Wolfe, director of PACs and coalitions of the NRCC. On committee strategy and decision making in previous elections, see Jacobson and Kernell, *Strategy and Choice,* 76-84; Paul S. Herrnson, "National Party Decision Making, Strategies, and Resource Distribution in Congressional Elections."
12. *Thornburg v. Gingles,* 478 U.S. 30 (1986).
13. Kathleen A. Frankovic, "Public Opinion in the 1992 Campaign," in *The Elections of 1992,* ed. Gerald M. Pomper (Chatham, N.J.: Chatham House, 1993), 111-112.
14. Personal interviews with Rob Engel on July 23, 1992, and February 23, 1993, and with Tom Cole on December 19, 1991, October 14, 1992, and February 23, 1993. See also the commentary of Les Frances, executive director of the DCCC, in *Machine Politics, Sound Bites, & Nostalgia,* ed. Michael Margolis and John Green (Lanham, Md.: University Press of America, 1993), 58.
15. Herrnson, "National Party Decision-Making."
16. Paul S. Herrnson, "Campaign Professionalism and Fundraising in Congressional Elections," *Journal of Politics* 54 (1992): 859-870.
17. Reps. Mike Synar (D-Okla.) and Barbara Kennelly (D-Conn.) took the lead in

recruiting female candidates for the DCCC. Rep. Jerry Lewis (R-Calif.) assumed this role for the NRCC.

18. Robert Biersack and Paul S. Herrnson, "Political Parties and the Year of the Woman," in *The Year of the Woman? Myths and Realities,* ed. Elizabeth Adell Cook, Sue Thomas, and Clyde Wilcox (Boulder: Westview Press, 1994), 173-174.

19. Presentation to students in the University of Maryland's Capitol Hill Internship Program, October 18, 1992.

20. These are considered separate elections under the FECA. Party committees, however, usually only give contributions to general election candidates.

21. The limits for Senate elections are higher than those for House elections. Presumably, the authors of the FECA believed that parties should be allowed to spend more in Senate elections since they typically involve larger constituencies than House elections.

22. Coordinated expenditures are occasionally referred to as 441a(d) spending, after the provision of the FECA that authorizes them.

23. The coordinated expenditure limit for states with only one House member was originally set at $20,000 and reached $55,240 in 1992.

24. See Herrnson, *Party Campaigning,* 43-44.

25. Party committees can also give "in-kind" services in lieu of cash contributions; however, they are more likely to use the coordinated expenditure route.

26. In 1982, for example, the NRCC spent just under $7.5 million on House elections, and the DCCC spent a total of $761,000. See also Frank J. Sorauf, *Inside Campaign Finance: Myths and Realities* (New Haven, Conn.: Yale University Press, 1992), figure 4.2.

27. The DCCC transferred about half as much money to Democratic state committees, and most of the money it transferred was hard money. Hard money consists of those funds that are raised within the FECA's guidelines and can be legally spent for or directly on behalf of federal candidates. "Soft" money flows outside the FECA's contribution and spending limits. Soft money comes about from a loophole in the law by which the FECA only regulates the money that is spent directly in conjunction with federal elections, leaving money spent in state and local elections and on "generic"party activities— such as registration and get-out-the-vote drives, bumper stickers and buttons, and party organizational development—that benefit a party's entire election ticket largely unregulated. On soft money see Elizabeth Drew, *Politics and Money: The New Road to Corruption* (New York: Macmillan, 1983), especially p. 15; and Frank J. Sorauf, *Money in American Elections* (Glenview, Ill.: Scott, Foresman/Little, Brown, 1988), 148-149, 320-324. The information on party transfers is from Federal Election Commission, "Democrats Narrow Financial Gap in 1991-92."

28. The transfers include both hard and soft money. See Federal Election Commission, "Democrats Narrow Financial Gap in 1991-92."

29. The figures include spending by all three national party organizations because they are subject to a common limit and thus must be made in coordination with one another. Crossover expenditures, such as those made by the senatorial campaign committees in House campaigns, usually consist of polls that are shared among House and Senate candidates. Separating Hill committee spending from all national party spending barely affects the figures in Table 4-2. Similarly, the patterns for the distribution of all party money, including state and local committee expenditures, are virtually identical to those in the table.

30. On the distribution of party funds in 1982 see Jacobson, "Party Organization and Campaign Resources," 604-625. On the distribution of party funds in 1984 see Herrnson, "National Party Decision-Making," 301-323.

31. Herrnson, "National Party Decision-Making," 301-323.

32. Rob Engel, telephone interview, August 2, 1993.

33. All of the open-seat Senate races are classified as prospects both because of their competitiveness and the fact that there were so few of them.

34. In some cases, the congressional campaign committees require candidates to use the services of one of their preferred consultants as a precondition for committee support. Although these cases are rare, they can arouse the ire of both candidates and political consultants. See Herrnson, *Party Campaigning,* 56-57; Stephen E. Frantzich, *Political Parties in the Technological Age* (New York: Longman, 1989), 82, 87-88; and Barbara G. Salmore and Stephen A. Salmore, *Candidates, Parties, and Campaigns: Electoral Politics in America,* 2d ed. (Washington, D.C.: CQ Press), 240-241.

35. See, for example, Jack Anderson and Michael Binstein, "Democrats: Playing Not to Lose," *Washington Post,* July 11, 1993, C7.

36. National Republican Congressional Committee, "NRCC Report '92: A Report Outlining Services and Activities of 1992" (Washington, D.C.: National Republican Congressional Committee, 1992), 16.

37. See especially Marjorie Randon Hershey, *Running for Office: The Political Education of Campaigners* (Chatham, N.J.: Chatham House, 1984), 215-216.

38. The allocatable costs of the polls varied by their type and size and by when they were released to the candidates. FEC regulations specify that candidates must pay 100 percent of the costs if they receive the poll results within 15 days of when the poll was completed, 50 percent if they receive them between 16 and 60 days, and 5 percent if the results are received between 61 and 180 days. After 180 days, a poll can be given to a candidate free of charge. General Services Administration, *Title 11-Federal Elections,* section 2 U.S.C. 106.4, pp. 77-78.

39. Kevin O'Donnell, director of survey research, NRCC, personal interview, June 11, 1992.

40. These figures probably underestimate the assistance distributed by the national parties because they include only campaign services that were given out as coordinated expenditures, exclude the small number of services that were given out as in-kind contributions and for other reasons described in the text. The figures are from Dwight Morris and Murielle E. Gamache, *Handbook of Campaign Spending* (Washington, D.C.: Congressional Quarterly, 1994), table 6-3.

41. See note 40.

42. Ibid., table 6-1.

43. Paul S. Herrnson, "The National Committee for an Effective Congress: Ideology, Partisanship, and Electoral Innovation," in *Risky Business? PAC Decision Making and Strategy in Congressional Elections,* ed. Robert Biersack, Paul S. Herrnson, and Clyde Wilcox (Armonk, N.Y.: M. E. Sharpe, 1994), chapter 4.

44. Democratic Caucus, U.S. House of Representatives, *Investing in America's Future,* ed. Paul S. Herrnson (Washington, D.C.: U.S. House of Representatives, 1990); *Taking Charge of America's Future,* ed. Kelly D. Patterson (Washington, D.C.: U.S. House of Representatives, 1991).

45. National Republican Congressional Committee, "NRCC Report '92," 26.

46. A small number of Senate candidates and other party officials also use the committee's media equipment.
47. Herrnson, *Party Campaigning*, 63.
48. See note 40.
49. See note 40.
50. Ibid., table 6-1.
51. Ibid., table 6-3.
52. Ibid., table 6-1.
53. Chuck Alston, "If Money Talks, Mr. Smith Won't Go to Washington," *Congressional Quarterly Weekly Report,* November 3, 1990, 3758; and Federal Election Commission, "Republicans Maintain 4-1 Spending Edge Despite Fundraising Decline over Prior Cycles," press release, November 1, 1990.
54. "DCCC Mid-Year Report," July 1992, 4.
55. Ibid.
56. PAC kits typically include information about the candidate's personal background, political experience, campaign staff, support in the district, endorsements, issue positions, and campaign strategy.
57. Kristine Wolfe, director of PACs and coalitions, NRCC, personal interview, June 8, 1992.
58. Matt Niemeyer, deputy PAC director, NRCC, personal interview, June 11, 1992.
59. For an excellent account of how Coelho solicited PAC contributions on behalf of other candidates, see Jackson, *Honest Graft,* 69-70, 77-81, 90-93.
60. Herrnson, *Party Campaigning*, 69-71.
61. Larry J. Sabato, *PAC Power: Inside the World of Political Action Committees* (New York: W. W. Norton, 1984), 144-149; Herrnson, *Party Campaigning;* Jackson, *Honest Graft,* 66-91.
62. In some cases the information exchange is a bilateral. The NCEC, BIPAC, and other "lead" and large, institutionalized PACs have information that they share with the committees. See Robert Biersack, "Introduction," in *Risky Business?* ed. Biersack, Wilcox, and Herrnson.
63. Herrnson, *Party Campaigning*, note 26, p. 158.
64. This generalization is drawn from questions 29, 31, 32, 33, 34, and 36 of the 1992 Congressional Campaign Study. See also Herrnson, *Party Campaigning in the 1980s,* chapter 4.
65. Cornelius P. Cotter, James L. Gibson, John F. Bibby, and Robert J. Huckshorn, *Party Organizations in American Politics* (Pittsburgh: University of Pittsburgh Press, 1989), 20-25; Cornelius P. Cotter and John F. Bibby, "Institutional Development and the Thesis of Party Decline," *Political Science Quarterly* 95 (Spring 1980): 1-27; "Party Organization at the State Level," in *The Parties Respond: Changes in the American Party System,* ed. L. Sandy Maisel (Boulder, Colo.: Westview Press, 1990), 21-40.
66. On local party organizations and voter mobilization see Cotter, et al., *Party Organizations in American Politics,* 45-54; Herrnson, *Party Campaigning,* 102-106; Robert Huckfeldt and John Sprague, "Political Parties and Electoral Mobilization: Political Structure, Social Structure, and the Party Canvass," *American Political Science Review* 86 (1992): 70-86; Gregory A. Caldeira, Samuel C. Patterson, and Gregory A. Markko, "The Mobilization of Voters in Congressional Elections," *Journal of Politics* 47 (1985): 490-509; Michael A. Krassa, "Context and the Canvass: The Mechanisms of Interactions," *Political Behavior* 10 (1988): 233-246; Peter W. Wielhower and Brad Lockerbie,

"Party Contacting and Political Participation, 1952-90," *American Journal of Political Science* 38 (1994): 211-229.

67. Figures calculated from "Democrats Narrow Financial GAP in 1991-1992," FEC press release.

68. This generalization is drawn from questions 29 through 36 of the 1992 Congressional Campaign Study.

69. Incumbents rarely have difficulty raising money, and, as Gary C. Jacobson notes, their fund-raising and spending are driven largely by their perception of the threat a challenger poses to their reelection. See Jacobson, *The Politics of Congressional Elections*, 3d ed. (New York: HarperCollins, 1992), 53; and Jacobson, *Money in Congressional Elections* (New Haven, Conn.: Yale University Press, 1980), 113-123.

70. State and local Democratic Party organizations spent an additional $50,764 in connection with Williams's campaign.

71. State and local Republican committees contributed an additional $660 to Marlenee's campaign.

72. The generalizations for the Senate campaigns are based on a questionnaire that is similar to the one in the appendix but is tailored to Senate elections. It is difficult to make generalizations about Senate campaigns because of the small number of Senate elections that occur in one election cycle, because of the tremendous diversity in the size and composition of the states, and because a different one-third of all Senate seats are up for election every two years. The fact that only twenty-eight (41 percent) of the Senate campaigns returned completed questionnaires is additional cause for concern. In order to improve the strength of the findings about Senate campaigns, the generalizations in this section are based on observations that span the 1984, 1986, and 1992 election cycles.

Chapter 5

The Interests Campaign

Organized interests, pejoratively referred to as "special" interests, have always been involved in American elections. Currently, they rely on political action committees (PACs) to carry out most of their campaign activities. A PAC can be best understood as the electoral arm of an organized interest. Interest groups form PACs to give campaign assistance to federal, or in some cases state or local, candidates with the hope of influencing election outcomes, the formation of public policy, or both. Most PACs have a sponsoring, or "parent," organization, such as a corporation, labor union, trade association, or other group. However, ideological and other "nonconnected" PACs are sometimes themselves the organizing agency.

The formation and campaign activities of any given PAC can best be understood by focusing on the interest or interests the PAC claims to represent, the goals it seeks to achieve, its history, organizational structure, resources, and decision-making process. Most PAC activity, like that of interest groups in general, is pragmatic. That pragmatism can be traced to the desire to advance a narrow set of goals by gaining access to and trying to influence powerful lawmakers. PAC activity is usually linked to a parent group's lobbying efforts. The activity of a select group of PACs, mostly nonconnected committees, can be explained by broader ideological goals, including a desire to change the composition of Congress.

This chapter examines the growth and development of the PAC community in Washington and the roles that PACs play in congressional elections. It discusses the motives that underlie PAC activity, strategies, methods of selecting candidates for support, and the distribution of contributions, independent expenditures, and other forms of campaign assistance.

The Rise of PACs

Interest groups have endorsed candidates, mobilized voters, and funded campaigns since the earliest days of the Republic. It was not until 1943, however, that the first political action committee, the Committee on Political Education (COPE), was founded by the Congress of Industrial Organizations (forerunner of the AFL-CIO).[1]

The Federal Election Campaign Act of 1974 (FECA) set the scene for the PAC explosion of the mid-1970s.[2] One of the goals of the act was to dilute the influence of moneyed interests on federal elections. The act limited individuals to a maximum contribution of $1,000 per candidate at each stage of the election—primary, general election, and runoff (if a runoff is required)—for a total of $3,000. It also imposed an aggregate limit of $25,000 on an individual's contributions to all federal candidates, parties, and PACs annually. Corporations, labor unions, trade associations, cooperatives, and other organized groups were barred from giving contributions directly to candidates for federal office. By limiting the size of the contributions that a candidate could collect from any one source, the act encouraged candidates to solicit smaller donations from a broader array of interests and individuals, including those of relatively modest means. The act also encouraged many interest groups to establish PACs. While never mentioning the term "political action committee," the FECA allowed for "a multicandidate committee" that raises money from at least fifty donors and spends it on at least five candidates for federal office to contribute up to $5,000 per candidate at each stage of the election.[3]

The FECA encouraged people to contribute to PACs by setting a low ceiling on individual contributions to candidates. The law's $1,000 ceiling on direct individual contributions to candidates and $5,000 ceiling on contributions to PACs make PAC contributions a popular vehicle among wealthy individuals who wish to use their money to influence congressional elections. The law also includes provisions outlining from whom PACs may solicit funds. Labor PACs, for example, may only solicit their members, whereas corporate PACs can solicit stockholders, executives, and administrative personnel.

In November 1975, in an advisory opinion written for Sun Oil Company, the Federal Election Commission (FEC) counseled the company that it could pay the overhead and solicitation costs of its PAC, thereby freeing the PAC to spend all of the funds it collected from donors on federal elections.[4] The SunPAC decision clarified a grey area in the law and, in the process, made PACs a much more attractive vehicle for collecting and disbursing funds. The advisory ruling contributed to an ex-

Figure 5-1   The Growth in the Number of PACs, 1974–1992

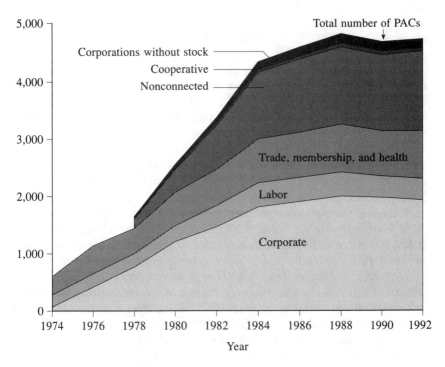

Source: Federal Election Commission.

plosion in the number of PACs that lasted from the mid-1970s to the mid-1980s.

The Supreme Court's ruling in *Buckley v. Valeo*,[5] allowing PACs to make unlimited independent expenditures (expenditures made without the knowledge or consent of a candidate or his or her campaign organization) in congressional and presidential elections, further stimulated the growth of federal PACs.[6] Both the FEC advisory opinion and the Supreme Court decision created new opportunities for organized groups to participate in politics. They encouraged a wide range of political leaders, business entrepreneurs, and others to form new PACs.

Between 1974 and the 1992 elections, the PAC community grew from just over 600 to 4,729 committees (see Figure 5-1).[7] Most of the growth occurred in the business sector, with corporate PACs growing in number from 89 in 1974 to 1,930 in 1992. Labor unions, many of which already had PACs in 1974, created the fewest new PACs, increasing in number from 201 to 372. The centralization of the labor movement into a relatively small number of unions greatly limited the growth of labor PACs. In addition, three new species of political action committee—the non-

Figure 5-2 The Growth of PAC Contributions in Congressional Elections

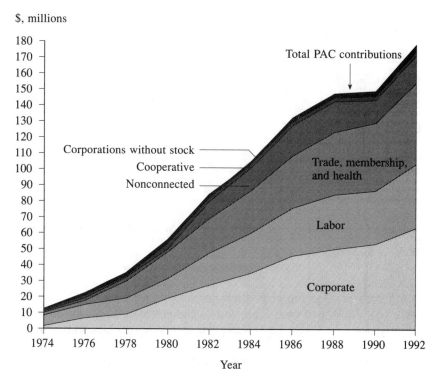

$, millions

Source: Federal Election Commission.

connected PAC (mostly ideological and issue-oriented groups), and PACs whose sponsors are either cooperatives or corporations without stock, such as the Southern Minnesota Sugar Cooperative and the Aircraft Owners and Pilots Association—were identified in 1977 but accounted for almost 1,600 PACs twenty-five years later.[8]

The growth in the number of PACs was accompanied by a tremendous increase in their activity. PAC contributions to congressional candidates grew from $12.5 million in 1974 to just under $178.3 million in 1992.[9] Corporate and other business-related PACs accounted for most of that growth (see Figure 5-2). In 1992 corporate PACs accounted for 36 percent of all PAC contributions to congressional candidates, followed by trade PACs, which accounted for 29 percent. PACs sponsored by cooperatives and corporations without stock contributed an additional 3 percent of the total amount spent by all political action committees. Union PACs gave 22 percent of all contributions received by congressional candidates, and nonconnected PACs accounted for the final 10 percent.

Table 5-1   The Concentration of PAC Contributions, 1991-1992

	PAC's total contributions					
	Over $250,000	$100,001-$250,000	$50,001-$100,000	$5,001-$50,000	$1-$5,000	$0
Percent of all PACs	3	5	6	28	22	35
(N)	(154)	(244)	(295)	(1,301)	(1,058)	(1,677)
Percent of all PAC contributions ($, millions)	55	20	11	13	1	0
	(102.9)	(38.1)	(20.9)	(24.6)	(2.1)	(0)

Source: Compiled by the author from Federal Election Commission, "PAC Activity Rebounds in 1991-92 Election Cycle: Unusual Nature of Contests Seen as Reason," press release, April 19, 1993.

Note: Includes contributions given in 1991 for debt retirement of 1990 campaigns, contributions given to special election candidates, and contributions given to Senate candidates who will be up for election in 1994 and 1996.

A very small group of PACs is responsible for most PAC activity. A mere 154 PACs, just over 3 percent of the entire PAC community, contributed roughly $103 million between 1991 and 1992, representing approximately 55 percent of all PAC money given in that election (see Table 5-1). Each of these committees, which are clearly the "big guns" of the PAC community, gave more than $250,000 to federal candidates. These include PACs sponsored by such corporations, trade associations, and unions as United Parcel Service, the National Association of Realtors, and the National Education Association, as well as nonconnected PACs such as EMILY's List, the National Abortion and Reproductive Rights Action League (NARAL), and Jesse Helms's National Congressional Club.

Another 5 percent of all PACs are "major players," each having contributed between $100,001 and $250,000 to congressional candidates in 1992. These committees, which include American Express's PAC, the International Longshoremen and Warehousemen's Union PAC, the National Right to Life PAC, and Washington PAC (or WASHPAC, a pro-Israel group), accounted for just over 20 percent of all PAC contributions. The big guns and major players are particularly influential because their wealth allows them to contribute to virtually every candidate whose election is of importance to them.

The "players" are those PACs that have the resources to give a significant contribution to many but not all of the candidates they wish to support. These PACs, which include the Brown and Williamson Tobacco

Employees' PAC, the Distilled Spirits Council PAC, the National Air Traffic Controllers' Association PAC, and the Conservative Victory Committee (CVC), each contributed between $50,001 and $100,000 in 1992, accounting for 11 percent of all PAC contributions.

The contributions of the next group of PACs, which might be labeled the "junior varsity," are clearly constrained by their size. These PACs each contributed between $5,001 and $50,000. They comprise 28 percent of the PAC community and gave almost 13 percent of all PAC contributions. Their donations tend to be significantly smaller than those of the larger PACs, and they find it impossible to give money to every candidate they wish to support. The managers of these PACs, such as the AMWAY PAC, the American Association of Publishers (AAP) PAC, the National Federation of Federal Employees (NFFE) PAC, and Republicans for Choice PAC, commonly have to answer requests for contributions by stating that they support the candidate and would like to give a contribution but don't have the money.

The next group, the "small fry," each gave between $1 and $5,000, accounting for just over 1 percent of all PAC contributions in 1992. They include the Lone Star Industries PAC, the Association of Independent Television Stations PAC, and the Committee of Concerned Italian Americans. These committees, which comprise about 22 percent of the PAC community, play a marginal role in the funding of congressional elections.

Finally, there are 1,677 inactive PACs, which gave no money in the 1992 elections. Of these, 910 are, for all practical purposes, defunct.[10] Although they registered with the FEC, they spent no money to collect contributions, pay off debts, or cover the costs of committee administration over the course of the 1992 election cycle.

Strategy, Decision Making, and Targeting

PAC goals and strategies are more diverse than those of the two major parties. Some PACs follow ideological strategies designed to increase the number of legislators who share their political views. These PACs, like political parties, view congressional elections as opportunities to alter the composition of Congress and view the electoral process as their primary vehicle for changing or reinforcing the direction of public policy. These PACs give money to incumbents, challengers, and open-seat candidates who share their broad ideology or positions on specific, often emotionally charged issues such as abortion.[11]

Ideological PACs give most of their contributions to candidates in close elections, where the PACs have the biggest chance of affecting an election outcome. However, some of these committees also make contributions and independent expenditures in connection with uncompetitive contests in order to attract attention to themselves or to a politician who shares the PAC's views. Gaining visibility for themselves and their views is important to many of these PACs because it helps them raise money.

PACs following ideological strategies rarely give money to members of Congress for the sake of securing access to the legislative process. The issues these PACs support are often linked to values so fundamental that legislators would not be expected to change their views in response to a contribution or visit by a lobbyist. Many of these PACs, and some others, require candidates to complete questionnaires that elicit their views on issues prior to giving a contribution.

Other types of PACs pursue "access" strategies designed to provide the group with the ability to gain at least an audience with members of Congress.[12] These PACs view elections pragmatically. For them, an election is a prime opportunity to shore up relations with members of Congress who work on legislation that is of importance to their parent organizations. Elections give these PACs the opportunity to create goodwill with powerful legislators or at least to minimize the enmity of legislators who disagree with them. Elections thus lay the groundwork for later lobbying efforts.

A PAC that follows an access strategy is likely to contribute most of its money to incumbents. Members of the House and Senate who chair committees or subcommittees, occupy leadership positions, or are policy entrepreneurs with influence over narrow pieces of legislation are likely to be given large contributions regardless of the competitiveness of their contests.[13] In fact, many access-oriented PACs give contributions to legislators who do not even have opponents. Giving to incumbents enables these PACs to accomplish their goal of ensuring access while also meeting such organizational imperatives as backing a large number of winners and giving money to candidates who represent districts that contain many of the PAC's supporters.

Access-oriented PACs also give significant sums to candidates for open seats. Most of these candidates have good chances of winning but need large amounts of money to run competitive campaigns. Giving an open-seat prospect a large contribution is useful to an access-oriented PAC because it can create tremendous goodwill, laying the groundwork for productive relations with a future member of Congress.

Access-oriented PACs tend to ignore challengers because most of them are likely to lose. Giving a challenger a contribution is often considered a waste of money, and such a contribution could also lead to serious repercussions from an incumbent. Moreover, backing challengers has a high probability of reducing a PAC's win-loss record and could lead to criticism of the PAC's manager.

PACs that use access strategies rarely make independent expenditures for or against candidates because of the publicity these expenditures can generate. Independent expenditures could be harmful to a corporate PAC, for example, if they anger congressional incumbents, upset some of the PAC's donors, or call undue attention to the group. Such publicity could lead to charges that a group is trying to buy influence and could hinder the achievement of its goals.

The last and largest group of PACs practice mixed strategies. They give contributions to some candidates because those candidates share the PAC's views, and they give to others because they wish to improve their access to legislators who work on policies the group deems important. Contributions motivated by the former reason are usually distributed to candidates in competitive contests—mostly to open-seat candidates, hopeful challengers, and incumbents who are in jeopardy. Contributions informed by the latter motive are given to incumbents who are in a position to influence legislation that is of importance to the PAC.

In some cases the two motives clash; for example, that happens when a highly qualified challenger who represents the PAC's views runs a competitive race against an incumbent in a position of power. In these situations PACs that use mixed strategies will usually support the incumbent, but in a few instances they will contribute to both candidates. Committees that follow mixed strategies and PACs that follow pure access strategies are less likely than ideological PACs to make independent expenditures.

PAC Strategy and the Political Environment

PACs, like most other groups and individuals involved in politics, are strategic actors that respond to their environment in ways that enable them to pursue their goals. During the 1970s most PACs used ideological strategies that followed partisan lines. They backed candidates who supported the positions adhered to by their organizational sponsors. Business-oriented PACs, including corporate and trade committees, largely supported Republican candidates. Labor organizations, which were and continue to be the most consistently partisan of all PACs, regularly gave 90 percent of their contributions to Democrats.[14] Over time, many business-oriented committees shifted from an ideological to access or mixed strategies. These PACs, with the encouragement of former DCCC chairman Tony Coelho, came to the realization that the Democrats would probably remain in firm control of the House and that it would be in their best interests to become more supportive of Democratic incumbents. As a result, many of these PACs redirected their support from Republican House challengers toward incumbents, many of whom were Democrats.[15] Perhaps the clearest strategic responses by PACs took place after partisan control of the Senate switched from the Democrats to the Republicans in 1981 and back to the Democrats in 1987. At these times, many access-seeking PACs switched their contributions to Senate candidates who belonged to the new majority party.[16]

Because of their desire to influence the composition of Congress, ideologically oriented PACs, mainly nonconnected committees, are the most likely to capitalize on the conditions peculiar to a particular election. A PAC that uses an access-seeking strategy, such as a corporate or trade committee, is less affected by electoral conditions, unless those conditions have the potential to influence its parent group's ability to meet with key legislators and their staffs.

The strategic changes in PAC behavior that occurred in the early 1980s were the result of committees learning how to participate more effectively in the electoral process and the increasing aggressiveness of fund-raising by incumbents.[17] Making strategic adjustments in anticipation of political change is difficult. The manager of an access-oriented PAC who believes that a member of Congress is likely to go from having little to major influence in a policy area, for instance, may have difficulty convincing the PAC's board of directors to raise the member's contribution from a token sum to a substantial donation. The manager's prospects of convincing the board to revamp totally its strategy because partisan control of Congress might change are extremely slim.

Given the conditions preceding the 1992 election, particularly the prospects for significant turnover in the House, a number of political observers surmised that many of the PACs that had adopted access strategies during the 1980s would return to ideological or mixed strategies. Corporate and trade PACs whose natural inclinations are to support politicians who prefer lower taxes, less government regulation, and policies designed to spur economic growth would support Republican nonincumbents who had real prospects for victory. Some of these candidates would be running in the multitude of open-seat races that were created as a result of redistricting and congressional retirements. Others would be challenging Democratic incumbents who had become vulnerable as a result of scandal, anti-Congress sentiments, or the redrawing of House districts. PAC managers who were attuned to the possibilities created by this confluence of forces may have wanted to change their committee's contribution patterns but been unable to do so because of their committee's decision-making process.

PAC Decision Making

The decision-making processes that PACs use to select individual candidates are affected by a PAC's overall strategy, wealth, organizational structure, and location.[18] Ideological PACs spend more time searching for promising challengers to support than do PACs that use access-seeking or mixed strategies. Ideological committees are also more likely than other PACs to support nonincumbents in congressional primaries. Wealthy PACs tend to spend more time searching for promising nonincumbents simply because they can afford to fund more candidates.[19] Federated PACs whose organizational affiliates are spread across the country typically have to respond to the wishes of these constituents when making contributions.[20] Nonconnected PACs and PACs that are sponsored by a single corporation or cooperative, on the other hand, are less constrained by the need to please a diverse and far-flung constituency. Committees located in the nation's capital have more information available to them about the relative competitiveness of individual races because they can plug into more communications networks than can PACs located in the hinterlands.[21]

PAC decision-making processes vary according to PACs' organizational capacities. The Realtors PAC, a large institutionalized committee with headquarters in Washington, was formed in 1969.[22] This federated PAC, which is sponsored by the National Association of Realtors (NAR), receives its money from PACs sponsored by NAR's 1,800 local affiliates and state associations located in all fifty states plus the District of Columbia, Guam, Puerto Rico, and the Virgin Islands. Realtors give donations to these affiliated PACs, which each pass 35 percent of their revenues to the national PAC. In 1992 NAR's national PAC distributed more than $2.9 million in contributions and just under $1 million in independent expenditures, making it the biggest "big gun" in that election.

The Realtors PAC utilizes a mixed strategy to advance the goals of the real estate industry. As do most other institutionalized PACs, it has explicit criteria for selecting candidates for support and uses a complex decision-making procedure. Incumbency and candidates' policy proclivities, electoral competitiveness, and local support are major factors that determine who gets a contribution. Party affiliation, ideology, and personal friendship are secondary concerns. Committee assignments, a member's voting record on real estate issues, and the ability to affect real estate interests are additional criteria used to evaluate incumbents, who are typically given preference over challengers.

The PAC's contribution decisions are made by a twenty-five-member board of trustees that is appointed by the president of the NAR. The decisions are guided by input from local realtors who interview candidates, evaluate congressional voting records and other policy-related information, assess the competitiveness of the election, consult with NAR political field staff, and then make a contribution recommendation to the Realtors PAC affiliate in their state. The state association reviews the material and then makes its recommendation to the PAC's board in Washington. PAC staff in the nation's capital prepare an analysis of every candidate who has been recommended for support by a state association, and the board then reviews the contests race-by-race. The board meets three or four times in nonelection years and up to eight times during an election year to make its contribution decisions.

Decisions on independent expenditures are made by a separate group that is also appointed by the NAR's president. Strong supporters of real estate issues who are involved in competitive races are targeted for this assistance. In deciding where to make its independent expenditures, the PAC commissions polls to evaluate the competitiveness of the election and to determine the kinds of expenditures that could be helpful in each situation. Most of the PAC's independent expenditures take the form of direct mail or mass media communications that address issues related to the price of homeownership and other real estate issues.

The decision-making process of the Realtors PAC is similar to that of other institutionalized committees, such as AT&T's PAC, the American Medical Association's PAC (AMPAC), and Clean Water Action-Vote Environment (CWAVE) PAC. It relies on a combination of factual information, local opinion, and national perspective to determine which candidates to support. The requirement that a board formally approve all recommendations is also typical of institutionalized PACs, as is the ability to conduct detailed research on individual elections. The PAC's lack of participation as either a source or a user of the information available in Washington communications networks is unusual for a PAC located in the nation's capital, but its size, federated structure, and tremendous resources enable it to make decisions with information it has collected independently of other PACs.

At the opposite end of the spectrum from the Realtors PAC are the noninstitutionalized PACs. The CVC is a fairly wealthy nonconnected ideological committee that was founded in 1987 by L. Brent Bozell to advance conservative causes and to help elect conservative candidates.[23] During the 1992 elections, the CVC contributed $95,200 to candidates for Congress; almost 90 percent of this money was given to challengers and open-seat contestants. WASHPAC, another nonconnected committee, was founded in 1980 by Morris J. Amitay, formerly the executive director of the American Israel Public Affairs Committee (AIPAC), to promote a secure Israel and strong American-Israeli relations.[24] It spent $201,500 in congressional elections in 1992, contributing the vast majority of its money to incumbents. The AAP PAC is a trade committee founded in 1973 to represent the interests of the publishing community. It is a relatively small PAC, having spent only $24,900 in 1992, all of which went to incumbents.[25] The AAP PAC is run by Dianne Rennert, who once worked for Sen. George McGovern (D-S.D.).

These three PACs—and thousands of other noninstitutionalized committees—are essentially one-person operations with one-person decision-making processes. Noninstitutionalized PACs rely primarily on personal contacts with candidates and other Washington insiders for the political information that guides their contribution decisions. The CVC's Bozell, for example, requires candidates who solicit CVC support to demonstrate their conservatism by pledging to support a balanced budget amendment, the line-item veto, and tax relief. He contacts the staffs of the Free Congress PAC, the National Right to Work PAC, and other conservative committees to learn about the competitiveness of different races.

Amitay, who started WASHPAC as a hobby, peruses candidates' speeches and press releases and incumbents' voting records and letters to constituents to gauge their support for Israel. He exchanges information about the competitiveness of different elections when meeting with other pro-Israel political activists. For Rennert, collecting the information needed to distribute AAP PAC's money is a simple task because the committee contributes almost all of its funds to incumbents who are in a position to influence legislation that affects the publishing community. She keeps abreast of developments in congressional contests through the many fund-raising events she attends or organizes. All three PAC managers are open to the suggestions of individuals who give donations to their committees, but they generally do not make contributions to candidates solely on the basis of donor suggestions.

Decision making for these PACs and multitudes of other one-person organizations can best be described as a consultative process. Their lack of formal rules and procedures allow their managers tremendous flexibility in choosing candidates for support. Their limited staff resources force the PAC managers to turn to others for much of the information they need to make contribution decisions. These PACs are in a better position than more institutionalized committees to adjust their initial strategies in response to changing electoral conditions. Of course, in the case of small committees such as the AAP's PAC, this is true only as long as their money holds out.

Between the institutionalized PACs and the small, one-person organizations are semi-institutionalized committees that possess some of the characteristics of the PACs in each of the other two groups. These PACs, which include NFFE and FHP Health Care PAC, usually have staffs of two-to-four people. The staffs are big enough to allow for a functional division of labor and to require the adoption of some concrete decision rules, but they are not big enough to rely solely on their own research when making contribution decisions. For instance, NFFE, a labor PAC that represents federal employees and regularly pursues a mixed strategy, has a three-person executive committee.[26] FHP PAC, a corporate committee that has consistently pursued an access strategy, has a two-person staff and a very active board of directors.[27] These PACs contributed $25,200 and $95,700, respectively, during the 1992 elections.

PACs with semi-institutionalized organizations typically rely on their staffs to learn where candidates stand on the issues and to collect information from other PACs and Washington-based party communities about the competitiveness of various races. NFFE collects information at meetings with the Federal Postal Coalition and other groups concerned with issues that affect federal employees. It also attends briefings held by the Democratic national, congressional, and senatorial campaign committees.[28] FHP PAC, which is located in California, gets its political intelligence from its donors, the company's Washington office, the National Association of Business PACs, the DNC, the RNC, and the four Hill committees. Both PACs and most other semi-institutionalized committees make their contribution decisions according to preestablished procedures. Many of these PACs require a board of directors to approve their general strategies but give their managers some discretion in making individual contribution decisions. These managers do not have as much flexibility as the managers of one-person committees, but they have more freedom than the managers of institutionalized PACs.

Lead PACs comprise a final group of committees. These PACs, which include the National Committee for an Effective Congress (NCEC), Business-Industry Political Action Committee (BIPAC), and Committee on Political Education (COPE), are as complex organizationally as the institutionalized PACs.[29] They are every bit as thorough in their research and decision making as are the institutionalized committees and are also motivated by ideological or policy goals. They differ from other committees in that they carry out research and select candidates for support with an eye toward influencing the decisions of other PACs. Much of the research conducted by lead PACs is oriented toward assessing the electability of individual candidates. Like the parties' congressional and senatorial campaign committees, these PACs spend tremendous time, money, and energy disseminating information about specific campaigns to other PACs. They occupy central positions in the networks of PACs, lobbyists, and individual contributors located in the Washington metropolitan area.

Contributions

PACs contributed a total of $178.4 million in the 1992 congressional elections. PAC contributions in two-party contested races were somewhat lower, reaching about $152.6 million (see Table 5-2). Corporate PACs accounted for the most PAC contributions, followed by trade groups, labor committees, and nonconnected PACs. Corporations without stock and cooperatives contributed the least, giving under 4 percent of the 1992 total.

As noted earlier, since the mid-1980s business-related PACs have adhered more closely to an access-oriented strategy than other committees. In 1992 corporate PACs gave 83 percent of their House and 73 percent of their Senate contributions to incumbents (see Tables 5-3 and 5-4). Forty-six percent of their House contributions went to shoo-ins, as did 35 percent of the contributions they gave in Senate elections. Corporate PACs

Table 5-2 PAC Contributions in Congressional Elections, 1992 (in thousands)

| | House | | Senate | | |
	Democrats	Republicans	Democrats	Republicans	Total
Corporate	$19,771	$16,671	$6,620	$11,580	$54,642
Trade, membership, and health	20,141	13,150	5,267	5,603	44,161
Cooperative	1,260	605	337	190	2,392
Corporations without stock	1,388	689	612	462	3,151
Labor	25,266	1,222	6,774	364	33,626
Nonconnected	5,713	2,962	3,430	2,540	14,645
All PACs	$73,539	$35,299	$23,040	$20,739	$152,617
(N)	(397)	(397)	(34)	(34)	(862)

Source: Compiled by the author from Federal Election Commission data.

Note: Figures are for general election candidates in major-party contested races, excluding those in incumbent-versus-incumbent House races.

contributed virtually nothing to challengers, but they gave 13 percent of their House contributions and 18 percent of their Senate contributions to open-seat candidates. Like corporate PACs, trade committees were fairly generous to incumbents, gave a mere pittance to congressional challengers, and spent considerable sums to help candidates in open-seat contests. PACs sponsored by cooperatives and corporations also allocated nearly all of their contributions in ways designed to give them continued access to powerful legislators and to develop relationships among the few nonincumbents who had a high probability of getting elected.

Labor PACs have consistently pursued highly partisan, mixed strategies. In 1992 they contributed virtually all of their money to Democrats. Labor contributions to House Democrats were almost equally divided between candidates in competitive and uncompetitive contests. Labor spending in Senate elections, on the other hand, was better targeted. Labor committees gave over three-fifths of their contributions to candidates in close or open-seat races. Labor's activity was clearly designed to maintain Democratic control of Congress.

Nonconnected PACs follow highly ideological strategies. In 1992 roughly 60 percent of their House spending went to candidates in close races, as did two-thirds of their spending in Senate elections. These PACs invested a relatively small portion of their funds in the races of incumbent shoo-ins and a large portion on hopeful challengers and open-seat prospects. As a group, nonconnected PACs treated Democrats somewhat

Table 5-3 The Allocation of PAC Contributions to House Candidates, 1992

	Corporate	Trade, membership, and health	Cooperative	Corporations without stock	Labor	Nonconnected
Democrats						
Incumbents						
In jeopardy	24%	22%	29%	28%	31%	24%
Shoo-ins	25	25	31	29	32	19
Challengers						
Hopefuls	—	2	1	2	8	5
Likely losers	—	—	—	—	3	1
Open-seat candidates						
Prospects	3	6	4	4	13	10
In one-party districts	2	4	2	2	8	6
Republicans						
Incumbents						
In jeopardy	13	11	11	9	1	8
Shoo-ins	21	18	18	13	3	10
Challengers						
Hopefuls	4	3	1	4	—	5
Likely losers	—	1	—	1	—	2
Open-seat candidates						
Prospects	6	6	2	4	—	6
In one-party districts	2	1	—	1	—	2
Total House contributions ($, thousands)	($36,441)	($33,292)	($1,865)	($2,076)	($26,488)	($8,705)

Source: Compiled by the author from Federal Election Commission data.

Notes: Figures are for general election candidates in major-party contested races, excluding those in incumbent-versus-incumbent races. The categories and numbers of candidates are the same as those in Table 4-2. Some columns do not add to 100 percent because of rounding.

Table 5-4 The Allocation of PAC Contributions to Senate Candidates, 1992

	Corporate	Trade, membership, and health	Cooperative	Corporations without stock	Labor	Nonconnected
Democrats						
Incumbents						
In jeopardy	14%	15%	20%	16%	16%	14%
Shoo-ins	15	17	16	23	23	16
Challengers						
Hopefuls	2	5	4	6	20	8
Likely losers	1	2	3	2	10	3
Open-seat candidates	4	10	21	11	25	15
Republicans						
Incumbents						
In jeopardy	24	19	22	18	3	17
Shoo-ins	20	18	10	18	2	13
Challengers						
Hopefuls	5	4	1	1	—	5
Likely losers	—	—	—	—	—	1
Open-seat candidates	14	10	3	5	—	7
Total Senate contributions ($, thousands)	($18,201)	($10,870)	($527)	($1,074)	($7,138)	($5,970)

Source: Compiled by the author from Federal Election Commission data.

Notes: Figures are for general election candidates in major-party contested races. The categories and numbers of candidates are the same as those in Table 4-2. Some columns do not add to 100 percent because of rounding.

better than Republicans, allocating 65 percent of their House and 56 percent of their Senate contributions to Democratic candidates.

Independent Expenditures

Independent expenditures usually take the form of direct communications from a PAC to voters advocating the election or defeat of one or more candidates. Independent expenditures made by PACs differ from the coordinated expenditures made by party committees in that independent expenditures must be made without the knowledge or consent of a candidate's campaign. Many independent expenditures take the form of television, radio, or newspaper advertisements that are directed toward the general public, but some take the form of direct mail or advertisements in trade magazines that are targeted at specific groups, such as realtors or voters who hold strong beliefs on highly charged issue like abortion.

The vast majority—fully 90 percent—of the $6.4 million in independent expenditures made in 1992 congressional elections were undertaken by nonconnected and trade PACs. Independent expenditures are consistent with the ideological or mixed strategies that these PACs follow. Moreover, because ideological PACs do not have traditional organizational sponsors, and because trade PACs are established to advance the political views of organizations that frequently have tens of thousands of members, these committees rarely worry about the retribution of an angry member of Congress or the negative publicity that might result from an independent expenditure. Unlike corporate PACs and labor committees, nonconnected and trade PACs are relatively safe from either outcome because they lack a single sponsor whose interests can be directly harmed.

More than $2.8 million of the $6.4 million in independent expenditures made in connection with the 1992 primaries and general elections advocated the election of specific House candidates, whereas just under $2.0 million was spent advocating the election of candidates to the Senate. PACs spent an additional $842,000 to detract from the election prospects of House candidates and another $363,000 to defeat candidates for the Senate.[30]

Most independent spending is made in connection with close election contests. In 1992 PACs spent roughly $2.4 million on House candidates who competed in general elections that were decided by 20 percent or less of the two-party vote (see Table 5-5). PACs spent a mere $486,000 in uncompetitive House races. Most of this spending favored incumbents. Open-seat contests were also the locus of significant independent spending, with more money being spent in connection with close than uncompetitive contests. The overall balance of PAC independent expenditures

Table 5-5 PAC Independent Expenditures in House Elections, 1992

	Democrats		Republicans	
	For	Against	For	Against
Incumbents				
In jeopardy	$585,938	$296,169	$429,498	$215,851
Shoo-ins	80,700	9,661	178,691	105
Challengers				
Hopefuls	74,405	9,555	264,287	365
Likely losers	9,791	0	27,280	10,837
Open-seat candidates				
Prospects	103,649	0	390,099	6,016
In one-party districts	148,522	0	19,683	325
Total	$1,003,005	$315,385	$1,309,538	$233,499

Source: Compiled by the author from Federal Election Commission data.

Notes: Figures are for general election candidates in major-party contested races, excluding those in incumbent-versus-incumbent races. The categories and numbers of candidates are the same as those in Table 4-2.

in two-party House races had a Republican tilt, favoring GOP candidates over Democrats by about $388,000.

PAC independent spending in contests for the Senate was similar to that for the House in that most of the activity—a total of $1,259,000—took place in competitive or open-seat races (see Table 5-6). PAC independent expenditures in races for the upper chamber differ from those for the lower chamber in that they favor challengers and Democrats. These differences reflect the comparatively slim majority Democrats hold in the Senate, the greater competitiveness of Senate elections, and the particular mix of candidates who were up for election in 1992.

Campaign Services

Although most of the journalistic reporting on PACs has focused on contributions and independent expenditures, some PACs do more than spend money. These committees carry out activities that have traditionally been conducted by political parties.[31] Some PACs (mainly ideological committees), including Clean Water Action-Vote Environment PAC and various PACs on both sides of the abortion rights issue, recruit candidates to run for Congress.[32] Others provide candidates with in-kind contributions of polls, campaign ads, issue research, fund-raising assistance, and strategic advice. AMPAC, for example, contributes polls to some can-

Table 5-6   PAC Independent Expenditures in Senate Elections, 1992

	Democrats		Republicans	
	For	Against	For	Against
Incumbents				
In jeopardy	$8,690	$844	$100,720	$63,387
Shoo-ins	61,655	31,925	309,508	945
Challengers				
Hopefuls	275,911	53,284	166,987	365
Likely losers	436,345	5	13,547	0
Open-seat candidates	267,943	24,242	220,502	75,921
Total	$1,050,544	$110,300	$811,264	$140,618

Source: Compiled by the author from Federal Election Commission data.

Notes: Figures are for general election candidates in major-party contested races. The categories and numbers of candidates are the same as those in Table 4-2.

didates. CWAVE helps its congressional, state, and local candidates frame environmental issues. The Free Congress PAC specializes in training conservative House challengers and open-seat contestants in grassroots mobilization techniques.[33] The NCEC provides Democratic House and Senate candidates and party committees with precinct-level demographic profiles, targeting assistance, and technical advice.[34] These and other PACs furnish campaign assistance in lieu of cash contributions because they want to influence how candidates' campaigns are run or to leave a more enduring impression than one can get from simply handing over a check.

One of the major forms of assistance that a PAC can give to a candidate, particularly a nonincumbent, is help with raising money. Lead PACs, such as BIPAC, COPE, and the NCEC, hold meetings to brief other PACs, circulate information about campaigns on their watch lists, and carry out other activities similar to those conducted by the Hill committees.[35] Even some smaller PACs, such as NFFE (representing federal employees) and the AAP PAC (representing publishers), help congressional candidates raise money by hosting fund-raising events or serving on candidates' fund-raising committees. The maturation of the Washington PAC community has led to the development of several networks of PACs, or PAC "families," which assist each other in selecting candidates for support.[36]

EMILY's List, whose name stands for "Early Money Is Like Yeast" and whose motto is "it makes the dough rise," is an example of a PAC that gives candidates fund-raising assistance. This nonconnected committee supports pro-choice Democratic women candidates, helping them raise money in the early, critical stage of the election. In addition to directly contributing $365,000, the PAC funneled roughly $5 million to women running in the 1992 congressional elections. It also donated more than $620,000 in soft money to Democratic state party committees.[37] EMILY's List requires its members to donate $100 to the PAC and to make minimum contributions of $100 to each of two candidates whom the PAC has designated for support. Members are instructed to write these checks to the candidates and then send them to the PAC, which in turn forwards the checks to the candidates with a letter explaining the PAC's role in collecting the money. This procedure, commonly referred to as "bundling," enables the PAC to act as a clearinghouse for individual campaign contributions. This enables a PAC to direct more money to candidates than it is otherwise legally allowed to contribute. Bundling also works well with individuals who wish to have a candidate acknowledge both their and the group's political support.

Organized interests besides PACs also provide candidates with help in congressional elections. Labor unions and church-based organizations in African American and ethnic communities have long histories of political activism and have made decisive contributions to Democratic candidates' field activities. Churches associated with the "new right" began to organize efforts to elect conservative Republicans in the 1970s. Some Elks Clubs, American Legion posts, and other fraternal organizations also endorse candidates and carry out voter mobilization activities. The National Chamber Alliance for Politics, which is a PAC sponsored by the U.S. Chamber of Commerce, distributes opportunity lists to pro-business PACs, and AIPAC provides information about candidates to PACs that support Israel.[38] Despite the fact that they carry out activities similar to those of lead PACs and the Hill committees, neither of these groups gives cash contributions to congressional candidates.[39]

Congressional candidates and their campaign aides generally evaluate the help they get from PACs and other interest groups less favorably than the assistance they get from party committees.[40] Democrats report receiving significant help with mobilizing voters and recruiting volunteers from labor unions and other groups, but they are not as helpful as state or local Democratic committees.[41] Senate candidates and campaign aides of both parties find PACs and other groups to be very helpful in fund-raising but not as helpful as the DSCC or NRSC. House campaigners, however, appraise the fund-raising assistance of organized interests somewhat more favorably than the help they get from the DCCC or NRCC.[42] The information provided by both House and Senate campaigns indicates that interest group activity tends to be more heavily focused in competitive contests and more important to the election efforts of hopeful challengers and open-seat prospects than incumbents. Finally, Democratic candidates get more campaign assistance from PACs and other groups than do Republicans.

Notes

1. Although it was referred to as a political action committee from its inception, COPE operated somewhat differently than modern (post-1974) PACs until the enactment of the FECA. COPE continues to occupy a prominent place among PACs and, as will be discussed later, is considered a lead PAC for many labor groups. See Clyde Wilcox, "Coping with Increasing Business Influence: The AFL-CIO's Committee on Political Education," in *Risky Business? PAC Decision Making and Strategy in Congressional Elections,* ed. Robert Biersack, Paul S. Herrnson, and Clyde Wilcox (Armonk, N.Y.: M. E. Sharpe, 1994), chapter 2.
2. For excellent discussions of the genesis and development of PACs, see Larry J. Sabato, *PAC Power: Inside the World of Political Action Committees* (New York: W. W. Norton, 1984), chapter 1; Joseph E. Cantor, *Political Action Committees: Their Evolution, Growth, and Implications for the Political System,* report 84-78 GOV, Congressional Research Service, Library of Congress (April 30, 1984); and Frank J. Sorauf, *Money in American Elections* (Glenview, Ill.: Scott, Foresman, 1988), chapter 4.
3. PACs that do not meet these requirements are subject to the same $1,000 spending limit as individuals.
4. FEC Advisory Opinion 1975-23 (December 3, 1975).
5. *Buckley v. Valeo,* 424 U.S. 1 (1976).
6. These expenditures can be made for or against a candidate and must be made without the knowledge or consent of either the candidate or members of the candidate's campaign organization.
7. Federal Election Commission, "Final Report Finds Slight Growth of PAC Activity," press release, October 31, 1993.
8. Federal Election Commission, "PAC Activity Rebounds in 1991-92 Election Cycle: Unusual Nature of Contests Seen as Reason," press release, April 29, 1993. It should be noted that there exists a small subset of nonconnected PACs, sometimes referred to as member PACs or leadership PACs, that are created by congressional leaders, other members of Congress, and other politicians to help these individuals advance their political careers, to help them build support for specific policies, or to enable them to help fellow party members get elected to or remain in Congress. On these PACs, see Ross K. Baker, *The New Fat Cats: Members of Congress as Political Benefactors* (New York: Twentieth Century Fund, 1989), especially chapters 3 and 4.
9. These figures include only congressional candidates who were seeking election during those election years. The figures would be slightly higher (roughly $187.9 million in 1992, for example) if candidates collecting money to pay for future or previous campaigns for Congress were included. The 1974 figure is taken from Gary C. Jacobson, *The Politics of Congressional Elections* (New York: HarperCollins, 1992), 67; the 1992 figure is from Federal Election Commission, "PAC Activity Rebounds in 1991-92 Election Cycle."
10. Removing the 910 "dead" PACs from the calculation reduces the number of inactive PACs to 21 percent of the total, but it does not affect the generaliza-

tion that a small portion of the PAC community accounts for the overwhelming majority of all PAC expenditures.

11. PAC strategies are discussed in several places. See, for example, Theodore J. Eismeier and Philip H. Pollock, III, *Business, Money, and the Rise of Corporate PACs in American Elections* (New York: Quorum Books, 1988), 27-30; J. David Gopoian, "What Makes PACs Tick? An Analysis of the Allocation Patterns of Economic Interest Groups," *American Journal of Political Science* 28 (May 1984): 259-281; Frank J. Sorauf, *Inside Campaign Finance: Myths and Realities* (New Haven: Yale University Press, 1992), 64-65, 74-75; and the case studies in *Risky Business?*, ed. Biersack, Herrnson, and Wilcox.

12. See for example, Laura Langbein, "Money and Access: Some Empirical Evidence," *Journal of Politics* 48 (1986): 1052-1062; Richard Hall and Frank Wayman, "Buying Time: Moneyed Interests and the Mobilization of Bias in Congressional Committees," *American Political Science Review* 84 (1990): 797-820; and Dan Clawson, Alan Neustadtl, and Denise Scott, *Money Talks: Corporate PACs and Political Influence* (New York: Basic Books, 1992), 169-173.

13. See, for example, John Frendreis and Richard Waterman, "PAC Contributions and Legislative Behavior: Senate Voting on Trucking Deregulation," *Social Science Quarterly* 66 (1985): 401-412; Janet M. Grenzke, "PACs and the Congressional Supermarket: The Currency is Complex," *American Journal of Political Science* 33 (February 1989): 1-24; John Wright, "Contributions, Lobbying, and Committee Voting in the U.S. House of Representatives," *American Political Science Review* 84 (1990): 417-438; Kevin B. Grier and Michael C. Munger, "Comparing Interest Group PAC Contributions to House and Senate Incumbents, 1980-1986," *Journal of Politics* 55 (August 1993): 615-643.

14. Labor PACs continued to give 90 percent or more of their money to Democratic congressional candidates throughout the 1980s and into the 1990s. See Norman J. Ornstein, Thomas E. Mann, and Michael J. Malbin, *Vital Statistics on Congress, 1993-1994* (Washington, D.C.: Congressional Quarterly, 1994), tables 3-14 and 3-15.

15. Eismeier and Pollock, *Business, Money, and the Rise of Corporate PACs,* 84-94; Theodore J. Eismeier and Philip H. Pollock, III, "The Tale of Two Elections: PAC Money in 1980 and 1984," *Corruption and Reform* 1 (1986): 189-207; Sorauf, *Inside Campaign Finance,* 67-77; Brooks Jackson, *Honest Graft: Big Money and the American Political Process* (New York: Alfred A. Knopf, 1988), 69-70, 77-81, 90-93.

16. See, for example, Ornstein, Mann, and Malbin, *Vital Statistics on Congress, 1993-1994,* tables 3-14 and 3-15.

17. Sorauf, *Inside Campaign Finance,* 61-71.

18. For a series of case studies examining the effects of all of these factors, see *Risky Business?*, ed. Biersack, Herrnson, and Wilcox.

19. Clyde Wilcox, "Organizational Variables and the Contribution Behavior of Large PACs: A Longitudinal Analysis," *Political Behavior* 11 (1989): 157-173.

20. John Wright, "PAC's, Contributions, and Roll Calls: An Organizational Perspective," *American Political Science Review* 79 (1985): 400-414.

21. Robert Biersack, "Introduction," in *Risky Business?* ed. Biersack, Herrnson, and Wilcox. See also Sabato, *PAC Power,* 44-49.

22. The information on the Realtors PAC is from Anne H. Bedlington, "The Realtors Political Action Committee," in *Risky Business?* ed. Biersack, Herrnson, and Wilcox, chapter 9. See also Wright, "PAC's, Contributions,

and Roll Calls: An Organizational Perspective," 400-414.

23. The information on the CVC is from Ronald G. Shaiko, "Le PAC, C'est Moi: Brent Bozell and the Conservative Victory Committee," in *Risky Business?* ed. Biersack, Herrnson, and Wilcox, chapter 16.

24. The information on Washington PAC is from Barbara Levick-Segnatelli, "WASHPAC: One Man Can Make a Difference," in *Risky Business?* ed. Biersack, Herrnson, and Wilcox, chapter 18.

25. The information on the AAP's PAC is from Julia Stronks, "The Association of American Publishers," in *Risky Business?* ed. Biersack, Herrnson, and Wilcox, chapter 14.

26. The information on NFFE is from William R. Pierce, "The National Federation of Federal Employees: Big Little Man?" in *Risky Business?* ed. Biersack, Herrnson, and Wilcox, chapter 12.

27. The information on FHP PAC is from John J. Pitney, "FHP Health Care PAC," in *Risky Business?* ed. Biersack, Herrnson, and Wilcox, chapter 13.

28. On rare occasions NFFE staff attend briefings organized by the Republican Party organizations in Washington.

29. On lead PACs see the introduction to part I in *Risky Business?* ed. Biersack, Herrnson, and Wilcox, pp. 17-18. On NCEC, see Paul S. Herrnson, "The National Committee for an Effective Congress: Liberalism, Partisanship, and Electoral Innovation," in *Risky Business?* ed. Biersack, Herrnson, and Wilcox, chapter 4; on BIPAC see Candice J. Nelson, "The Business-Industry PAC: Trying to Lead in an Uncertain Climate," in *Risky Business?* ed. Biersack, Herrnson, and Wilcox, chapter 3; and on COPE see Wilcox, "Coping with Increasing Business Influence."

30. Federal Election Commission, "PAC Activity Rebounds in 1991-92 Election Cycle."

31. William J. Crotty, *American Parties in Decline* (Boston: Little, Brown, 1984), 172-173; Edwin Epstein, "Business and Labor Under the Federal Election Campaign Act of 1971," in *Parties, Interest Groups, and Campaign Finance Laws,* ed. Michael J. Malbin (Washington, D.C.: American Enterprise Institute, 1980), 110-112; Theodore J. Eismeier and Philip H. Pollock, III, "Political Action Committees: Varieties of Organization and Strategy," in *Money and Politics in the United States: Financing Elections in the 1980s,* ed. Michael J. Malbin (Washington, D.C.: American Enterprise Institute, 1984), 122-141; Margaret Ann Latus, "Assessing Ideological PACs: From Outrage to Understanding," in *Money and Politics in the United States,* ed. Malbin, 150-160; Sabato, *PAC Power,* 93-95; Edwin M. Epstein, "The PAC Phenomenon: An Overview—Introduction," *Arizona Law Review* 22 (1980): 355-372; Frank J. Sorauf, "Political Parties and Political Action Committees: Two Life Cycles," *Arizona Law Review* 22 (1980): 445-464.

32. On CWAVE see Robyn Hicks, "Grassroots Organization in Defense of Mother Nature: Clean Water Action Vote Environment," in *Risky Business?,* ed. Biersack, Herrnson, and Wilcox, chapter 15; on NARAL see Sue Thomas, "NARAL PAC: Reproductive Choice in the Spotlight," in *Risky Business?,* ed. Biersack, Herrnson, and Wilcox, chapter 10. See also Crotty, *American Parties in Decline,* 173.

33. James G. Gimpel, "Peddling Influence in the Field: The Direct Campaign Involvement of the Free Congress PAC," in *Risky Business?* ed. Biersack, Herrnson, and Wilcox, chapter 5.

34. Herrnson, "The National Committee for an Effective Congress."

35. AMPAC, the American Medical Association's PAC, also carries out similar

activities. See Linda L. Fowler and Robert D. McClure, *Political Ambition: Who Decides to Run for Congress* (New Haven: Yale University Press, 1989), 111-112.

36. See, for example, Sabato, *PAC Power,* 44-49.
37. See Rachel E. Stassen-Berger and Charles R. Babcock, " 'Soft Money' Role of EMILY's List," *Washington Post,* May 30, 1993, A25.
38. On the National Chamber Alliance for Politics see Sabato, *PAC Power,* 47.
39. The National Chamber Alliance spends very small sums ($10,000 or less in each of the last three election cycles) to help congressional candidates raise money from other PACs, and these sums are categorized by the FEC as in-kind contributions. AIPAC, which is not a political action committee, gives no cash or in-kind contributions to federal candidates.
40. These generalizations are drawn from responses to questions 29 through 36 of the 1992 Congressional Campaign Study.
41. See questions 30 and 35 of the 1992 Congressional Campaign Study.
42. See question 32 of the 1992 Congressional Campaign Study.

Chapter 6

Campaigning for Resources

Vice President Hubert Humphrey described fund-raising as a "disgusting, degrading, demeaning experience." [1] This is a sentiment with which few candidates would disagree. Congressional elections are costly undertakings, and raising the funds needed to wage them has evolved into a campaign in and of itself. Part of this campaign takes place in the candidate's state or district, but many candidates are dependent on resources that come from party committees and PACs located in and around Washington, D.C., and from wealthy individuals who typically reside in major metropolitan areas.

The campaign for resources begins earlier than the campaign for votes. It requires that a candidate attract the support of sophisticated, goal-oriented groups and individuals who have strong preconceptions about what it takes to win a congressional election. Theoretically, all congressional candidates can turn to the same sources and use the same techniques to gather campaign funds and services. In fact, however, candidates begin and end on uneven playing fields. The level of success that candidates achieve with different kinds of contributors or fund-raising techniques depends largely on whether they are incumbents, challengers, or candidates for open seats. It also depends on the candidates' party affiliation and on whether they are running for the House or the Senate. This chapter explores the fund-raising strategies and successes of different kinds of candidates.

The 1992 congressional elections broke almost all records for campaign spending. Expenditures soared by 52 percent over 1990 levels to reach $678 million. [2] Fifty House candidates each spent more than $1 million, while the number of Senate candidates topping $3 million reached twenty-one. Challenger Michael Huffington broke all barriers in House elections by spending more than $5 million of his own money to defeat incumbent Robert Lagomarsino in the Republican primary and Democrat Gloria Ochoa in the general election in California's 22nd district.[3] Majority Leader Richard Gephardt (D-Mo.) spent the second most of House candidates—in excess of $3.3 million—and crushed Republican challenger Malcolm Holekamp by a 32 percent margin. The record for Senate spending was set by Democrat Barbara Boxer, who spent nearly $10.4 million in her successful open-seat race against Bruce Herschensohn, who spent $7.9 million. In addition to their direct expenditures, Boxer received $1.7 million in party coordinated expenditures and Herschensohn nearly $2.5 million, bringing the total campaign resources at their disposal to $12.1 million and $10.4 million, respectively.

Inequalities in Resources

Significant inequalities exist in the resources, including money and party coordinated expenditures, that different kinds of candidates are able to raise. The typical House incumbent involved in a two-party contest raised approximately $566,000 in cash and party coordinated expenditures in 1992, which is over three times more than the typical House challenger.[4] Open-seat candidates also gathered significant resources, accruing an average of $465,000 in two-party contests.

The resource discrepancies in competitive House races are great. Incumbents in jeopardy raised over two times as much in cash and party coordinated expenditures as did hopeful challengers during the 1992 elections (see Figure 6-1). Perceiving themselves as vulnerable, the incumbents followed the standard practice of collecting enough resources to swamp their opponents. Competitive open-seat contests were much more equal financially. The differences in spending between Democratic and Republican open-seat prospects were trivial.

The resource discrepancies in uncompetitive House contests are even greater than those in competitive ones. Incumbents, who begin raising funds early (often before they know who they will face in the general election), raise much more money than their opponents (see Figure 6-2). Incumbent shoo-ins raised five and one-half times more than likely-loser challengers in 1992. The spread among open-seat candidates running in one-party districts tends to be smaller. Democratic candidates in these contests typically outspent their opponents by a margin of more than two-to-one. The Democrats' financial advantage stemmed from two facts: most noncompetitive open seats were previously occupied by members of their party, and their districts contained more Democratic than Republican voters.

The typical Senate incumbent raised $1.7 million more than the typi-

Figure 6-1   Average Campaign Resources in Competitive House Elections, 1992

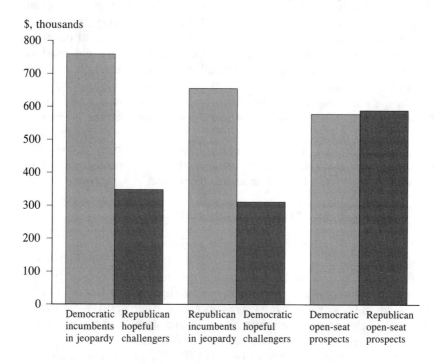

\$, thousands

Source: Compiled by the author from Federal Election Commission data.

Notes: Figures include receipts and party-coordinated expenditures for all two-party contests that were decided by margins of 20 percent of the vote or less, except incumbent-versus-incumbent races. The categories and numbers of candidates are the same as in Table 4-2.

cal challenger during the 1992 election (see Figure 6-3). Open-seat Senate contests were fairly well funded, with the average contestant spending just over \$3.1 million. The differences in the amounts spent by Democratic and Republican candidates were trivial. Finally, electoral competitiveness was important in attracting campaign resources. Candidates who defeated their opponents by 20 percent of the two-party vote or less spent more than twice as much as candidates involved in one-sided races.

House Incumbents

Sources of Funds

Most incumbents rely on individuals, PACs, and party committees for support. Individuals who make contributions of less than \$200, many of whom reside in a candidate's state or district, are an important source

Figure 6-2 Average Campaign Resources in Uncompetitive House Elections, 1992

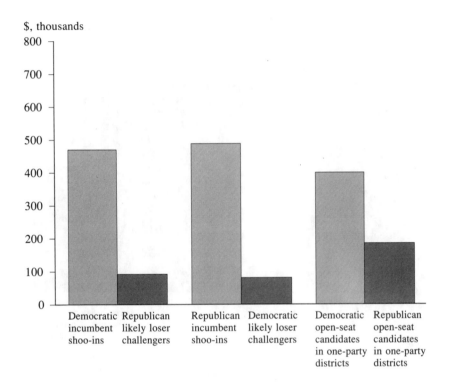

$, thousands

Democratic incumbent shoo-ins | Republican likely loser challengers | Republican incumbent shoo-ins | Democratic likely loser challengers | Democratic open-seat candidates in one-party districts | Republican open-seat candidates in one-party districts

Source: Compiled by the author from Federal Election Commission data.

Notes: Figures include receipts and party-coordinated expenditures for all two-party contests that were decided by margins over 20 percent of the vote, except incumbent-versus-incumbent races. The categories and numbers of candidates are the same as in Table 4-2.

of funds (see Figure 6-4). They account for approximately $104,000, or 18 percent, of the average incumbent's campaign chest.[5] Symbolically, they are often viewed as an indicator of grass-roots support.

Individuals who contribute $200 or more account for an additional $147,000, or 26 percent, of the typical incumbent's funds. Many make contributions across district or state lines. Over half of all individual large contributions given in the 1990 congressional elections came from donors in California, New York, and the Washington, D.C., area.[6] Individuals living in just one opulent community—defined by Manhattan, New York's 10021 ZIP code—contributed $1.48 million to candidates in other states.[7] These contributions, along with those of parties and PACs, have helped to form a national market for campaign contributions.[8]

Individual contributions that cross state lines are controversial be-

Figure 6-3   Average Campaign Resources in Senate Elections, 1992

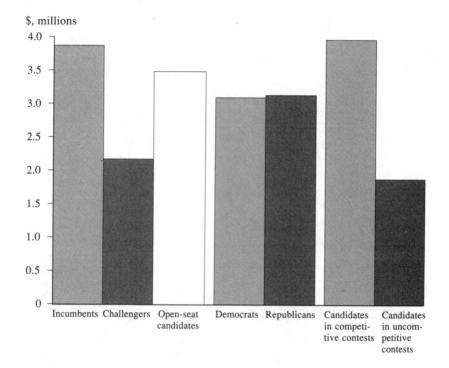

$, millions

Source: Compiled by the author from Federal Election Commission data.

Notes: Figures include receipts and party-coordinated expenditures for all two-party contests. N=68.

cause many are given by lobbyists who seek access to legislators for whom they are not entitled to vote.[9] Democrats from low-income urban and rural districts have become particularly dependent on out-of-state money, leading some to fear that these legislators may not be representing the interests of poorer voters as well as they should.

PACs provide $262,000, or 46 percent, of a typical incumbent's bankroll. Another $14,000 in campaign contributions and coordinated expenditures, a mere 3 percent of the candidate's total resources, is supplied by the incumbent's party. Most of this support is provided by the party's congressional campaign committee. Finally, House members contribute an average of $7,000 of their own money to help fund their campaigns.

Democratic House members collect a greater portion of their funds from PACs than do Republicans, who rely more heavily on individual contributors, particularly those who make small donations (see Table 6-1). The Democrats' procedural control of the House gives them greater

Figure 6-4   Sources of House Incumbents' Campaign Receipts, 1992

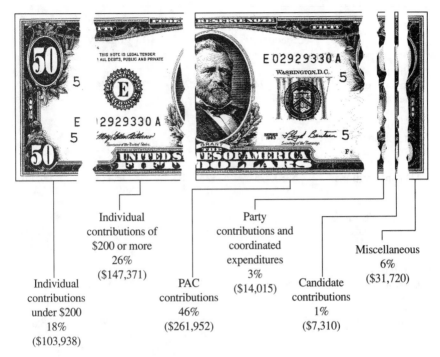

Individual
contributions of
$200 or more
26%
($147,371)

Individual
contributions
under $200
18%
($103,938)

PAC
contributions
46%
($261,952)

Party
contributions and
coordinated
expenditures
3%
($14,015)

Candidate
contributions
1%
($7,310)

Miscellaneous
6%
($31,720)

Source: Compiled by the author from Federal Election Commission data.

Notes: The dollar values in parentheses are averages. Candidate contributions include loans candidates made to their own campaigns. Miscellaneous includes interest from savings accounts and revenues from investments. Figures are for general election candidates in major-party contested elections, excluding incumbent-versus-incumbent races. N=313.

influence over the substance and scheduling of legislation, which provides them with an advantage in raising money from PACs. The Republicans, who typically do not have as much clout with PACs, are able to turn to their largely middle- and upper-middle-class supporters for the small contributions that make up a quarter of their campaign treasuries.

Fund-raising Activities

Incumbents routinely complain about the time, effort, and indignities associated with asking people for money. Personal discomfort figures prominently in how they raise their funds. A fear of defeat and a disdain for fund-raising have two principal effects: they encourage incumbents to raise large amounts of money and to place the bulk of their fund-raising in the hands of others, mainly professional consultants.

The need to raise large sums of money every two years and their lack

Table 6-1 Sources of Support for House Incumbents, 1992

	Democrats		Republicans	
	In jeopardy	Shoo-ins	In jeopardy	Shoo-ins
Individual contributions under $200	$111,724 (15%)	$73,721 (16%)	$164,934 (25%)	$111,445 (23%)
Individual contributions of $200 or more	$184,844 (24%)	$118,285 (25%)	$173,820 (26%)	$144,041 (29%)
PAC contributions	$383,428 (51%)	$237,695 (51%)	$239,473 (36%)	$200,061 (41%)
Party contributions and coordinated expenditures	$18,151 (2%)	$10,360 (2%)	$35,751 (5%)	$4,563 (1%)
Candidate contributions	$19,884 (3%)	$2,088 (0.4%)	$12,937 (2%)	$930 (0.2%)
Miscellaneous	$40,401 (5%)	$26,193 (6%)	$38,729 (6%)	$28,637 (6%)
(N)	(72)	(121)	(41)	(79)

Source: Compiled by the author from Federal Election Commission data.

Notes: Figures are averages for general election candidates in major-party contested races, excluding those in incumbent-versus-incumbent races. Candidate contributions include loans candidates made to their own campaigns. Miscellaneous includes interest from savings accounts and revenues from investments. Some columns do not add to 100 percent because of rounding.

of enthusiasm for doing so have encouraged many incumbents to develop permanent fund-raising organizations. These organizations consist of direct-mail specialists and PAC fund-raising experts who are kept on retainer or are allowed to keep a portion of the money they raise. These consultants write direct-mail appeals, update contributor lists, identify and solicit potentially supportive PACs, and organize fund-raising events. They enable incumbents to minimize their involvement in the fund-raising process. In many cases, all a House member has to do is show up at fund-raising events or make telephone calls to potential contributors who insist on having a word with the member prior to giving a donation.

Incumbents raise small contributions by making appeals through the mail, over the telephone, or at fund-raising events. Direct mail can be a relatively reliable method of fund-raising for an incumbent because the solicitations are usually made from lists of previous donors that indicate which appeals garnered earlier contributions.[10] Most direct mail generates contributions of less than $100 and is targeted at the candidate's constituents. However, a number of prominent House members, including Majority Leader Gephardt and Minority Whip Newt Gingrich (R-Ga.), have huge direct-mail lists that include individuals who reside across the United States. Telephone solicitations, which also require a list of likely contributors, are also used to raise funds.

Traditional fund-raising events are another popular means for raising small contributions. Cocktail parties, barbecues, and picnics with admission costs ranging from $10 to $50 that are held in the candidate's district are useful ways to raise money. They are also helpful in generating favorable press coverage and building goodwill among voters.

Incumbents can ensure the success of their fund-raising events by establishing fund-raising committees comprising business executives, labor officials, civic leaders, and political activists who live in their districts. The "Lion's Den," a group of individuals who raise campaign money for Sen. Carl Levin (D-Mich.), is an example of a well-organized network of fund-raisers. The Lion's Den began as a group of a dozen or so Levin supporters who first helped Levin campaign for the House and later the Senate. They created committees to organize fund-raising events and make telephone solicitations on Levin's behalf. Lion's Den members have traditionally given contributions of all sizes, often purchasing enough tickets to fill a table at fund-raising dinners. They have also encouraged guests at one event to become the sponsors of others. Over time, the Lion's Den has grown from a small group to a large network of fund-raisers, each of whom has made a substantial contribution to Levin's reelection efforts. Most House and Senate incumbents have developed fund-raising committees and networks similar to Levin's, often relying on individuals and groups located in Washington as well as in their district or state.

Individual large contributions and some PAC money are also raised at fund-raising events and through networks of supporters such as the Lion's Den. Events that feature the president, congressional leaders, or other national leaders help bring in individual large contributions. Some of these are held in the candidate's state, but most are held in Washington, D.C., New York City, or Hollywood—the nation's political, financial, and entertainment centers.

Traditional fund-raising events can satisfy the goals of a variety of contributors. They give individuals who desire proximity to power the opportunity to speak with members of Congress and other political elites. Persons and groups that contribute for ideological reasons get the opportunity to voice their specific issue concerns. Individuals and organizations that are motivated by material gain, such as a tax break or federal funding for a project, often perceive these events as opportunities to build a relationship with a member of Congress.

In raising individual large contributions House members have advantages over challengers that extend beyond the prestige and political clout that come with incumbency and an ability to rely on an existing group of supporters. Incumbents also benefit from the fact that many wealthy individuals have motives that are similar to those of party committees and PACs. Moreover, information that parties and PACs mail to their big donors often focuses on incumbents' campaigns, further leading some wealthy individuals to contribute to incumbents in jeopardy over hopeful challengers. More than one-quarter of all individuals who donated $200 or more to each of four congressional candidates or $4,000 or more to two candidates in 1990, for instance, gave all of their contributions to incumbents. Another 45 percent of these individuals gave between 67 percent and 99 percent of their funds to incumbents.[11]

The rise of Washington, D.C.-based cue-givers and the FECA's ceilings on campaign contributions have led to the replacement of one type of "fat cat" with another. Individuals and groups that directly gave candidates tens or hundreds of thousands of dollars have been replaced with new sets of elites that do not directly give these large sums but instead help candidates raise them from others.[12]

Incumbents consciously use the influence that comes with holding office to raise money from PACs. Legislators first identify those PACs that are most likely to respond favorably to their solicitations. These include PACs that supported the incumbent in a previous race, those that agree with an incumbent's policy positions on specific issues, or access-oriented or mixed-motive PACs sponsored by groups that are affected by legislation that the incumbent is in a position to influence.

Members of Congress who serve in party leadership positions, who serve on powerful committees, or who are recognized entrepreneurs in certain policy areas can easily raise large amounts of money from wealthy PAC constituencies. Majority Leader Gephardt, for example, raised more than $1.2 million from a wide variety of PACs in 1992. Rep. Pete Stark (D-Calif.) raised most of his PAC money from a much narrower constituency. Stark was able to capitalize on his chairmanship of the House Ways and Means Committee's Health Subcommittee, which writes tax laws that affect the health and insurance industries, to collect more than $328,000 (93 percent of his total PAC dollars) from health and insurance PACs.[13]

Once an incumbent has identified his or her "PAC constituency," the next step is to ask for a contribution. This is usually done at fund-raising events, through the mail, or over the telephone. The most effective solicitations state the member's background, legislative goals, accomplishments, sources of influence (including committee assignments, chairmanships, or party leadership positions), the nature of the competition they face, and the amount of money they need. Incumbents frequently convey this information through PAC kits they mail to PACs.

Some PACs require a candidate to meet with one of their representatives who personally delivers a check. A few require incumbents to complete questionnaires on specific issues, but most PACs rely on members' prior roll-call votes or interest group ratings as measures of their policy proclivities. Some PACs, particularly ideological committees, may want evidence that a representative or senator is facing serious opposition before giving a contribution. Party leaders and Hill committee staff are sometimes called to bear witness to the competitiveness of an incumbent's race.

Parties are a third source of money and campaign services. The most important thing incumbents can do to win party support is demonstrate that they are vulnerable. The Hill committees have most of the information they need to make such a determination, but incumbents can give details on the nature of the threat they face that might not be apparent to a party operative who is unfamiliar with the nuance of a member's seat. The NRCC gives incumbents who request extra party support the opportunity to make their case before a special Incumbent Review Board composed of NRCC House members. Once a Hill committee has made an incumbent a priority, it will go to great efforts to supply the candidate with money, campaign services, and assistance in collecting resources from others.

The financing of Rep. David Price's 1992 reelection effort in North Carolina's 4th district is typical of that of most incumbents. The Price campaign raised nearly $140,000 (30 percent of its total receipts) in small contributions using campaign newsletters, direct-mail solicitations, and a number of "low-dollar" fund-raising events held in the district. It collected another $45,400 (roughly 10 percent of its receipts) in individual contributions of $200 or more at high-dollar events, including a fund-raising dinner attended by House Speaker Tom Foley (D-Wash.).[14]

The Price campaign raised approximately $278,000 (59 percent of its money) from PACs.[15] Nearly 70 percent of this money was contributed by corporate, trade, and other business-related committees,[16] while 30 percent was raised from labor PACs. Some of this money was raised at the event that featured Speaker Foley, but much of it was raised at Washington, D.C.-based events and through solicitations coordinated by the fund-raising specialists at Creative Campaigns. Price had little difficulty raising money from these groups because of his membership on the House Appropriations Committee, which plays a major role in the funding of federal projects. Finally, the campaign received nearly $10,000 in contributions and coordinated expenditures from the DCCC (roughly 2 percent of its resources). Had Price faced strong opposition the party would undoubtedly have spent more on his race, as it had in previous years. Like most congressional incumbents, Price contributed none of his own money to his reelection effort.

With only two-year terms, House incumbents usually begin raising money almost immediately after they are sworn into office. Sometimes they have debts to retire, but often they use money left over from previous campaigns as seed money for their upcoming election. Fifty-three percent of all House incumbents closed out the 1990 and began the 1992 election cycle with more than $100,000 in their possession. Nearly one-third of all House incumbents completed their 1992 campaigns with more than $100,000, which they will use to jump start their 1994 bids for reelection. Much of this money will be used as seed money to raise more funds.

Early fund-raising is carried out for strategic reasons. Incumbents build substantial war chests early in the election cycle to try to discourage potential challengers.[17] An incumbent who spent several hundreds of thousands or even millions of dollars to win by a narrow margin in the last election will have a greater compulsion to raise money early than someone whose previous election was a landslide. Once they have raised enough money to reach an initial comfort level, however, incumbents appear to be driven largely by the threat posed by an actual challenger.[18] Incumbents under duress seek to amass huge sums of money regardless of source, while those who face weak opponents may weigh other considerations, such as developing a "diversified portfolio of contributors." [19]

A typical incumbent's campaign—one waged by a candidate who faces stiff competition in neither the primary nor general election—will generally engage in heavy fund-raising early and then allow this activity to taper off as it becomes clear the candidate is not in jeopardy. The 1992 Price campaign exemplifies this pattern. As a result of his prior experience—his previous reelection contests were highly competitive—Price began raising funds for 1992 almost immediately after his 1990 victory. He kept his direct-mail and PAC fund-raising operations active in the hope of raising enough money to deter another well-funded challenger or defend himself against one should the need have arisen. Between January 1 and June 30 of 1991 the Price campaign raised $56,441 (12 percent of its total funds). It then collected an additional $128,501 (27 percent) by the year's end. All of this money was raised before Price had an opponent. Between January 1 and June 30 of 1992 the campaign raised an additional $199,230 (45 percent). In then slowed its fund-raising activities significantly, raising only $79,000, or 16 percent of its funds, between July 1 and election day.

The campaign reduced its fund-raising efforts when it became apparent that the candidate's opponent, Vicky Goudie, would not be able to raise the funds needed to mount a strong challenge. As Price's campaign manager explains,

> We did not coast or take things for granted. But at the same time, given that the opposition was severely underfunded, reluctant to appear in public, or to hold a press conference, it didn't make sense to "cry wolf" and try to convince our supporters, contributors, and everyone else that "the sky was falling" and we needed help.

Price's 1992 campaign finances demonstrate that a good deal of incumbent fund-raising is challenger-driven.[20] Early money is raised to deter a strong opponent from entering the race. Later money is raised in response to the threat posed by an actual challenger. If a strong challenger does not materialize, then an incumbent's fund-raising will usually slow down. Because he lacked significant opposition in 1992, Price spent just over half of what he had spent to get reelected in 1990.

The 1992 Fazio campaign also supports the generalization that incumbent spending is heavily influenced by the nature of the threat a challenger poses. The campaign began soliciting contributions early and aggressively because of the expectation that redistricting would draw a strong challenger into the race. By June 30, 1991, it had amassed a treasury of more than $282,500 (roughly 14 percent of its total funds). Between July 1 and December 31 of that same year, the campaign collected another $136,500 (7 percent of its funds). All of this money was raised despite the fact that Fazio was unchallenged in the Democratic primary and a Republican had yet to officially step forward to challenge him.

Following Republican Bill Richardson's declaration of candidacy, Fazio's fund-raising picked up. By March 31, 1992, the campaign had raised an additional $307,500 (15 percent of its receipts). During this same period Richardson raised nearly $162,000, encouraging the Fazio campaign to further step up its fund-raising efforts. Between April 1 and June 30 Fazio collected another $344,400 (roughly 17 percent of his funds). The pace of the Fazio campaign's fund-raising continued to accelerate in response to the opponent's efforts, resulting in the campaign collecting nearly $515,000 (26 percent of its funds) between July 1 and October 14. Another $394,700 (20 percent) was collected between October 15 and November 23. Finally, the campaign raised just under $13,000 by the end of the year to help close out its debts.

The Fazio campaign's fund-raising was driven by the threat the candidate had anticipated and the one that actually arose once the campaign began. Just as a lack of competition enabled Price to scale back his fund-raising efforts, stiff competition encouraged Fazio to set a personal fund-raising record.

Figure 6-5 Sources of House Challengers' Campaign Receipts, 1992

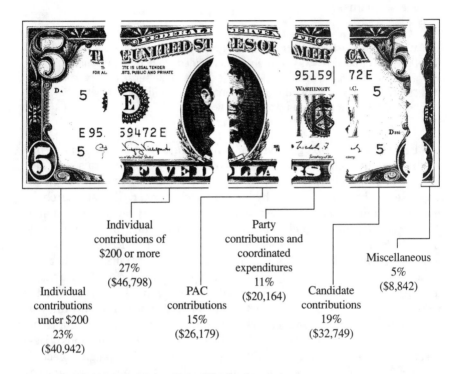

Individual
contributions of
$200 or more
27%
($46,798)

Party
contributions and
coordinated
expenditures
11%
($20,164)

Miscellaneous
5%
($8,842)

Individual
contributions
under $200
23%
($40,942)

PAC
contributions
15%
($26,179)

Candidate
contributions
19%
($32,749)

Source: Compiled by the author from Federal Election Commission data.

Notes: The dollar values in parentheses are averages. Candidate contributions include loans candidates made to their own campaigns. Miscellaneous includes interest from savings accounts and revenues from investments. Figures are for general election candidates in major-party contested elections. N=313.

House Challengers

Sources of Funds

Challengers raise less money than incumbents, and their mix of funding sources differs from that of incumbents. House challengers raise a greater portion of their funds from individuals. In 1992 challengers raised an average of $41,000, or 23 percent of their campaign budgets, in individual contributions of less than $200 (see Figure 6-5). Challengers collected roughly the same portion of their funds as incumbents in the form of individual large contributions ($200 or more), but the $47,000 that the typical challenger raised was less than one-third the amount raised by a typical incumbent. Challengers raised roughly one-tenth the money that incumbents collected from PACs, and PAC money only ac-

Table 6-2   Sources of Support for House Challengers, 1992

	Democrats		Republicans	
	Hopefuls	Likely losers	Hopefuls	Likely losers
Individual contributions under $200	$71,931 (23%)	$19,253 (24%)	$83,381 (24%)	$19,349 (21%)
Individual contributions of $200 or more	$59,869 (19%)	$17,551 (22%)	$102,515 (30%)	$28,310 (31%)
PAC contributions	$87,732 (28%)	$14,289 (18%)	$237 (11%)	$5,910 (6%)
Party contributions and coordinated expenditures	$26,706 (9%)	$15,033 (19%)	$43,343 (12%)	$7,505 (8%)
Candidate contributions	$36,267 (12%)	$9,780 (12%)	$67,636 (19%)	$25,795 (28%)
Miscellaneous	$27,876 (9%)	$2,743 (3%)	$12,387 (4%)	$4,264 (5%)
(N)	(41)	(79)	(72)	(121)

Source: Compiled by the author from Federal Election Commission data.

Notes: Figures are averages for general election candidates in major-party contested races, excluding those in incumbent-versus-incumbent races. Candidate contributions include loans candidates made to their own campaigns. Miscellaneous includes interest from savings accounts and revenues from investments. Some columns do not add to 100 percent because of rounding.

counted for 15 percent of the typical challenger's budget. Party money, on the other hand, played a greater role in challenger than in incumbent campaigns. Challengers, on average, received $6,000 more in party contributions and coordinated expenditures than did incumbents. Finally, challengers dug far deeper into their own wallets than did incumbents. The typical challenger contributed or loaned the campaign $33,000, which is over four times more than the typical incumbent.

Democratic challengers, especially Democratic hopefuls, raised more money from PACs than did their Republican counterparts (see Table 6-2). GOP challengers collected more money from individuals who made large contributions. Republican challengers, particularly those in close races, received more party support than did Democrats. Republicans also invested more in their own campaigns. Richardson, for example, contributed more than $23,000 to his race.

Fund-raising Activities

Challengers have the greatest need for money, but they encounter the most difficulties in raising it. The same factors that make it difficult for challengers to win votes also harm their abilities to gather resources, especially in the nation's capital. A lack of name recognition, limited campaign experience, a relatively untested organization, and a high probability of defeat haunt the typical challenger who comes to the nation's capital in search of support. The fact that their opponents are established Washington operators who possess political clout does not make challengers' quests for support any easier.

Most competitive challengers start raising money early and at home.[21] They begin by donating or loaning to their campaigns the initial funds that are needed to solicit contributions from others. They then turn to relatives, friends, professional colleagues, local political activists, and virtually every individual whose name is in their Rolodex or on their holiday card list. Some of these people are asked to chair fund-raising committees and host fund-raising events. Candidates who have previously run for office are able to turn to past contributors for support. Competitive challengers frequently obtain lists of contributors from members of their party who have previously run for office or from private vendors. In some cases, challengers receive lists from party committees or PACs; however, these organizations usually send out a fund-raising letter on behalf of the candidates rather than physically turn over their contributor lists. In 1986, then-House challenger David Price made use of former North Carolina governor and senate candidate Jim Hunt's contributor list.

Only after enjoying some fund-raising success locally do most nonincumbents set their sights on Washington. Early fund-raising success improves their prospects of raising more money.[22] Seed money raised from individuals is especially helpful in attracting funds from PACs, particularly for candidates who have not previously held elective office.[23] The endorsements of local business, labor, party, or civic leaders have a similar effect. If it can be obtained, the assistance of congressional leaders or members of a candidate's state delegation can be very helpful to challengers who hope to raise money from their party's congressional campaign committee, PACs, or individual large contributors.[24] When powerful incumbents organize luncheons, attend meet and greets, and appear at fund-raising events for nonincumbents, contributors usually respond favorably. Unfortunately for most challengers, their long odds of success make it difficult for them to enlist the help of incumbents. House members prefer to focus their efforts on candidates who have strong electoral prospects and may someday be in a position to return the favor by supporting the member's leadership aspirations or legislative goals in Congress.

Challengers can use their knowledge of how party leaders and PAC managers make contribution decisions to improve their fund-raising prospects. Political experience and a professional campaign staff can be very helpful in this regard.[25] Candidates who have put together feasible campaign plans, hired reputable consultants, and can present polling figures indicating that they enjoy a reasonable level of name recognition are more likely to capture the attention of party officials, PAC managers, and the inside-the-beltway journalists who handicap elections than are political amateurs who wage largely volunteer efforts. Political experience and a staff of seasoned campaign professionals can help challengers articulate their campaign's specific needs and make a convincing case for support.

During the 1992 congressional elections, House challengers who had previously held an elective office, an appointive position, or a state party chairmanship or who had previously run for Congress or were congressional, presidential, or statehouse aides benefited by an average of $17,138 more in national party contributions and coordinated expenditures than political amateurs. They also received more election services from their party's congressional campaign committee. Challengers who relied on paid staffers or consultants to manage their campaigns and carry out other important campaign activities received approximately $22,600—four times more party support than those who waged less professional campaigns.[26] Bill Richardson, who had a great deal of political experience and ran a professional campaign, received more than $35,300 in NRCC and RNC contributions and coordinated expenditures and an additional $35,000 in support from the California Republican party. Vicky Goudie, who had only limited political experience and ran a volunteer-based campaign, received a mere $2,000 in total party support.

Given that challengers are at such a great disadvantage in raising money from PACs, one of the keys to a successful PAC fund-raising strategy is for them to identify the few committees that are likely to give them support. For Democrats, this includes labor groups. Challengers can improve their prospects of attracting labor PAC money by showing they have strong ties to the labor community, have previously supported labor issues in the state legislature, or support labor's current goals.[27]

Challengers of both parties may be able to attract support from PACs, particularly ideological committees, by convincing PAC managers that they are committed to the group's cause. A history of personal support in behalf of that cause is useful. Challengers, and in fact most nonincumbents, typically demonstrate this support by pointing to roll-call votes they cast in the state legislature, to the backing of PAC donors or affiliated PACs located in their state or district, or to the support of Washington-based organizations that share some of the PAC's views.

Nonincumbents who make a PAC's issues among the central elements of their campaign message and communicate this information in their PAC kits enhance their odds of winning a committee's backing. Properly completing a PAC's questionnaire or having a successful interview with a PAC manager is usually crucial. Political experience and professional expertise can help a nonincumbent accomplish these objectives. In 1992 experienced challengers raised an average of $33,308 more in PAC money than amateurs, and challengers who fielded professional campaign organizations raised $29,300—over four times more PAC money than was raised by those who relied mostly on volunteers.[28]

Ideological causes were in the forefront of many candidates' PAC fund-raising strategies in 1992. Women challengers were able to capitalize on their gender and attract large amounts of money and campaign assistance from EMILY's List, the WISH List (the Republican counterpart of EMILY's List), and other pro-women's groups.[29] Challengers who came down on either side of the abortion issue were frequently able to raise money from PACs that shared their positions. By taking a side on such emotionally laden issues as handgun control or support for Israel some challengers are able to attract the support of ideological PACs.

A perception of competitiveness is critical to challenger fund-raising, and a scandal involving an incumbent can help a challenger become competitive. The 1992 elections were notable for the huge number of legislators who were implicated in some form of scandal. Clearly not every incumbent who bounced a check at the House bank had to worry about being accused of committing a major ethical transgression, but any House member who wrote twenty-five or more bad checks or was the subject of a major federal investigation probably had a great deal to worry about. These incumbents typically drew stronger opponents who had more fund-raising success. Challengers who ran against scandalized incumbents raised an average of $33,000 more than those who did not, including nearly $5,000 more from parties and almost $10,000 more from PACs.[30]

The experiences of Vicky Goudie and Bill Richardson demonstrate the impact that perceptions of competitiveness have on challenger fund-raising. Almost from the beginning, Goudie's campaign to unseat David Price was in trouble. While Goudie had announced that she intended to run a competitive, well-financed campaign, her fund-raising records told a different story. The Goudie campaign began collecting money a full year after Price, which is typical of most incumbent-challenger races. Between January 8 and September 30, 1992, the Goudie campaign raised only $8,605 (70 percent of its total funds), including $3,205 that came out of the candidate's pocket. The campaign would collect another $3,725 by the close of the election cycle and spend a total of $12,270 in the race.

Goudie's fund-raising troubles typify those of most House challengers, including virtually all of those who would be classified as likely losers.

The candidate disliked asking people for money and had no professional fund-raising operation to solicit contributions for her. Her desire to make campaign finance a political issue, which is fairly common among challengers, also created some fund-raising difficulties. As her campaign manager explained, Goudie decided to emphasize her "outsider" status by refusing money from all but a few selected PACs and by turning away any individual contributions of more than $100.[31] This decision enabled Goudie to contrast herself with Price, who had collected in excess of $323,000 in PAC and individual large contributions, but it left her campaign without the money needed to deliver its populist message.

As a former elected official and a major player on the boards of a number of interest groups, Bill Richardson had little reason to limit his campaign to small individual contributions raised at low-dollar events. His campaign exemplifies that of most hopeful challengers in that it solicited money from a broad array of individuals and groups using a variety of techniques, including fund-raising events, direct mail, and PAC solicitations. Experience, a professional organization, and a good strategy enabled Richardson to raise a total of $856,853 in his 1992 congressional race against Vic Fazio.

The Richardson campaign, like the Goudie organization, began collecting money a full year after its opponent. The campaign's initial solicitations were very successful. It raised $161,610 (roughly 19 percent of its funds) between January 1 and March 31 of 1992. It collected an additional $194,000 (23 percent of its receipts) during the months of April, May, and June. The campaign's fund-raising picked up between July 1 and October 14, during which it collected another $290,000 (34 percent of its funds). An additional $211,400 (24 percent of its total money) was raised in the remaining three weeks of the election.

The growing competitiveness of the race helped Richardson attract the support of party committees, PACs, and individuals who were captivated by the opportunity to defeat a Democratic House leader. Unfortunately for Richardson, Fazio's supporters also responded to the competitiveness of the race, enabling the incumbent to raise $2.33 for every $1.00 the challenger collected. The dynamics of the race were similar to those in many close incumbent-challenger contests: a hopeful challenger was able to raise enough funds to run a competitive campaign, but the incumbent was able to collect many times more.

Candidates for Open House Seats

Sources of Funds

Candidates for open seats possess few of the fund-raising advantages of incumbents but also lack the liabilities of challengers. Open-seat candi-

Figure 6-6 Sources of House Open-Seat Candidates' Campaign Receipts, 1992

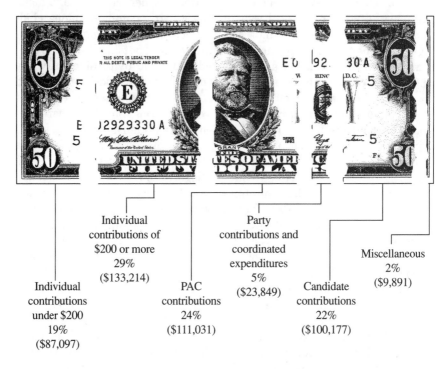

Individual
contributions of
$200 or more
29%
($133,214)

Party
contributions and
coordinated
expenditures
5%
($23,849)

Miscellaneous
2%
($9,891)

Individual
contributions
under $200
19%
($87,097)

PAC
contributions
24%
($111,031)

Candidate
contributions
22%
($100,177)

Source: Compiled by the author from Federal Election Commission data.

Notes: The dollar values in parentheses are averages. Candidate contributions include loans candidates made to their own campaigns. Miscellaneous includes interest from savings accounts and revenues from investments. Figures are for general election candidates in major-party contested elections. N=168.

dates rely on many of the same fund-raising strategies as challengers but usually have considerably more success. Because most open-seat contests are competitive, they receive a great deal of attention from parties, PACs, and other informed contributors. This places open-seat candidates in a position to convince Washington insiders that their campaigns are worthy of support. For this reason their campaign receipts resemble those of incumbents in a number of ways. In 1992 open-seat contestants and incumbents raised just under half of their funds from individuals and around 5 percent of their resources from parties (see Figure 6-6). The major differences in funding between the two types of campaigns are that open-seat candidates depend more heavily on their own money and less on PAC funds than do incumbents.

Democratic open-seat candidates collected more PAC money than Republicans in 1992 (See Table 6-3). Moreover, Democrats who ran in one-

Table 6-3   Sources of Support for House Open-Seat Candidates, 1992

	Democrats		Republicans	
	Prospects	One-party seats	Prospects	One-party seats
Individual contributions under $200	$111,820 (19%)	$82,047 (20%)	$90,771 (15%)	$50,385 (25%)
Individual contributions of $200 or more	$162,399 (28%)	$108,677 (27%)	$171,709 (29%)	$58,223 (29%)
PAC contributions	$149,390 (26%)	$146,341 (37%)	$100,391 (17%)	$34,956 (17%)
Party contributions and coordinated expenditures	$21,867 (4%)	$9,804 (2%)	$42,908 (7%)	$12,783 (6%)
Candidate contributions	$110,997 (19%)	$46,865 (12%)	$168,136 (29%)	$37,637 (19%)
Miscellaneous	$19,449 (3%)	$6,800 (2%)	$15,400 (3%)	$7,128 (4%)
(N)	(50)	(34)	(50)	(34)

Source: Compiled by the author from Federal Election Commission data.

Notes: Figures are averages for general election candidates in major-party contested races, excluding those in incumbent-versus-incumbent races. Candidate contributions include loans candidates made to their own campaigns. Miscellaneous includes interest from savings accounts and revenues from investments. Some columns do not add to 100 percent because of rounding.

party Democratic districts relied far more on PAC dollars than others. Republican candidates, on the other hand, received more party support and bankrolled larger portions of their own campaigns than did Democrats.

Fund-raising Activities

Open-seat candidates can help their cause by informing potential contributors of the experience and organizational assets they bring to the race, but these factors have less impact on open-seat candidates' than on challengers' fund-raising prospects. Experienced candidates raised an average of $5,346 more in party money than political amateurs in 1992, and candidates who mounted professional campaigns raised $24,400 in PAC contributions—about one-and-one-half times more money than those who mounted largely volunteer efforts.[32] Open-seat contestants who meet the goals that Hill committee staffers set are among the top recipients of party money, campaign services, and transactional assistance. Getting the endorsement of the congressional delegation and other incumbents can also be very helpful.

Winning support from PACs can be a little more challenging. Open-seat candidates use the same techniques as challengers to identify PAC constituencies and to campaign for PAC support but usually have greater success. Because their odds of victory are greater, open-seat candidates have an easier time gaining an audience with PAC managers and are able to raise more PAC money. Similarly, open-seat candidates point to the same kinds of information as do challengers to make the case that their campaigns will be competitive. Experienced open-seat contestants collect more PAC money—nearly twice as much in 1992—than amateurs.[33] Open-seat candidates who wage professional campaigns collect substantially more PAC money than those who wage largely volunteer efforts. In 1992 they collected an average of $117,000 in PAC contributions, nearly three times as much.[34]

The fund-raising experiences of Democrat Corrine Brown and Republican Don Weidner in Florida's 3rd district exemplify those of open-seat candidates in competitive races. Brown collected roughly $157,000 (54 percent of her money) from PACs. She was able to use her position in the Florida statehouse and the pro-Democratic nature of her district to attract significant funds from PACs. Labor committees furnished Brown with $52,000. Trade association PACs and corporate committees contributed an additional $50,000 and $27,000, respectively. Liberal ideological committees gave her an additional $27,000; all but $5,000 of these contributions came from pro-choice groups and PACs formed with the explicit purpose of supporting women candidates.

Weidner, who had never held an elective position but had served as executive director of the state GOP, was unable to break the $29,000 mark in PAC funds, raising only 11 percent of his money from these committees. He raised $21,000 from trade PACs, most of which was given by medical associations who saw a natural ally in Weidner, who has worked for various medical associations. The candidate raised only $2,000 from corporate committees and nothing from labor. He also collected just over $2,000 from nonconnected committees, including $650 given by a PAC sponsored by Rep. Bill McCollum, a fellow Floridian. Even though McCollum's support undoubtedly helped Weidner raise PAC money, it was not enough to help him overcome the skepticism with which many PACs viewed his race. Weidner's limited political experience probably hurt his ability to raise money from corporate PACs, and his probusiness posture (and Brown's support for labor) eliminated his opportunities to raise money from unions. The fact that he was a Republican, white male running against a Democratic, African American woman in a black-majority district that leaned Democratic during the "year of the woman" especially hurt Weidner's ability to raise funds from PACs and individuals who are motivated primarily by access.

Both candidates raised significant sums through the mail and at low-dollar receptions; Brown collected about $94,000 in contributions of less than $200 and Weidner collected just under $88,000. These figures accounted for about one-third of each candidate's campaign funds. Weidner raised $121,000 (about 47 percent of his funds) in individual contributions of $200 or more. Brown, on the other hand, raised only $31,000 (11 percent of her money) in individual large contributions. Party support for the candidates was roughly even: the DCCC contributed $450 to the Brown campaign and spent $4,200 on her behalf; the NRCC spent $3,500 on behalf of Weidner but gave him no direct contributions. The endorsements of members of their state delegations and other congressional party leaders helped these candidates secure party funds. Both candidates also invested $15,000 in their own campaigns, accounting for about 5 percent of their total funds.

The uncertainties surrounding the redrawing of Florida's 3rd district delayed both Brown's and Weidner's declarations of candidacy and fund-raising activities, but both were able to collect large amounts of money quickly. By the September preceding the election each candidate had raised approximately $128,000. These sums, which represent half of Weidner's receipts and 42 percent of Brown's, were spent largely on their primary campaigns. Between primary day and the October 1 runoff, Weidner raised $18,200 (7 percent of his total funds) and Brown collected $58,200 (19 percent of her entire war chest). During the final stretch to election day, Weidner was able to raise $106,600 (41 percent of his funds) and Brown collected $97,800 (32 percent of her funds). The evenness of the candidates' fund-raising reflects the uncertainty surrounding their race, which is common in competitive open-seat contests.

Senate Campaigns

The differences in the campaigns that Senate and House candidates wage for resources reflect the broader differences that exist between House and Senate elections. Candidates for the Senate need more money and start requesting support earlier. They often meet with party officials, PAC managers, wealthy individuals, and other sources of money or fund-raising assistance three years before they plan to run. As a result of the monumental size of their task, Senate candidates need to rely more on others for fund-raising. Nonincumbent Senate candidates are more likely than their House counterparts to hire professional consultants to manage their direct-mail, individual big donor, and PAC solicitation programs.

Table 6-4 Sources of Support for Senate Candidates, 1992

	All	Party		Status			Competitiveness	
		Democrats	Republicans	Incumbents	Challengers	Open-seat candidates	Competitive	Uncompetitive
Individual contributions under $200	$688,117 (22%)	$736,275 (24%)	$639,958 (20%)	$605,169 (16%)	$522,924 (24%)	$1,091,346 (31%)	$903,392 (23%)	$380,582 (20%)
Individual contributions of $200 or more	$1,127,097 (36%)	$1,161,775 (37%)	$1,092,419 (35%)	$1,567,065 (40%)	$824,924 (38%)	$903,180 (26%)	$1,441,351 (36%)	$678,164 (35%)
PAC contributions	$643,806 (20%)	$677,644 (22%)	$609,968 (19%)	$1,110,766 (29%)	$233,295 (11%)	$552,076 (16%)	$698,630 (17%)	$565,486 (29%)
Party contributions and coordinated expenditures	$406,220 (13%)	$336,813 (11%)	$475,627 (15%)	$395,085 (10%)	$358,631 (16%)	$501,648 (14%)	$609,680 (15%)	$115,563 (6%)
Candidate contributions	$161,391 (5%)	$79,159 (3%)	$243,624 (8%)	$29,974 (1%)	$176,091 (8%)	$351,057 (10%)	$210,430 (6%)	$91,336 (5%)
Miscellaneous	$114,086 (4%)	$126,251 (4%)	$101,920 (3%)	$172,643 (4%)	$58,008 (3%)	$110,055 (3%)	$128,761 (3%)	$93,121 (5%)
(N)	(68)	(34)	(34)	(26)	(26)	(16)	(40)	(28)

Source: Compiled by the author from Federal Election Commission data.

Notes: Figures are averages for general election candidates in major-party contested races. Candidate contributions include loans candidates made to their own campaigns. Miscellaneous includes interest from savings accounts and revenues from investments. Some columns do not add to 100 percent because of rounding.

Figure 6-7 Sources of Senate Candidates' Campaign Receipts, 1992

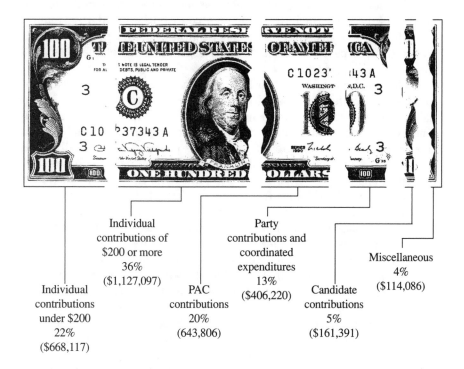

Individual contributions of $200 or more
36%
($1,127,097)

Individual contributions under $200
22%
($668,117)

PAC contributions
20%
(643,806)

Party contributions and coordinated expenditures
13%
($406,220)

Candidate contributions
5%
($161,391)

Miscellaneous
4%
($114,086)

Source: Compiled by the author from Federal Election Commission data.

Notes: The dollar values in parentheses are averages. Candidate contributions include loans candidates made to their own campaigns. Miscellaneous includes interest from savings accounts and revenues from investments. Figures are for general election candidates in major-party contested elections. N=68.

Senate candidates raised on average more than $1.1 million from individual large contributions in 1992, accounting for 36 percent of their campaign resources (see Table 6-4). Individual small contributions and donations from PACs each accounted for another fifth of the typical Senate candidate's war chest, while party contributions and coordinated expenditures accounted for another 13 percent. The candidates themselves provided roughly 5 percent of the money spent directly in Senate campaigns.

Compared with candidates for the House, candidates for the Senate rely more heavily on individuals, particularly those who give large contributions. Senate candidates also rely more heavily on party committees, particularly the DSCC and NRSC for contributions and coordinated expenditures. PAC money, on the other hand, is a less important component of the typical Senate candidate's war chest (see Figure 6-7).

Party affiliation has less of an impact on fund-raising for the upper than the lower chamber of Congress. Democratic Senate candidates depend slightly more on individual large contributions and PAC money than do Republicans. GOP candidates collect a greater portion of their resources from party committees and contribute more of their personal funds to their campaigns.

The differences between incumbent, challenger, and open-seat candidates are significant, especially in terms of the total dollars the candidates receive. Senate incumbents rely more on PAC money than challengers and open-seat contestants, but the differences are smaller than those for the House. Senate incumbents also depend less on individuals who give small contributions, party committees, and personal funds than do Senate challengers. Open-seat contestants draw the greatest portion of their funds in individual contributions, particularly those less than $200.

The in-state fund-raising of Senate candidates differs from that of House candidates in scope and professionalism but not in goals or techniques. Senate candidates merely send out more direct-mail solicitations and hold more fund-raising events than House contestants. The campaigns that Senate candidates conduct to win the support of parties, PACs, and wealthy individuals, however, differ from those for the House in some important respects. Senate challengers are more likely than their House counterparts to win the backing of PACs because their races are generally more competitive. The fact that many of them are current officeholders helps Senate challengers leverage money from PACs and wealthy individuals whose contributions are motivated by political access. The greater visibility and competitiveness of their races also give Senate challengers advantages in raising money from individuals or groups that pursue ideological goals.

This is not to imply that incumbency does not provide members of the Senate with fund-raising advantages. Senators, like House members, often begin their quest for reelection with significant sums left over from their previous campaigns. Forty-one percent of all Senate incumbents had in excess of $500,000 left from their 1990 campaigns, and 21 percent had this much left after 1992. Leftover funds give incumbents a significant head start in fund-raising. Senators also have political clout that challengers do not possess. Republican senator Orrin Hatch of Utah, for example, was able to use his membership on the Senate Finance Committee and Labor and Human Resources Committee to raise more than $430,000 from health and insurance PACs and $160,000 from health and insurance executives in preparation for his 1994 reelection campaign.[35]

A final difference between House and Senate elections concerns how candidates obtain support from their Hill committees. All four Hill committees rely on members of Congress to help them raise funds, but candidate assistance in fund-raising has become an informal criterion for senatorial campaign committee support. The DSCC and NRSC have created special accounts for elections held in different regions. The DSCC also created the Democratic Women's Council to provide support to women candidates for the Senate. These accounts give Senate candidates incentives to participate in fund-raising events held for their region (or gender), making it possible for the senatorial campaign committees to meet, or come close to meeting, the high ceilings that the FECA sets for coordinated expenditures in Senate elections.

Notes

1. Quoted in David Adamany and George E. Agree, *Political Money: A Strategy for Campaign Finance in America* (Baltimore: Johns Hopkins University Press, 1975), 8.
2. Federal Election Commission, "1992 Congressional Spending Jumps 52% to $678 Million," press release, March 4, 1993.
3. Huffington, who won 52 percent of the general election vote, defeated Democrat Gloria Ochoa and independent Melinda Lorenz, who received 37 percent and 10 percent of the vote, respectively.
4. These figures and those that follow include all candidate receipts and party coordinated expenditures for all two-party House and Senate contests, except incumbent-versus-incumbent House races.
5. The base used in calculating the percentages is the candidates' total receipts plus any coordinated spending the parties made on the candidates' behalf. Coordinated spending is included in the calculations whereas PAC independent expenditures are not. This is because candidates have some control over the activities that are paid for by coordinated expenditures but have no influence over PAC independent expenditures. Calculations are for candidates in major-party contested races excluding incumbent-versus-incumbent races.
6. Citizen Action, "Hidden Power: Campaign Contributions of Large Individual Donors, 1989-1990" (Washington, D.C.: Citizen Action, 1991), 15-16.
7. Citizen Action, "Hidden Power," 14.
8. For an excellent discussion of the nationalization of campaign finance see Frank J. Sorauf, *Inside Campaign Finance: Myths and Realities* (New Haven: Yale University Press, 1992), 47.
9. Robert Biersack, Paul S. Herrnson, Wesley Joe, and Clyde Wilcox, "The Allocation Strategies of Congressional High Rollers: A Preliminary Analysis," paper presented at the annual meeting of the Midwest Political Science Association, Chicago, Illinois, April 14-16, 1994.
10. On direct-mail fund-raising, see Kenneth R. Godwin, *One Billion Dollars of Influence: The Direct Marketing of Politics* (Chatham, N.J.: Chatham House, 1988).
11. Biersack et al., "The Allocation Strategies of Congressional High Rollers."
12. See, for example, Sorauf, *Inside Campaign Finance*, 124-127.
13. The figure on health PACs is calculated from a Citizen Action study cited in Charles R. Babcock, "Health Interests and Lawmakers," *Washington Post*, December 28, 1993, A13.
14. The dinner was held in December 1991, when it was expected that Price would once again face a well-financed opponent.

15. The remaining 1 percent of Price's campaign chest came from miscellaneous sources, including interest earned on bank accounts.

16. This figure also includes $10,875 that Price received from PACs sponsored by corporations without stock or cooperatives. The candidate received about .05 percent of his PAC contributions from nonconnected committees.

17. Some argue that preemptive fund-raising by incumbents may not discourage quality challengers from running. See Jonathan S. Krasno and Donald Philip Green, "Preempting Quality Challengers in House Elections," *Journal of Politics* 50 (1988): 920-936; Peverill Squire, "Preemptive Fundraising and Challenger Profile in Senate Elections," *Journal of Politics* 53 (1991): 1150-1164.

18. Gary C. Jacobson, *Money in Congressional Elections* (New Haven: Yale University Press, 1980), 113-123; Jonathan S. Krasno, Donald Philip Green, and Jonathan A. Cowden, "The Dynamics of Fundraising in House Elections," *Journal of Politics* 56 (1994): 459-474.

19. Sorauf, *Inside Campaign Finance*, 75.

20. Gary C. Jacobson, *The Politics of Congressional Elections,* 3d ed. (New York: HarperCollins, 1992), 53-54.

21. Over 50 percent of all challengers who raised more than $400,000 in the elections held between 1982 and 1984 began raising money before the beginning of the election year. See Clyde Wilcox and Robert Biersack, "Research Update: The Timing of Candidacy Decisions in the U.S. House, 1982-1988," *Legislative Studies Quarterly* 15 (1990): 115-126.

22. Robert Biersack, Paul S. Herrnson, and Clyde Wilcox, "Seeds for Success: Early Money in Congressional Elections," *Legislative Studies Quarterly* 18 (1993): 535-553; Krasno, Green, and Cowden, "The Dynamics of Fundraising in House Elections."

23. Biersack et al., "Seeds for Success."

24. Paul S. Herrnson, *Party Campaigning in the 1980s* (Cambridge, Mass.: Harvard University Press, 1988), 75.

25. The impact of campaign professionalism on campaign receipts persists when controls are introduced to factor out the impact of campaign money on campaign professionalism. See Paul S. Herrnson, "Campaign Professionalism and Fundraising in Congressional Elections," *Journal of Politics* 54 (1992): 859-870.

26. The challengers who relied on paid staff or consultants to perform three or more of the nine campaign activities listed in Table 3-1 raised an average of $22,600 in party money; those who relied on staff to perform fewer than three of those activities received an average of $5,400.

27. Clyde Wilcox, "Coping with Increasing Business Influence: The AFL-CIO's Committee on Political Education," in *Risky Business? PAC Decisionmaking in Congressional Elections,* ed. Robert Biersack, Paul S. Herrnson, and Clyde Wilcox (Armonk, N.Y.: M. E. Sharpe, 1994), chapter 2; Denise L. Baer and Martha Bailey, "The Nationalization of Education Politics: The National Education Association PAC and the 1992 Elections," in *Risky Business?* ed. Biersack, Herrnson, and Wilcox, chapter 6.

28. The challengers who relied on paid staff or consultants to perform three or more of the nine campaign activities listed in Table 3-1 received an average of $29,300 in PAC contributions; those who relied on staff to perform fewer than three of those activities received an average of $6,800.

29. The WISH List's name is an acronym for Women In the Senate and House.

30. Challengers who ran against scandalized incumbents raised $186,000, which includes almost $25,800 from parties and $34,000 from PACs.
31. Goudie accepted $1,486 from PACs; most of it was from the Women's Leadership Network, a group created to help elect Republican women candidates. Richard Goudie, campaign manager, Vicky Goudie for Congress Committee, telephone interview, April 8, 1994.
32. The open-seat candidates who relied on paid staff or consultants to perform three or more of the nine campaign activities listed in Table 3-1 received an average of $24,400 in PAC contributions; those who relied on staff to perform fewer than three of those activities received an average of $17,600.
33. Experienced open-seat candidates collected an average of $60,130 in 1992.
34. Open-seat candidates who relied on paid staff or consultants to perform seven or more of the nine campaign activities listed in Table 3-1 received an average of $117,000 in PAC contributions; those who relied on staff to perform fewer than three of those activities received an average of $39,400.
35. Hatch raised this money between January 1, 1987, and October 30, 1993. It is anticipated that he will raise even more from the health and insurance industries before the 1994 election. The figures are from a Citizen Action study cited in Charles R. Babcock, "Health Interests and Lawmakers," *Washington Post*, December 12, 1993, A21.

Chapter 7

Campaign Strategy

Successful candidates craft a message with broad appeal, set the political agenda that defines voters' choices, and get their supporters to the polls on election day. These candidates win because of the partisan makeup of their district and because their targeting, message, communications, and field work enable them to become popular with voters and to capitalize on district conditions and national events. This chapter focuses on how voters decide to cast their ballots in congressional elections and on the strategies campaigns use to affect those decisions. Campaign information, targeting, and message are discussed in this chapter, and campaign communications and field work are covered in the next.

Voting Behavior

Traditional democratic theory holds that citizens should make informed choices when voting in elections. It holds that they should be knowledgeable about the candidates, be aware of the major issues, and take the time to discern rigorously which candidate is more likely to represent their views and govern in the district's and the nation's best interests. The weight of the evidence, however, suggests that the vast majority of voters in congressional elections fall short of these expectations.[1]

Most voters make their congressional voting decisions on the basis of relatively little information. In a typical House contest between an incumbent and a challenger, for example, only about 20 percent of all voters can recall the names of the two major-party candidates. In open-seat House contests, about one-third of all voters can remember the names of the major-party contestants. Voters tend to possess more information about candidates in Senate elections: roughly 30 percent can recall the names of both candidates in contests involving an incumbent and a challenger, and about two-thirds can identify both candidates in open-seat races.[2] Clearly, many individuals arrive at the voting booth without much information about the candidates.

When put to the less-stringent test of merely recognizing the candidates' names, just over half of all voters recognize the names of both major-party contestants in incumbent-challenger House races, and almost 80 percent recognize the names of both candidates in open-seat contests. The levels of name recognition are higher in Senate contests, where roughly 80 percent recognize the names of both the incumbent and challenger, and more than 90 percent recognize the names of candidates in open-seat races.[3] Thus, the name recognition test, which demands roughly the same, minimal amount of information from voters as does actually casting a ballot, shows that a substantial portion of the electorate lacks the information needed to make what scholars refer to as "an informed vote choice." This is particularly true in House elections.

The inability to recall or recognize the candidates' names is indicative of a lack of substantive information in congressional elections. In most House elections, voters generally do not have enough information about the candidates' ideological orientations or policy positions on which to base their voting decisions.[4] Voters tend to have more substantive information about candidates in Senate elections, but issue voting is limited primarily to hard-fought campaigns.[5]

Incumbency and Voter Information

By and large, the candidates who suffer most from voter disinterest are challengers, particularly those running for the House. Whereas more than 90 percent of all voters recognize their House member's name, only 54 percent recognize the name of the challenger. Incumbents also tend to be viewed favorably. Half of those voters who recognize their representative's name indicate they like something about that person; only 12 percent mention something they dislike. The corresponding figures for House challengers are 21 percent and 14 percent.[6] As the high reelection rates for House members indicate, the name recognition and voter approval ratings of most incumbents are difficult for their opponents to overcome. Only those challengers who can break through the name recognition barrier and overcome their "invisibility problem" stand a chance of winning.

Senate challengers tend to be less handicapped by voter inattentiveness than are challengers for the House. Their greater political experience and skill, the superiority of their campaign organizations, and the greater interest of the media and voters in their races result in better name recognition for Senate challengers than for their House counterparts. Voters are also more aware of Senate than House challengers' ideological orientations and issue positions.[7] Even though Senate challengers' name recognition is lower than the near-universal recognition enjoyed by Senate incumbents, it is high enough to make the typical incumbent-challenger race competitive. This helps explain why there is more electoral turnover in the upper than in the lower chamber of Congress.

The inequalities in candidate information that characterize most incumbent-challenger races generally do not exist in open-seat contests. The major-party candidates typically begin an open-seat race as relative equals and have similar opportunities to convey their messages to voters. The greater competitiveness of these contests results in more extensive press coverage, which in turn helps both candidates become better known to voters. The result is that more voters make informed choices in open-seat races than in incumbent-challenger contests.

Voting Decisions

Given their ignorance of candidates and issues, how do voters make a decision on election day? Only those voters who know something about both candidates' backgrounds, political qualifications, party affiliation, and stands on the issues are in a position to sift through the information, weigh the benefits of voting for one candidate over another, and cast their ballots in accordance with classical democratic theory.[8]

Voters who do not meet this threshold level of knowledge tend to utilize "voting cues"—shortcuts that enable them to cast a ballot without engaging in a lengthy decision-making process. The most frequently utilized voting cue is incumbency. Knowing only an incumbent's name is sufficient for an individual to cast an adequately informed vote, some scholars argue. Reasoning that the incumbent should be held accountable for the government's performance, the state of the economy, the nation's foreign involvements, or other issues, these voters quickly determine whether to support the status quo—and vote for the incumbent—or to advocate change—and cast their ballot for the challenger.[9]

Other voters pin the responsibility for the state of the nation on the president and reward or punish the congressional candidate who belongs to the president's party. When these individuals are satisfied with how things are being run in Washington, they support the congressional candidate who belongs to the president's party. And when they are dissatisfied with the state of the nation's affairs, they vote for the candidate whose party does not occupy the White House. Presidential coattails can help a congressional candidate when a popular president is running for reelection, but belonging to the president's party usually has more harmful than beneficial effects in midterm elections.[10] The party cue, like the incumbency cue, enables voters to make retrospective voting choices without having much knowledge about the candidates or their positions on the issues.

The party cue also enables voters to speculate about a candidate's ideological orientation and issue positions. Republicans are generally identified as more conservative than Democrats and are associated with free market economics, lower taxes, family values, hawkish foreign policy, and the wealthier elements of society. Democrats are associated with greater economic intervention, government regulation, a more dovish foreign policy, minorities, the poor, and working people. Some voters project the parties' images to candidates and use these projections to guide their congressional voting decisions. Others habitually support a party's nominees regardless of their credentials, issue positions, or opponents.

Partisanship and incumbency can affect the voting decisions of individuals who possess even less political information than do those individuals described above. The voting behavior of individuals who go to the polls out of a sense of civic responsibility or out of habit and who lack much interest in or knowledge about politics can in many ways be equated with the behavior of shoppers at a supermarket. Individuals in both situations select a product—either a consumer good or a congressional candidate—with little relevant information. Except for first-time shoppers and newly enfranchised voters, these individuals have made similar selections before. Previous decisions, established preferences, and habits often have a decisive impact on their current decisions. The shopper, lacking a good reason to try a new product, such as a sale or a two-for-one give-away, is likely to purchase the same brand name product that he or she previously purchased. The voter is likely to cast a ballot for the candidate or party that he or she supported in previous elections.[11] If the voter recognizes one candidate's name, which is almost always the incumbent's, that candidate will usually get the individual's vote. If the voter recognizes neither candidate but tends to be favorably predisposed toward one party, then he or she will probably vote for that party's candidate. Only in the rare case when the recognized candidate or favored party is associated with a scandal, a domestic or foreign policy failure, or some other problem will relatively uninformed voters cast their ballots against that candidate or party. Situations in which voters have little information, then, work to the advantage of incumbents and candidates who belong to the district's or state's dominant party.

Voters and Campaign Strategy

Candidates and political consultants generally do not plan election campaigns on the basis of abstract political theories, but they do draw on a body of knowledge about why people vote and how they make their voting decisions. Their notions about voting behavior have many points in common with the generalizations discussed above. Among these are: 1) most voters have only limited information about the candidates, their ideologies, and the issues; 2) voters are generally more familiar with and favorably predisposed toward incumbents than challengers; and 3) most voters cast their ballots based on party identification. These beliefs account for some of the differences that exist among the campaigns waged by incumbents, challengers, and open-seat candidates as well as many of the differences that exist between House and Senate campaigns.

Generally, House members use strategies that capitalize on the advantages of incumbency. They discuss the services and the federal projects they have delivered to their constituencies.[12] They focus on elements of their public persona that have helped make them popular with constituents and draw on strategies they have used successfully in previous campaigns.[13]

Some incumbents capitalize on their advantages in name recognition and voter approval by virtually ignoring their opponents. They deluge the district with direct mail, radio advertisements, television commercials, yard signs, or other communications that completely ignore their opponent in order to minimize the attention the challenger gets from the local media and voters. An alternative strategy is to take advantage of a challenger's relative invisibility by attacking his or her experience, qualifications, or positions on the issues early in the campaign. Incumbents who succeed in defining their opponents leave them in the unenviable position of being invisible to most voters and negatively perceived by others. The Price campaign pursued the former strategy in 1992, going so far as refusing to debate its opponent.[14] The Fazio campaign pursued the latter approach, attacking Bill Richardson's record in the California state senate early in the campaign season.[15]

House challengers are in the least enviable position of any candidates. Not only are they less well known and less experienced, but they are also without the campaign resources of their opponents. In order to win, challengers need to force their way into voters' consciousness and to project a message that will give voters reasons to cast a ballot for a largely unknown quantity.

Many challengers seek to make the election a referendum on some negative aspect of the incumbent's performance. They portray the incumbent as incompetent, corrupt, or out of touch with the district. They magnify the impact of any unpopular policy or scandal with which the incumbent can be associated. Challengers often try to link the current officeholder to unpopular policies or trends and to tout themselves as agents of change, often using negative or "comparative" ads to do so.

Lacking the advantages of an incumbent or the disadvantages of a challenger, open-seat candidates frequently begin the election as relative equals. Both candidates face the challenge of making themselves familiar to voters and becoming associated with themes and issues that will attract electoral support. They also have the opportunity to define their opponents. Some open-seat candidates seek to define themselves and their opponents on the basis of issues. Others, particularly those running in districts that favor their party, emphasize partisan cues.

Gauging Public Opinion

Campaigns use many different instruments to take the public's pulse. Election returns from previous contests are analyzed to locate pockets of potential strength or weakness. Geodemographic analysis enables campaigns to identify individuals who voted in previous elections and to classify them according to their gender, age, ethnicity, race, religion, and economic background. By combining census data with previous election returns, campaigns are able to identify potential supporters and to formulate messages that will appeal to them.

Polls are among the most commonly used means of gauging public opinion. During the 1992 election cycle, every Senate campaign and 86 percent of all House campaigns used some form of polling to learn about voters. Benchmark polls, which are taken early in the election cycle, inform campaigns about the issue positions, partisanship, and initial voting preferences of people living in their state or district. House campaigns commonly commission benchmarks a year prior to the election, and Senate candidates have been known to commission them as early as two years before election day.[16] Benchmark polls also measure the levels of name recognition and support that the candidates and their opponents or prospective opponents enjoy. Benchmarks also help campaigns learn about the kinds of candidates voters prefer, the types of messages that are likely to attract support, and to whom specific campaign advertisements should be directed.

Campaigns also use benchmark polls to generate support. Challenger and open-seat candidates disseminate favorable benchmarks to attract press coverage and the support of campaign volunteers and contributors. Incumbents typically publicize benchmarks to discourage potential challengers. When poll results show a member of Congress to be in trouble, however, the incumbent uses them to convince parties, PACs, and other potential contributors that they need extra help to win.

Trend polls are taken intermittently throughout the campaign season to discover changes in the voters' attitudes. Some senators use them to chart their public approval throughout their six-year terms. These polls are more narrowly focused than benchmarks. They feature detailed questions designed to reveal whether a campaign has been successful in getting voters to associate their candidate with a specific issue or theme. Trend polls help campaigns determine whether they have been gaining or losing ground with different segments of the electorate. They can reassure a campaign that its strategy is working or indicate that a change in message is needed.

Just as trend and benchmark polls present "snapshots" of public opinion, tracking polls provide campaigns with a "motion picture" overview. Tracking polls ask small samples of voters to discuss their reactions to a few key advertisements, issue statements, or campaign events. Each night a different group of voters is interviewed. The interviews are pooled into "rolling averages" that usually consist of the responses from the three most recent nights. Changes in rolling averages can be used to reformulate a campaign's final appeals. Because tracking polls are very expensive, campaigns rarely use them prior to the last two months of the election; most tracking polls are used during the last three weeks of the campaign.

A few candidates supplement their polling with focus groups. Focus groups usually consist of one-to-two-dozen participants and a professional facilitator, who meet for two-to-three hours. The participants are selected not to be a scientifically representative sample but to represent segments of the population whose support the campaign needs to reinforce or attract. Campaigns use focus groups to learn how voters can be expected to respond to different images and themes or to pre-test actual campaign advertisements. Some of the more sophisticated consultants, such as the Wirthlin Group, a prominent Republican firm, employ computerized audience response techniques to obtain a precise record of how focus group participants react to specific portions of campaign advertisements.[17] These techniques enable an analyst to plot a line that represents the participants' reactions onto the ad itself, pinpointing exactly which portions participants liked or disliked. Focus group research is very useful in fine-tuning campaign communications.

Finally, campaigns learn about public opinion through a variety of approaches that do not require the services of public opinion experts. Newspaper, magazine, radio, and television news stories provide information about voters' positions on major issues. Exchanges with local party leaders, journalists, political activists, and voters can also be helpful in getting a sense of the public mood.

When asked about the significance of different forms of information, House candidates and campaign aides typically rank direct contact with voters first, indicating that they consider it to be very-to-extremely important (see Table 7-1). Voter contact is followed by public opinion polls, which are generally considered to be moderately-to-very helpful in learning about voters' opinions. News stories come next, followed by discussions with local party activists and mail from voters. Although they play a bigger role than PACs and other interest groups, national party officials and the materials they publish are less important than local information sources.

Table 7-1 Campaigners' Perceptions of the Importance of Different Sources of Information for Gauging Public Opinion in House Campaigns, 1992

Source	All	Party		Status			Competitiveness	
		Democrats	Republicans	Incumbents	Challengers	Open-seat candidates	Competitive	Uncompetitive
Candidate contact with voters	4.37	4.32	4.42	4.34	4.44	4.29	4.28	4.45
Public opinion surveys	3.53	3.69	3.37	3.82	3.19	3.68	3.95	3.17
Newspaper, radio, TV	3.05	3.16	2.94	2.95	3.19	2.96	2.88	3.20
Local party activists	2.63	2.63	2.63	2.66	2.52	2.76	2.64	2.61
Mail from voters	2.45	2.45	2.46	3.11	2.07	2.10	2.28	2.60
National party publications	2.28	2.17	2.40	1.91	2.61	2.29	2.12	2.42
National party leaders	2.14	2.02	2.26	1.89	2.31	2.23	2.11	2.16
(N)	(325)	(164)	(161)	(118)	(134)	(73)	(149)	(176)

Source: Question 14 of the 1992 Congressional Campaign Study.

Notes: Candidates and campaign aides were asked to assess the importance of each source on the following scale: 1 = not important or not used; 2 = slightly important; 3 = moderately important; 4 = very important; 5 = extremely important. The values listed are the arithmetic means of the scores. Figures include responses from House general election candidates and campaign aides in major-party contested races, excluding those involved in incumbent-versus-incumbent races.

Incumbents, candidates for open seats, and candidates in competitive contests report making greater use of surveys than do challengers and candidates in lopsided races, reflecting the fact that many in these latter groups cannot afford to purchase surveys. Democrats rely more heavily on polls than do Republicans, mainly because more Democratic candidates are incumbents and more Republicans are challengers. Challengers and candidates involved in one-sided contests are forced to rely more heavily than others on news reports, party publications, and the advice of national party leaders. Incumbents, who are often sensitized to issues by the constituent mail that floods their offices, consider letters to be a more significant indicator of public sentiment than does any other group of candidates.

Targeting

Campaigns are not designed to reach everyone. Targeting involves categorizing different groups of voters, identifying their political preferences, and designing appeals to which they are likely to respond. It is the foundation of virtually every aspect of campaign strategy. Candidates and their campaign managers consider a number of factors when devising their targeting strategies, including the groups that reside in the district, the groups' underlying partisan and candidate loyalties, their size and turnout level, and the kinds of issues and appeals that will attract their support.[18] Using this information, they formulate a strategy designed to build a winning coalition.

Partisanship is an important consideration in the voter targeting of roughly three-fifths of all campaigns (see Table 7-2). Most campaigns focus on members of their party and independent voters. Challengers and open-seat candidates are slightly more likely than incumbents to focus on these voters, reflecting the fact that most incumbents have built a measure of bipartisan support during their tenure in office.

Candidates in uncompetitive races are the least likely to focus their efforts on a combination of independents and members of their own party. Underdogs running in one-party districts need to pursue votes from members of the opposing party as well as from their party's loyalists and independents. Their opponents are in a position to seek support from all corners because most district voters identify with the dominant party. In some cases, candidates in uncompetitive districts do not have the resources needed to carry out even a basic party-oriented targeting strategy. For instance, lacking a poll or a precinct-by-precinct breakdown of where Republican, Democratic, and independent voters resided, Vicky Goudie's campaign resorted to focusing on districts that had the highest turnout levels in the previous congressional election.

Other factors that campaigns consider when designing targeting

Table 7-2 The Partisan Component of Targeting Strategies in House Campaigns, 1992

Target	All	Party		Status			Competitiveness	
		Democrats	Republicans	Incumbents	Challengers	Open-seat candidates	Competitive	Uncompetitive
Members of own party	8%	10%	6%	10%	6%	8%	7%	9%
Members of opposing party	3	4	2	2	4	1	3	3
Independents	3	4	2	2	4	4	5	2
Members of both parties	3	2	5	2	4	4	5	2
Members of own party and independents	37	36	38	33	40	38	42	32
Members of opposing party and independents	5	6	4	3	6	7	6	4
All voters	40	38	43	47	36	38	32	48
(N)	(334)	(165)	(169)	(123)	(136)	(75)	(156)	(178)

Source: Question 16 of the 1992 Congressional Campaign Study.

Notes: Figures include responses from House general election candidates and campaign aides in major-party contested races, excluding those involved in incumbent-versus-incumbent races. Some columns do not add to 100 percent because of rounding.

strategies include demography and issues. Sixty-three percent of all House campaigns base their targeting efforts on demographic, geographic, or occupational groups (see Table 7-3). One-third concentrate on specific ethnic, racial, religious, gender, or age groups. Seventeen percent focus on counties, suburbs, cities, or other geographic locations. Another 12 percent target union members, blue-collar workers, small-business owners, or voters involved in particular industries. Issues and political attitudes, including partisanship and whether voters can be classified as undecided, play a central role in the targeting strategies of the remaining one-third of all campaigns.

Group-oriented and issue/attitudinal-oriented targeting strategies each offer campaigns some distinct advantages. The group-oriented approach is based on the idea that there are identifiable segments of the population whose support the campaign needs to attract and that specific communications can be tailored to win that support. Just as soliciting money from a readily identifiable fund-raising constituency is important in the campaign for resources, communicating a message to identifiable groups of supporters and undecided voters is important in the campaign for votes. Campaigns that utilize group-based or segmented targeting strategies emphasize one aspect of their message in literature that is distributed to one group and different aspects in literature that is distributed to others. By tailoring their messages to attract the votes of readily identifiable population groups, these campaigns hope to build a winning coalition. In 1992, for example, many campaigns stressed the impact of the economy on children and families in literature that was mailed to women, while they emphasized economic growth issues in literature that was mailed to business executives and upper-class and upper-middle-class voters.

The issue/attitudinal approach is based on the premise that issues and ideas should drive the campaign. Campaigns that target on the basis of specific policies or a broad ideology, such as conservatism or progressivism, hope to win the support of single-issue or ideological voters who favor these positions. In many cases, one or two specific issues are emphasized in order to attract the support of swing voters whose ballots a campaign believes will have a decisive impact on the election outcome. Some candidates targeted pro-life or pro-choice voters in 1992, believing their ballots would be decisive. Others targeted pro-environment or anti-gun control voters.

Targeting strategies that are based on issues or voter attitudes more readily lend themselves to the communication of a coherent campaign message than do group-oriented strategies. They are especially effective at mobilizing single-issue voters and political activists who have strong ideological predispositions. Campaigns that target on the basis of issues, however, run the risk of alienating moderate voters who agree with the

Table 7-3 The Geodemographic and Attitudinal Components of Targeting Strategies in House Campaigns, 1992

	All	Party		Status			Competitiveness	
		Democrats	Republicans	Incumbents	Challengers	Open-seat candidates	Competitive	Uncompetitive
Demography	34%	37%	30%	34%	31%	37%	35%	32%
Geography	17	15	18	30	9	11	12	22
Occupation	12	13	10	7	16	11	14	10
Issues	14	8	21	11	20	9	13	16
Party affiliation	12	10	13	7	14	15	14	10
Persuadable voters	5	7	2	4	2	11	8	1
Perot supporters	1	0	2	0	2	0	0	2
Miscellaneous	7	9	4	7	7	6	5	9
(N)	(334)	(165)	(169)	(123)	(136)	(75)	(156)	(178)

Source: Question 17 of the 1992 Congressional Campaign Study.

Notes: Figures include responses from House general election candidates and campaign aides in major-party contested races, excluding those involved in incumbent-versus-incumbent races. Some columns do not add to 100 percent because of rounding.

candidate on most policy matters but disagree on the issues the campaign has stressed. Campaigns waged by policy amateurs and ideologues are the most likely to suffer from this problem. Often these candidates become boxed in by their own strategy and message, are labeled "ultra-liberals" or "right wingers" by their opponents, and ultimately lose.

More Democrats than Republicans target specific demographic and occupational groups. Senior citizens and women are the segments of the population most frequently targeted by Democratic candidates. In 1992 Corrine Brown, whose north central Florida district contains many elderly people and African Americans, focused most of her efforts on these two groups.[19] Republicans, on the other hand, were more likely to make issues the major consideration underlying their targeting strategies in the hope of peeling away Democratic voters. Republicans focused primarily on voters who were concerned about the national deficit, declining job prospects, and taxes. Ron Weidner, Brown's opponent, targeted conservative voters who were concerned about crime and victim's rights, wasteful government spending, and spiraling health-care costs. The Republicans traditionally focus on issues and make policy-based appeals to win the Democratic and independent votes that GOP candidates need to overcome their minority status in most congressional districts. The Democrats' focus on groups reflects the fact that their party is an amalgamation of many diverse segments of the population.

Geography plays a far greater role in the targeting strategies of incumbents than of challengers or open-seat candidates. Many challengers target on the basis of issues in order to peel away voters from their opponent. Occupation, which is often related to issues, plays a greater role in the strategic planning of challengers than of any other group. Open-seat candidates and contestants in competitive races are the most likely to go after independents. Often referred to as "persuadable" or "swing" voters, independents can make the difference between winning and losing in elections where neither candidate has a huge base of support.

Message

The message gives substance to a campaign and helps to shape the political agenda, mobilize backers, and win votes. In a well-run campaign, the same coherent message pervades every aspect of the candidate's communications—from paid television advertisements to impromptu remarks. Campaign messages can be an essential ingredient to victory in competitive elections because they have a big impact on the decisions of persuadable voters.

Campaign messages are a mix of imagery and issue information. The most successful messages are thematic. They use some combination of factual information about a candidate's qualifications to hold office, party affiliation, personal accomplishments and issue positions to produce a coherent image of the candidate. According to Joel Bradshaw, president of the Democratic consulting firm Campaign Design Group, good campaign themes have six characteristics: they are clear and easy to communicate; they are short; they convey a sense of emotional urgency; they reflect voters' perceptions of political reality; they establish clear differences between the candidate and the opponent; and they are credible.[20]

The precise mix of personal characteristics, issues, and broad themes that candidates project depends on their political views, the groups they target, and the messages that they anticipate their opponents will communicate. Good strategic positioning results from the transmission of a message that most voters will find appealing; when that result is achieved, an election becomes what strategists refer to as a "battle for the middle ground."[21] In designing a message, campaign decision makers consider a variety of factors, which Fred Hartwig of Peter Hart and Associates refers to as "the Seven P's of Strategy": performance, professional experience, positioning, partisanship, populism, progressivism, and positivity.[22] Ladonna Lee, a leading Republican political strategist, emphasizes the importance of consistency. The different components of the message must produce a coherent public image or persona.[23]

Campaigns endeavor to create a favorable image for their candidates by identifying them with decency, loyalty, honesty, hard work, and other cherished values.[24] Campaign communications interweave anecdotes about a candidate's professional success, family, or ability to overcome humble origins to portray him or her as the living embodiment of the American dream—someone who voters should be proud to have represent them in Washington. Campaigns frequently emphasize elements of their candidate's persona that point to an opponent's weakness. Veterans who run against draft-dodgers, for example, commonly emphasize their war records.

Incumbents frequently convey image-oriented messages. They seek to reinforce or expand their base of support by concentrating on those aspects of their persona and performance that make them popular with constituents.[25] Their messages convey images of competent, caring individuals who work tirelessly in Washington to improve the lives of the folks they represent back home. Incumbents' campaign communications often describe how they have helped constituents resolve problems, brought federal programs and projects to the district, and introduced or co-sponsored legislation that is supported by most district voters. Some discuss bills they have introduced to help the local economy or efforts they have made to prevent the closing of a military base or a factory. Those whose districts have experienced the ravages of floods, earthquakes, riots, or other disasters almost always highlight their roles in bringing federal relief to victims.

Many challengers and open-seat contestants also seek to portray themselves as caring, hard-working, and experienced. Nonincumbents who have previously held elective office frequently contrast their accomplishments with those of their opponent. In 1992 many challengers who were state legislators blamed their opponents for contributing to the federal deficit while pointing to their own budget-cutting activities as the correct way to solve the nation's economic problems.

Political amateurs usually discuss their successes in the private sector, seeking to make a virtue of their lack of political experience. Many blame the "mess in Washington" on the "career politicians" and discuss how someone who has succeeded in the private sector is needed to make government work for the people again. Nevertheless, a challenger who focuses on experience rarely wins. As one consultant explained, "By virtue of their being the current officeholder, an incumbent can 'out-experience' a challenger to death."

Issues

Most House candidates and campaign aides maintain that the bulk of their messages focus on policy concerns rather than the candidate's personality—a claim that has been borne out by examinations of their campaign materials.[26] In 1992 roughly 47 percent of all House campaigns reported that issues were the primary focus of their message; 25 percent, most of which were incumbents' campaigns, emphasized candidate imagery (see Table 7-4). Challengers run the most opposition-oriented campaigns. They point to incumbents' ethical lapses, congressional roll-call votes that are out of sync with constituents' views, or federal policies that have disadvantaged local voters or harmed the national interest. More than one-third of all challengers tried to make their opponent or their opponent's actions in office a defining campaign issue in 1992.

Candidates turn to a number of sources for ideas and information about public policies. Incumbents have many sources of information at their disposal. Although congressional staffs, the Congressional Research Service of the Library of Congress, and the General Accounting Office are not allowed to carry out issue research for campaigns, the fruits of their labors help incumbents keep abreast of the major issues affecting their constituents and the nation. Party organizations, PACs, and Washington-based lobbyists also help incumbents stay on top of the issues. Parties and some PACs furnish similar assistance to nonincumbents, who are generally less well versed on the issues and in greater need of factual information and rhetorical devices to refine their messages. Most campaigns find newspaper and magazine articles useful for generating ideas on policy stands.

Almost all candidates take policy stands that identify them with "valence" issues, such as a strong economy, job creation, domestic tranquil-

Table 7-4 The Major Focus of Advertising in House Campaigns, 1992

Focus	All	Party		Status			Competitiveness	
		Democrats	Republicans	Incumbents	Challengers	Open-seat candidates	Competitive	Uncompetitive
Candidate's image	25%	27%	22%	40%	12%	20%	23%	26%
Candidate's issue positions	47	50	44	44	46	53	41	53
Candidate's image and issue positions	2	2	2	2	3	3	3	2
Opponent's image	12	6	17	6	14	16	19	6
Opponent's issue positions	11	12	11	7	18	6	11	11
Opponent's image and issue positions	2	1	3	1	4	1	3	2
All of the above	1	2	1	1	2	0	1	1
(N)	(338)	(171)	(167)	(129)	(136)	(73)	(155)	(183)

Source: Question 24 of the 1992 Congressional Campaign Study.

Notes: Figures include responses from House general election candidates and campaign aides in major-party contested races, excluding those involved in incumbent-versus-incumbent races. Some columns do not add to 100 percent because of rounding.

ity, and international security, which are universally viewed in a favorable light. Some make these the centerpiece of their campaign, either ignoring or soft-pedaling "position issues" that have two or more sides.[27] When both candidates campaign mainly on valence issues, the dialogue becomes what might be described as a conversation between "Tweedle-dee" and "Tweedle-dum"—two mythical candidates between whom there is "not a dime's worth of difference."

When candidates communicate dissimilar stands on position issues, however, political debate becomes more meaningful. The politics of gun control, abortion, and civil rights have for several years had the potential to affect elections in which substantial numbers of voters discerned differences in the candidates' stances. Prayer in school, family values, social entitlement programs, senior citizens' concerns, illegal immigration, policy toward Cuba, and environmental issues—which were also stressed by one or more candidates in 1992—have also had the potential to affect the numbers of votes that candidates have won.

Challengers are especially likely to benefit by emphasizing position issues. By stressing points of disagreement between themselves and the incumbent, challengers can help their images crystallize, attract media attention, and strip away some of their opponent's support.[28] Incumbents may not derive the same electoral benefits from running on position issues because they are usually evaluated in personal terms.[29] Candidates who campaign on position issues hope to attract the support of single-issue or ideological voters or to overcome some weakness in their image. Some liberal Democrats emphasize crime to project "tougher" images. Some conservative Republicans discuss health care to show their compassion.

Candidates try to anticipate the issues their opponents will emphasize before taking a strong policy stance. Candidates who run against police officers rarely mount "law and order" campaigns because of the obvious disparities in credibility that they and their opponents have on crime-related issues. Candidates who learn that their opponent holds an unpopular position on a salient issue generally try to make it the central focus of the campaign in order to pry voters from their opponent's camp. In 1992, which was widely proclaimed the "Year of the Woman," many Democrats and some liberal Republicans sought to attract women's votes by making the right to have an abortion a major part of their campaign platform. Democrats who adopted this position got the added benefit of being able to coordinate their message with the Clinton-Gore campaign. Divisions within the Republican Party made abortion an issue to avoid for many GOP candidates. Women who were running against men were the most likely to campaign as pro-choice and to run on women's issues in general, but some male candidates also used their position on abortion to attract the support of women and liberal voters.[30]

The economy has been the dominant issue in most elections since the Great Depression and continues to be a major focus of most candidates, reflecting the fact that economic issues—whether they be inflation, unemployment, or the national deficit—are usually the number one concern of voters. In 1992 34 percent of all House candidates and campaign aides answered, "the economy," when asked to name the most important issue in their campaign (see Table 7-5). Another 34 percent named the deficit, taxes, jobs, the budget, or some other specific economic issue.

Democratic candidates blamed the Reagan and Bush administrations for the nation's economic woes. Many followed the Clinton-Gore campaign's lead and discussed the economy as a fairness issue, pointing to the increased tax burdens that Reagan-Bush policies placed on the middle class and the tax breaks they gave to wealthy Americans. Vic Fazio pressed for balancing the federal budget through spending cuts and tax reductions that would stimulate the economy and proclaimed: "It's time to replace the Lifestyles of the Rich and Famous with a new Fanfare for the Common Man." [31] David Price advocated education and worker training as two of the keys to the nation's economic recovery. He capitalized on his previous efforts to pass workplace literacy legislation and the widespread support for education that exists in North Carolina's Research Triangle, which lies largely in his district.[32]

Republican candidates focused on slow economic growth and the deficit, attributing both to wasteful government subsidies, excessive regulation, and profligate pork-barrel spending approved by the Democratic-controlled Congress. Bill Richardson called for $500 billion in federal spending cuts and argued that a balanced budget amendment was needed because the "government got the [country] into this economic mess." [33] Ron Weidner's ads called for the government to "spend less, save more" and for the elimination of "pork-barrel" projects.[34]

The importance of the economy is further demonstrated by the number of candidates who made it a secondary or tertiary focus of their campaign. Every 1992 House campaign that did not make economics its number one issue made the economy its second-most-important issue. Some campaigns named specific economic concerns as their first-, second-, and third-most-important issues.

Health care was also an important policy concern in 1992. Forty percent of all House campaigns made the nation's health-care system an important issue.[35] More Democratic than Republican candidates campaigned on health-care reform, following the lead of the Clinton-Gore campaign and the Democrats' traditional activism on social welfare programs. More Democrats than Republicans also focused on abortion rights, civil rights, and other social and cultural issues. Many of the Republicans (and some conservative Democrats) who campaigned on social and cultural issues championed the right-to-life side of the abortion de-

Table 7-5 Campaigners' Perceptions of the Most Important Issues in House Campaigns, 1992

	All	Party		Status			Competitiveness	
		Democrats	Republicans	Incumbents	Challengers	Open-seat candidates	Competitive	Uncompetitive
Economy	34%	39%	30%	37%	30%	36%	37%	32%
Economic-related	34	31	36	33	30	40	31	35
Political reform	7	4	10	5	10	3	8	5
Incumbent-related	6	8	5	11	4	3	4	8
Candidate's persona	4	2	6	4	5	4	4	3
Social or cultural issues	5	5	5	4	6	5	5	4
Health care	4	4	5	2	6	5	5	4
Political change	2	2	2	2	2	3	2	2
Foreign policy	1	1	—	—	2	—	1	1
Miscellaneous	1	2	1	1	2	1	1	2
(N)	(334)	(165)	(169)	(123)	(136)	(75)	(156)	(178)

Source: Question 13 of the 1992 Congressional Campaign Study.

Notes: Figures include responses from House general election candidates and campaign aides in major-party contested races, excluding those involved in incumbent-versus-incumbent races. Some columns do not add to 100 percent because of rounding.

bate, stressed traditional family values, and promoted other concerns that have recently been brought to the political agenda by the Christian Coalition and other groups associated with the "New Right." Some also ran on law and order issues.

Political reform was also an important issue in 1992, reflecting the anti-Washington-establishment mood of the country. Nearly 30 percent of all House campaigns focused on term limits, campaign finance, or some other reform-related issue. Challengers concentrated most heavily on the need for reform, often coupling their reformist message with attacks on their opponent. Many tried to link their opponent's bounced checks, vote for a congressional pay raise, or PAC contributions to calls for government reform. Richardson punctuated his call for political reform with the accusation that Fazio was the "Prince of PACs" and a "captive of special interests." [36]

Though most incumbents prefer not to have to defend the political institutions in which they serve, they often have no choice, especially when a challenger attempts to label them as "part of the problem." Political reform played a significant role in just under one-fifth of all 1992 incumbent campaigns. Some incumbents sought to defend Congress, while others tried to impress upon voters that they were part of the solution and not the problem. One candidate said he "neutralized" the reform issue by arguing he "was constructively working to improve government from the inside, while [his opponent] was content to merely lob stones from a distance."

Even though most candidates prefer that they, not their opponents, are the ones whom voters associate with valence issues, a number of candidates find it profitable to stake out strong stands on position issues. Thirteen percent of all House candidates made abortion, gun control, or one or more other position issues a central focus of their campaigns in 1992.[37] The percentages of Democrats, Republicans, incumbents, challengers, and open-seat candidates who staked out position issues were virtually identical. There were also no differences in the percentages of candidates in competitive and uncompetitive contests who made position issues a central element of their campaign messages.

Partisanship, Populism, and Progressivism

Candidates who run in districts that are made up overwhelmingly of members of their party normally emphasize partisan themes and messages. They frequently mention their party in speeches and campaign literature. They also run "tag lines" stating "This ad was paid for by 'Candidate X,' Democrat (or Republican) for Congress" at the end of their television or radio advertisements. They highlight their party affiliation on their billboards, newspaper ads, mass mailings, and other campaign literature. Campaigns that are run in "hostile" or divided districts typically use nonpartisan strategies, avoiding any mention of party affiliation.

Progressive strategies have become increasingly popular with Democrats in recent years. Democrats who run as progressives advocate using government as an agent of change. They avoid the term "liberal" because voters associate it with government regulations and high taxes, which are very unpopular.[38] Instead, many opt to call themselves progressives or "new" Democrats.

Populist strategies are commonly used by candidates of both parties. Republican populists, like Newt Gingrich of Georgia and other members of the Conservative Opportunity Society, campaign against government, taxes, and special interests in Washington. They maintain that they are for the "little guy." Democratic populists, such as Byron Dorgan, who was elected North Dakota's at-large representative in 1980 and its junior senator in 1992, also champion the cause of the ordinary American. Rather than oppose big government, these candidates run against big business. Dorgan built his reputation as a populist when, as state tax commissioner, he sued out-of-state corporations doing business in North Dakota to force them to pay taxes there.[39]

Negative Campaigning

The last element of campaign strategy is concerned with negative campaigning. Just as positive campaigning attempts to build up a candidate, negative campaigning endeavors to tear down an opponent. Negative campaigning is a legitimate form of campaign communication that has the potential to enhance the electoral process. Campaign ads that question a candidate's qualifications or point to unpopular, wasteful, or unethical practices bring a measure of accountability to the political system.[40] Yet, much negative campaigning amounts to little more than character assassination and mudslinging, which have always been and will probably always remain a part of American political campaigns.

Negative campaigning was used by one or both candidates in 71 percent of all House and virtually every Senate election held in 1992. Roughly nine out of every ten House contests that were decided by 20 percent or less of the vote featured negative campaigning, and as elections got closer the probability that they would feature negative ads went up.[41] The sense of urgency that pervades a close contest encourages the contestants to "tar and feather" each other because it is easier to discredit an opponent than to build loyalty.[42]

Negative advertising is believed to be a very important component of challenger campaigns because they must break voters of the habit of casting their ballots for the incumbent. As Joel Bradshaw explains, "Challengers cannot prevail unless they convince voters to replace the incumbent."[43] Nevertheless, many incumbents have made negative advertising a central element of their strategies in recent years, using early attacks on their challengers to define them for voters before they can define themselves.[44] Because of their competitiveness, open-seat campaigns tend to be the most negative of all.

The most effective negative ads are grounded in fact, document their sources, focus on some aspect of the opponent's policy views rather than personality, use ridicule, and are delivered by a surrogate.[45] Republican House challenger Rick Lazio of New York had tremendous success with a television ad that featured a room full of people voting themselves a huge pay raise to ridicule nine-term House Democrat Tom Downey for voting for a congressional pay raise. The ad, which ran on local cable television stations, helped Lazio generate substantial free media coverage and undercut Downey's support among voters. Other candidates aired commercials that featured bouncing checks or flip-flopping candidates. Ridicule is a powerful weapon in politics because it is difficult for people to vote for a candidate at whom they have just laughed.

Campaign attacks that do not adhere to the preceding guideposts tend to be less effective and can backfire, making the candidate who levies the charges look dishonest or mean spirited. Democratic House member James Moran of Virginia learned this lesson during his 1992 reelection campaign when, after attacking Republican challenger Kyle McSlarrow for using illegal drugs while in college, he had to confess later that he also used illegal drugs as a youth.[46] Moran went on to defeat McSlarrow by a fourteen-point margin, but his drug-related accusations and admissions harmed his standing with some voters. When both candidates in an election attack one another, the effects of negative campaigning can cancel each other out, dampening voter enthusiasm for both contestants and for participating in the electoral process.

Opposition research provides the foundation for negative campaigning. Campaigns begin with a thorough examination of an opponent's personal and professional background. Current members of Congress are qualified by virtue of their incumbency, although in some cases, such as 1992, incumbency can be used as a weapon against them. The backgrounds of challengers and open-seat candidates are usually more open to question, especially if they have no political experience or have pursued a career that most constituents would view with skepticism. Junk bond traders and dog catchers are at risk of being attacked as unqualified because of their professions.

The candidate's public record is the next thing that is usually explored. Challenger campaigns often study their opponent's attendance records, roll-call votes, floor speeches, and other congressional activities. Incumbent and open-seat campaigns study their opponent's political record if that person has previously held office. If an opponent has never held office, then a campaign will usually turn to newspaper or trade magazine accounts of speeches made to civic organizations, trade associations, or other groups.

Virtually all campaigns search for activities that can be construed as illegal or unethical. Federal indictments for influence peddling, the Keating Five scandal in the Senate, and the banking and Post Office scandals in the House provided many challengers with grist for the attack portions of their campaigns in 1992. Similarly, incumbents and open-seat contestants routinely search for unethical business transactions, evidence of tax-dodging, and other questionable activities that could be used to discredit their opponents. Sometimes ex-spouses, estranged children, former friends, colleagues, and neighbors are interviewed to find examples of improper behavior or character flaws.

Most opposition research is tedious. Researchers scour the *Congressional Record,* records of the floor proceedings of state legislatures, newspapers, and other public sources to show that a candidate is out of touch with the district, has flip-flopped on an issue, has taken an inordinate number of government-financed trips, or has committed some other questionable act. Opposition researchers often pore over campaign finance reports so they can make the claim that an opponent has raised too much campaign money from PACs or wealthy individuals who do not live in the candidate's district or state. This information is used to substantiate the claim that the opponent has or is likely to represent their interests instead of those of constituents.

The widespread use of negative advertising has encouraged most campaigns to search for their own candidate's weaknesses. As one campaign manager explained, "We need to be prepared for the worst. We have to spend a lot of time looking at the things our opponent may try to pin on us." Campaigns investigate their own candidates, often with the help of their party, in anticipation of attacks they expect to be levied against them. Sometimes campaigns discuss a potential liability before an opponent has had a chance to raise it. They seek to "inoculate" their candidates by preempting an attack. Well-financed Senate and House contenders have gone so far as to record television commercials containing their responses to particular charges before their opponent makes them. Others hire consulting firms that stake their reputations on their ability to prepare a televised response to an attack in less than one day.

Many of the most effective negative campaigns run in the last few elections blamed incumbents for a poor economy, for supporting tax increases, or for losing touch with their districts. Most 1992 challengers added congressional pay raises, political scandal, congressional perks, and the acceptance of PAC contributions to that list. Some personalized their attacks by counting the number of checks a member bounced at the House bank or the number of junkets he or she had taken at taxpayer or corporate expense. A common attack message played off the question, "If a person can't balance their own checkbook, even after gaining a pay raise, how can they be expected to balance the federal budget or resist raising taxes?" Bill Richardson tried to blame Vic Fazio for the House banking and Post Office scandals by pointing out that, as a Democratic congressional leader, Fazio was partially responsible for running those institutions. Fazio defused the attacks by carrying around a sign that read "No Bounced Checks." [47]

Notes

1. Angus Campbell, Philip E. Converse, Warren E. Miller, and Donald E. Stokes, *The American Voter* (New York: John Wiley and Sons, 1960), 541-548; and Donald R. Kinder and David O. Sears, "Public Opinion and Political Action," in *Handbook of Social Psychology*, 3d ed., ed. Gardner Lindzey and Elliot Aronson (New York: Random House, 1985), 659-741.
2. Gary C. Jacobson, *The Politics of Congressional Elections* (New York: HarperCollins, 1992), 117-118. See also Alan I. Abramowitz and Jeffrey A. Segal, *Senate Elections* (Ann Arbor: University of Michigan Press, 1992), 39.
3. See note 2.
4. Alan I. Abramowitz, "A Comparison of Voting for U.S. Senator and Representative in 1978," *American Political Science Review* 74 (1980): 633-640.
5. Gerald C. Wright and Michael B. Berkman, "Candidates and Policy in United States Senate Elections," *American Political Science Review* 80 (1986): 567-588; and Mark C. Westlye, *Senate Elections and Campaign Intensity* (Baltimore: Johns Hopkins University Press, 1992), 122-151.
6. Jacobson, *The Politics of Congressional Elections*, 119-120. See also Abramowitz and Segal, *Senate Elections*, 42.
7. Abramowitz, "A Comparison of Voting for U.S. Senator and Representative in 1978," 633-640; Wright and Berkman, "Candidates and Policy in United States Senate Elections," 567-588; and Westlye, *Senate Elections and Campaign Intensity*, chapter 6.
8. See, for example, Raymond E. Wolfinger and Steven J. Rosenstone, *Who Votes?* (New Haven: Yale University Press, 1980), 34-36, 58-60, 102-114.
9. See Morris P. Fiorina, *Retrospective Voting in American National Elections* (New Haven: Yale University Press, 1981); Gerald H. Kramer, "Short-Term Fluctuations in U.S. Voting Behavior, 1986-1964," *American Political Science Review* 65 (1971): 131-143; Edward R. Tufte, "Determinants of the Outcomes of Midterm Congressional Elections," *American Political Science Review* 69 (1975): 812-826; James E. Campbell, "Explaining Presidential Losses in Midterm Congressional Elections," *Journal of Politics* 47 (1985): 1140-1157; Richard D. McKelvey and Peter C. Ordeshook, "Information and Elections: Retrospective Voting and Rational Expectations," in *Information and Democratic Processes*, ed. John A. Ferejohn and James H. Kuklinski (Urbana: University of Illinois Press, 1990), 281-312; Samuel C. Popkin, *The Reasoning Voter: Communication and Persuasion in Presidential Campaigns* (Chicago: University of Chicago Press, 1991), especially chapters 3 and 4.
10. Alan I. Abramowitz, Albert D. Cover, and Helmut Norpoth, "The President's Party in Midterm Elections: Going from Bad to Worse," *American Journal of*

Political Science 30 (1986): 562-576; Samuel Kernell, "Presidential Popularity and Negative Voting: An Alternative Explanation of the Midterm Congressional Decline of the President's Party," *American Political Science Review* 71 (1977): 44-66. See also the studies cited in note 9.

11. Abramowitz, "A Comparison of Voting for U.S. Senator and Representative in 1978," 633-640; Raymond E. Wolfinger, "Candidates and Parties in Congressional Elections," *American Political Science Review* 74 (1980): 622-629; Barbara Hinckley, "House Re-Elections and Senate Defeats: The Role of the Challenger," *British Journal of Political Science* 10 (1980): 441-460; and Jacobson, *The Politics of Congressional Elections,* 132-136.

12. David R. Mayhew, *Congress: The Electoral Connection* (New Haven: Yale University Press, 1974), 49-68.

13. See Richard F. Fenno, Jr., *Home Style: House Members in Their Districts* (Boston: Little, Brown, 1978), especially chapters 3 and 4.

14. Eugene Conti, Price's campaign manager and administrative assistant, personal interview, July 8, 1993.

15. Caryn R. Sagal, "1992: The Year of the Challenger or the Year of the Incumbent? The Showdown in California's 3rd Congressional District," independent honors thesis, University of Maryland, 1994.

16. For an excellent discussion of polls see Barbara G. Salmore and Stephen A. Salmore, *Candidates, Parties, and Campaigns: Electoral Politics in America,* 2d ed. (Washington, D.C.: Congressional Quarterly, 1989), 116-119.

17. Bryce Bassett, director of marketing support, The Wirthlin Group, presentation to the Taft Institute Honors Seminar in American Government, June 15, 1993.

18. See for example, Robert Axelrod, "Where the Votes Come From: An Analysis of Presidential Election Coalitions, 1952-1968," *American Political Science Review* 66 (1972): 11-20.

19. Katina Rae Stapleton, "The Wild Race to Washington: The Making of Florida 3," unpublished paper, University of Maryland, 1992.

20. Joel C. Bradshaw, "Who Will Vote for You and Why: Designing Campaign Strategy and Theme," paper presented at the Conference on Campaign Management, The American University, Washington, D.C., December 10-11, 1992.

21. The logic behind the battle for the middle ground is presented in Anthony Downs, *An Economic Theory of Democracy* (New York: Harper and Row, 1957), chapter 8.

22. Fred Hartwig, vice president, Peter Hart and Associates, presentation to the Taft Institute Honors Seminar in American Government, June 15, 1993.

23. Ladonna Y. Lee, "Strategy," in *Ousting the Ins: Lessons for Congressional Challengers,* ed. Stuart Rothenberg (Washington, D.C.: Free Congress Research and Education Foundation, 1985), 18-19.

24. Kathleen Hall Jamieson, *Dirty Politics: Perception, Distraction, and Democracy* (Oxford: Oxford University Press, 1992), especially chapter 2.

25. Fenno, *Home Style,* chapters 3 and 4.

26. See Peter Clarke and Susan H. Evans, *Covering Campaigns: Journalism and Congressional Elections* (Stanford: Stanford University Press, 1983), 38-45; and Paul Bradford Raymond, "Shaping the News: An Analysis of House Candidates' Campaign Communications," in *Campaigns in the News: Mass Media and Congressional Elections,* ed. Jan Pons Vermeer (New York: Greenwood Press, 1987), 15.

27. On the differences between valence issues and position issues see Donald E. Stokes, "Spatial Models of Party Competition," in *Elections and the Politi-*

cal Order, ed. Angus Campbell, Philip E. Converse, Warren E. Miller, and Donald E. Stokes (New York: John Wiley and Sons, 1966), 161-169.

28. See, for example, Gary C. Jacobson and Samuel Kernell, "National Forces in the 1986 U.S. House Elections," *Legislative Studies Quarterly* 15 (1990): 72-85.
29. See Gary C. Jacobson, *The Politics of Congressional Elections* (New York: HarperCollins, 1993), 139-141.
30. This generalization is drawn from question 13 of the 1992 Congressional Campaign Study.
31. Amy Chance, "Fazio: Time for a 'New Economics,'" *Sacramento Bee,* July 14, 1992, A5.
32. Eugene Conti, Price's campaign manager and administrative assistant, personal interview, July 8, 1993.
33. Laura Mecoy, "California Budget Campaign," *Sacramento Bee,* A1; Martin Smith, "Bill Richardson Rides Again," *Sacramento Bee,* February 4, 1992, B4.
34. Stapleton, "The Wild Race to Washington."
35. The 40 percent figure includes campaigns that named health care as their first-, second-, or third-most-important issue.
36. Sagal, "1992: The Year of the Challenger or the Year of the Incumbent?"
37. In addition to abortion and gun control, the following were classified as position issues: prayer in school and other religion-based issues, illegal immigration, family values, social entitlement programs, civil rights and racial issues, senior citizens' issues, policy toward Cuba, the preservation of endangered species, nuclear power, and other environmental issues.
38. Hartwig presentation, June 15, 1993.
39. Phil Duncan, ed., *Politics in America, 1992: The 102nd Congress* (Washington, D.C.: Congressional Quarterly, 1991), 1133.
40. See, for example, James Innocenzi, "Political Advertising," in *Ousting the Ins,* ed. Rothenberg, 53-61; Salmore and Salmore, *Candidates, Parties, and Campaigns,* 159; Jay Bryant, "Paid Media Advertising in Political Campaigns," paper presented at the Conference on Campaign Management, The American University, December 10-11, 1992.
41. These generalizations are drawn from question 28 of the 1992 Congressional Campaign Study.
42. Richard R. Lau, "Negativity in Political Perception," *Political Behavior* 4 (1982): 353-377; and Richard R. Lau, "Two Explanations for Negativity Effects in Political Behavior," *American Journal of Political Science* 29 (1985): 110-138; Jamieson, *Dirty Politics,* 41.
43. Bradshaw, "Who Will Vote for You and Why."
44. Ladonna Y. Lee, "Strategy," 22.
45. See, for example, Jamieson, *Dirty Politics,* 103.
46. Peter Baker, "Moran Tried Marijuana in His Early Twenties," *Washington Post,* October 20, 1992, D1, D6.
47. Sagal, "1992: The Year of the Challenger or the Year of the Incumbent?"

Chapter 8

Campaign Communications

Campaign communications range from sophisticated television advertisements to old-fashioned knocking on doors. The resources at a candidate's disposal, the types of media available, and the competitiveness of the election are the factors that most strongly influence how campaigns reach voters. This chapter examines the techniques that campaigns use to disseminate their messages and get their supporters to the polls.

Campaign communications are meant to accomplish six objectives: to improve a candidate's name recognition, project the candidate's image, set the campaign agenda, exploit the issues, undermine the opponent's credibility and support, and defend the candidate against attacks. These objectives, of course, are designed to advance the campaign's broader goals of shoring up and expanding its bases of support and getting its supporters sufficiently interested in the election to vote.

Campaign communications usually proceed through four short phases which begin in late summer and continue until election day. In the first, often called the biography phase, candidates introduce themselves to voters by highlighting their experiences and personal backgrounds.

Next, candidates use issues to attract the support of uncommitted voters, energize their supporters, and further define themselves to the public. The attack phase often begins after one candidate learns that he or she is slipping in the polls or failing to advance on an opponent. At this time, candidates contrast themselves with their opponent, point to inconsistencies between an opponent's rhetoric and actions, try to exploit unpopular positions that the opponent has taken, or just plain sling mud at one another. In the final weeks of the campaign, most successful candidates pull their message together by reminding voters who they are, why they are running, and why they are more worthy of being elected than their opponent. At this final, or summation, phase they commonly emphasize phrases and symbols that were presented earlier in the campaign.

Television Advertising

Virtually every household in the United States possesses at least one television set, and the average adult watches more than three and one-half hours of television per day.[1] Fifty-four percent of all voters maintain that television is their most important source of information in senatorial and other statewide races. Forty-nine percent cite television as their most important source of information on House candidates.[2]

Television is the best medium for conveying image-related information to voters. It is also extremely useful in setting the campaign agenda and associating a candidate with valence issues.[3] Television ads enable candidates to transmit action-oriented videos that demonstrate such desirable qualities as leadership. Pictures of candidates meeting with voters or attending groundbreaking ceremonies convey more powerfully than do written or verbal statements the message that these individuals are actively involved in community affairs and have close ties to voters. Visuals are what make television an important campaign medium. As Republican strategist Robert Teeter explains, "80 or 90 percent of what people retain from a TV ad is visual. . . . If you have the visual right, you have the commercial right. If you don't, it almost doesn't matter what you're saying." [4] Television advertisements have the added advantage of giving the campaign full control over the message that is presented. Unlike interactive modes of communication, such as debates and speeches, paid advertisements do not allow an opponent or disgruntled voter to interrupt.

Roughly nine out of ten Senate campaigns and 70 percent of all House campaigns used television advertising during the 1992 elections.[5] More campaigns would have used television if the costs were not so high. Campaigns must pay the same rates as commercial advertisers for nonpreemptible advertising slots, and these can be prohibitive, especially during prime time. Democratic representative José Serrano or Michael Walters, his Republican opponent, would have had to spend $25,000 to broadcast one thirty-second prime-time ad to reach voters living in New York's 16th district during the 1992 election. The cost of broadcasting an ad to this South Bronx district is exorbitant because the district is in a media market that spans the entire New York metropolitan area. Candidates in Maine's 1st district, on the other hand, paid only $260 to air a thirty-second prime-time television ad that blanketed virtually the entire district.[6]

Some campaigns save money by forgoing the certainty that their ads will be broadcast during prime time. Those who purchase preemptible broadcast time are guaranteed a television station's lowest unit rate by federal law but run the risk of their ads being aired at some less desirable time. That is a risk few campaigns take. Other campaigns, including many in major metropolitan areas, save money by substituting cable TV for broadcast stations.

High costs and the mismatch between media markets and the boundaries of congressional districts discourage House candidates in the highly urbanized areas of the Middle Atlantic, West Coast, and southern New England from using television advertising. The distribution of media markets and relatively low advertising rates in most southwestern states and many rural areas, however, enable many House candidates to use television extensively.[7] Senate candidates tend to make greater use of television than candidates for the House because the configuration of state borders and media markets make television a relatively cost-efficient communications medium for candidates in statewide contests. Senate campaigns' greater funding levels and the expectation that Senate candidates will use television also contribute to its greater use in contests for the upper chamber.

Televised campaign advertisements have come a long way since the days when candidates appeared as talking heads that spouted their political experiences and issue positions. Six trends define the evolution of the modern television campaign commercial. They are a movement toward greater emphasis on imagery and valence issues, the use of action-oriented themes and pictures, the employment of emotionally laden messages, a decrease in the length of ads, an increase in negative advertising, and a reduction in the amount of time required to create an ad. Gimmicky, ten- and fifteen-second spots punctuated by twenty or so words have recently become extremely popular with House candidates. An ability to counterattack within twenty-four hours has become a major selling point for many media firms.[8]

Typically, incumbents' ads during the biography stage of the campaign depict them as experienced leaders who know and care about their constituents. Challengers and candidates for open seats also try to present themselves as capable and honorable by pointing to their accomplishments in politics, family life, or the private sector. All candidates broadcast advertisements that repeatedly mention and display their names and frequently end their commercials with the line "Vote for [candidate's name] for Congress."

Candidates who have led remarkable lives often broadcast what are called "mini-docudramas" to showcase their war record, community activism, or road to professional success. The biographical ad designed by Joe Slade White and Company for Ben Nighthorse Campbell's 1992 Democratic Senate primary in Colorado had a major impact on voters because it told how the candidate had triumphed over adversity to become a national leader and connected his personal experiences to his issue positions, thereby increasing his credibility on the issues. The two-minute ad opens with the words "Imagine this" printed in white on a black background. A narrator begins by reading the following text:

> Imagine this.... A young Native American; his mother a victim of tuberculosis, his father of chronic alcoholism. Early on, the young boy is to learn first-hand what happens when people are divided from one another. His sister and he are placed in separate orphanages; the odds are against them. But the odds themselves cannot rob the boy of his most valuable possessions—his dreams and his courage. At seventeen, he dons his country's uniform in the Korean War. In 1964, he again wears the uniform of his country as a member of the U.S. Olympic Team. His fellow athletes choose the young Native American to carry the flag in the closing ceremonies. His name: Ben Nighthorse Campbell.

As this portion of the script is read, black-and-white and color photographs show Campbell as a young boy in a sailor suit, then as a young man in a military uniform, and next in an Olympic uniform wearing a medal. The narration continues:

> Throughout his life, he has known how important real jobs are—a lesson he learned early loading and hauling crates of tomatoes and pears from the fields to the market. He taught high school during the day, and rode in the back of an ambulance as a young deputy at night. His strong pro-choice stand comes from seeing a young woman in the back of that ambulance one night, the victim of a back-alley abortion.

During this segment of the ad, Campbell is shown saddling a horse, and then some ambulance workers are shown unloading an emergency victim, over which the words "Pro-Choice" are faded in to the picture. The sound and images are designed to show how Campbell's pro-worker, pro-choice positions reflect his life experiences. This theme is continued:

> And as a man who saw his own family broken by poverty and illness, Ben Nighthorse Campbell's commitment to affordable, quality health care for all Americans is real. And as a chief of the northern Cheyenne his respect for the earth, the land, and the water is also real. As a husband and father, as a lawmaker and representative who has made a difference in people's lives, Ben Nighthorse Campbell knows that you cannot lead unless you can heal. And he has put the real lessons of an extraordinary life to work, to heal, to lead and to bring us together. And while the politics of the past have sought to divide us, Ben Nighthorse Campbell has united us. Real life. Real work. Real leadership. Ben Nighthorse Campbell for Colorado's U.S. senator. The time is now.

Here, the visuals are of the young Campbell in a sailor suit and the adult Campbell wearing a wide-rimmed, western-style hat, which is followed by a fade-in of the words "Pro-Health Care." When the narrator discusses Campbell's respect for the earth, he is shown on horseback adorned in a feathered headdress, staff, and other ceremonial, Native American garb. When Campbell's roles as a husband and father are raised, a photograph of him sitting on the front step of a house with his wife, son, and daughter is presented. The photographs that follow are a full-face close-up of the candidate and a picture of him speaking with an elderly female constituent. Then, there is a moving shot of Campbell sitting at a picnic table speaking with young teenagers, which is followed by a black screen with white letters that deliver the message:

"Real Life"
"Real Work"
"Real Leadership"

Finally, Campbell is shown riding a spotted horse in the Colorado landscape, and the words "Ben Nighthorse Campbell for U.S. Senator" are superimposed on the image, along with a small print tag line that reads "Paid for by Campbell Victory Fund '92."

Not many candidates have origins as humble or accomplishments as impressive as those of Senator Campbell, and few can present themselves in such heroic terms. Most House candidates cannot afford the broadcast time or production costs associated with a two-minute biographical ad. Nevertheless, candidates for both chambers can use television to make the point that they are resourceful, caring, effective leaders whose personal experiences underscore their commitment to certain issues and qualify them to serve in Congress. Some rely on the testimonials of popular national leaders. Others use what Republican political consultant Frank Luntz calls "sainthood spots," which commonly feature a mother or other family member turning the pages of the candidate's scrapbook or a photo album and discussing how even as a child the candidate showed great discipline and ideals.[9] One of the most popular kinds of testimonial features "man on the street" interviews that show average people giving their reasons for supporting a candidate.

Some House and Senate candidates use "community action" spots to show their involvement in local functions. These image-oriented ads are designed to demonstrate that the candidate cares enough about the district or state to represent it in Washington. "Feel good" ads are virtually devoid of substance and are designed to appeal to the electorate's sense of community pride or nationalism. They feature visuals of a candidate marching in parades, on horseback in the countryside, or involved in some other popular local activity. "Passing the torch" ads manipulate symbols to show the candidate to be the right person for the job. The most effective of these spots aired in recent years was broadcast by a presidential rather than a congressional candidate. It featured a youthful Bill Clinton shaking hands with President John F. Kennedy on the grounds of the White House.

During the issue phase, campaign ads communicate general policy positions on valence or position issues. David Price broadcast ads in 1992 discussing the importance of education and the role that workplace literacy plays in economic revitalization. Other candidates focused on taxes, abortion, illegal immigration, or other divisive issues. Although most voters have only a limited interest in any single issue, ads that focus on position issues can help a candidate pick up crucial support among single-issue voters or emphasize certain elements of his or her image.[10]

In the attack phase of the campaign, candidates use televised ads that often feature fancy graphics to point to their opponent's shortcomings. Television is ideally suited to comparative ads because it enables candidates to present pictures of themselves and their opponents side-by-side and to roll lists of issues down the screen showing themselves on the popular and their opponent on the unpopular sides of salient policies. Sometimes the opponent's head is reduced in size, "phased out," or distorted to keep voters' attention and to subtly imply that faulty issue positions are only one of an opponent's weaknesses.

Television is also an effective medium for portraying inconsistencies in an opponent's positions. Ads that feature images of the opponent somersaulting back and forth across the screen or debating himself or herself are useful in highlighting inconsistencies among an opponent's congressional roll-call votes, speeches, and campaign positions. They are especially useful for delivering the message that an incumbent has failed to represent constituents' views in Congress.

Challengers often use televised ads to criticize an incumbent's performance. Some present pictures of empty desks with "voice-overs" decrying poor attendance records. Pictures of airliners or beaches are frequently used to make the case that legislators have been vacationing at the public's or some interest group's expense rather than performing their jobs in Washington. Dozens of challengers capitalized on scandal and voter alienation in 1992 by broadcasting ads that featured bouncing checks, bouncing heads, or legislators voting themselves a pay raise. Both congressional campaign committees created generic ads designed to help challengers exploit both their opponents' ethical problems and voter frustration with Congress.

One attack ad often begets another, though television is ideal for alternative, often theatrical strategies. An ad in which a candidate criticizes an opponent for dragging the race into the mud can effectively answer negative charges while enhancing the candidate's image of sincerity as he or she appears to take the high road. Humorous ads can also be very effective and memorable. Russ Feingold responded to the negativity of his opponents' campaigns in the 1992 Senate Democratic primary in Wisconsin by airing an ad that featured him ducking to avoid being hit by mud thrown by his opponents, House member Jim Moody and millionaire business executive Joe Checota. Feingold's humorous, low-budget ads enabled him to overcome Moody's and Checota's spending advantages in the primary and to go on to win the general election.

In the summation stage of the campaign, eleventh-hour television blitzes are used to solidify a candidate's message in the minds of voters. Key phrases and visuals from earlier commercials are repeated as candidates who are ahead shore up support and those running behind appeal to undecided voters.

Radio Advertising

Radio is an extremely popular medium for congressional campaign communications. More than 90 percent of all House candidates and virtually every Senate contestant purchased radio ads during the 1992 elections.[11] Inexpensive to record and broadcast, radio commercials are ideal for building a candidate's name identification. Another advantage is that some candidates—whether intimidated by the television camera, untelegenic, novices to the spotlight, or products of the pre-television era—perform better on radio. For many incumbents, taping radio commercials is an easy extension of the radio shows they regularly send back to stations in their districts. Like television, radio is an excellent vehicle for emotion-laden messages.[12]

Radio allows candidates to target voters with great precision. Radio stations broadcast to smaller, more homogeneous audiences than television, enabling campaigns to tailor their messages to different segments of the population. Campaigns can reach Hispanic voters in the Southwest, Florida, or the inner cities of the Northeast by advertising on Spanish-language stations. "Golden oldies stations," which feature music from the 1960s and 1970s, are ideal for reaching middle-aged voters. Radio talk programs, such as the "Rush Limbaugh Show," are excellent vehicles for reaching voters who are committed to particular ideologies. Commuting hours furnish near-captive audiences of suburbanites who travel to work. In 1992 House Democrat George Brown, Jr., who is not reputed to be a fan of country and western music, placed ads on a country and western station to reach the hundreds of thousands of music enthusiasts who commute to and from work in his California district.[13]

Newspaper Advertising

Newspaper advertisements dominated campaign communications for much of American history but fell in importance with the decline of the partisan press in the late 1800s.[14] Congressional campaigns still purchase newspaper ads, but they are not as widely used as radio and many other media. Seventy percent of all House and 80 percent of all Senate campaigns purchased ads in local or statewide newspapers during the 1992 elections.[15]

Newspapers have a number of shortcomings as a campaign medium. They do not lend themselves to emotional appeals, are not as good as television for portraying imagery, and cannot be used to deliver a personalized message. Only a few congressional districts and states have large enough minority communities to sustain independent newspapers that can be used to target communications to these groups. The plethora of advertisements that appear in newspapers also limits their effectiveness as a tool for reaching voters.[16]

So why do most campaigns place ads in newspapers? One reason is that they are inexpensive. Newspaper advertisements cost less than ads transmitted via television, radio, mail, and virtually all other media. Newspaper ads can also be useful in announcing the times and locations of campaign events. Finally, some candidates and campaign aides believe that purchasing advertising space from a local newspaper can help them secure the paper's endorsement.

Direct-Mail Advertising

Mail can be used to raise money, convey a message, or encourage people to vote, but the key to success in all three areas is a good mailing list. A good fund-raising list is made up of previous donors or persons who have a history of contributing to like-minded candidates; a good advertising list includes supporters and persuadable voters; and a good voter mobilization list includes only the candidate's supporters.

Direct mail (sometimes referred to as persuasion mail) is one of the most widely used methods of campaign advertising in congressional elections, having been used by 94 percent of all House and nearly all Senate candidates in 1992.[17] Mail is a one-way medium which offers tremendous advantages in message control and delivery. Its main advantage is in targeting. Campaigns can purchase lists that include such information as a voter's name, address, gender, age, race or ethnicity, employment status, party registration, voting history, and estimated income.[18] This information enables campaigns to tailor the candidate profiles, issue positions, and photographs they include in their mailings such that they appeal to specific segments of the population. This makes mail an excellent medium for staking out position issues and for campaigning in heterogeneous states or districts. Campaigns waged in highly diverse areas, such as New York's 12th district, which is 58 percent Hispanic and includes most of Chinatown, often use the mail to campaign in more than one language.

A second advantage of mail is that it is a relatively inexpensive medium. Letters that are produced using personal computers and laser printers can be mailed to voters for little more than the price of a first-class stamp. Campaigns can also take advantage of Post Office discounts for pre-sorted mailings.

Nevertheless, direct mail is not without its disadvantages, including the fact that it is often tossed out as junk mail. Another disadvantage is that it rests principally on the power of the printed word. While television enables campaigns to embellish their messages with visual images and radio allows them to use sound effects for the same purpose, mail depends primarily on written copy to hold voters' attention and get a message across. This makes it a less effective medium for communicating image-related information.

Direct-mail experts rely on a number of techniques to combat the weaknesses of their medium. Personalized salutations, graphs, and pictures are often used to capture and hold voters' attention. Other gimmicks include the use of postscripts that are designed to look as though they were handwritten.

Direct mail is an especially powerful medium for challengers and candidates who have strong ideological positions because it is ideal for negative advertising or making appeals that stir voters' emotions. Yet mail also offers some advantages to incumbents. Many members of Congress send out letters early in the election cycle to reinforce voter support without mounting a highly visible campaign.[19] These mailings often include messages reinforcing those that incumbents communicate in congressionally franked mass mailings to constituents, which are prohibited after September 1 in election years.

Direct mail played a prominent role in a number of congressional elections, but its greatest impact was probably felt in the race for California's 3rd district seat. Bill Richardson struck the first blow in what could be called the "contest of dueling mail" when he sent to 100,000 voters copies of two issues of the *Valley Messenger,* a newspaper created by his campaign. The *Valley Messenger* looked very much like an ordinary newspaper. It had articles, letters to the editor, and an editorial page and bore the motto: "Serving the Communities of Northern California." The pseudo-newspaper attacked Fazio's "connections to Capitol Hill's perks and PACs" and his votes on appropriations for federal programs. The first issue's headline declared "Fazio Named #1 Big Spender in Congress." The second issue featured a photograph of Fazio below the caption, "Stop Me Before I Mail Again." It was printed on standard newsprint, and the only direct reference to the fact that the *Valley Messenger* was not an actual newspaper was a tiny disclaimer at the bottom of the front page stating: "Paid for by H. L. 'Bill' Richardson for Congress."[20]

Not to be outdone by the Richardson campaign, the Fazio organization printed its own issue of the *Valley Messenger.* This issue, however, carried a far different message. It featured the headline "Fazio Best for Congress" and included a front page editorial that endorsed Fazio and apologized for printing untrue stories about him in previous issues. Other articles criticized Richardson's campaign record and extolled Fazio's performance in Congress.[21] The Fazio campaign's response, which was widely admired by political consultants for its one-upmanship, caught the Richardson campaign off guard and without the time to respond. It contributed to the incumbent's 11 percent margin of victory.

Free Media

One of the major goals of any campaign is to generate free, or "earned," media—radio, television, newspaper, or magazine coverage that candidates receive when news editors consider their activities newsworthy. Earned media has other advantages besides the free publicity it gives to candidates. It also has greater credibility than campaign-generated communications because it is delivered by a neutral observer.[22] The major disadvantage of free media is that campaigns cannot control what news correspondents report. Misstatements and blunders are more likely to appear in the news than are issues raised in major policy speeches.

News coverage of congressional elections consists of stories based on press releases issued by campaigns; stories about events, issues, or time that a reporter has spent with a candidate; and analytical or editorial stories about a candidate or campaign.[23] Most analysis focuses on the "horse-race" aspect of the election. Those stories that get beyond handicapping the race usually discuss candidates' political qualifications, personal characteristics, or campaign organizations. Fewer stories focus on the issues.[24] Coverage by the electronic media tends to be shorter, more action-oriented, and less detailed and features less editorializing than print journalism.

Most journalists strive to cover politics objectively, but this does not mean that all candidates are treated the same. Reporters follow certain norms when pursuing leads and researching and writing their stories— norms that usually work to the advantage of certain kinds of candidates, most notably incumbents. Moreover, editorial boards are exempt from the norms of objectivity that govern political reporting. Newspaper owners and their editorial boards make no bones about voicing their opinions on editorial pages. Radio and television stations also air programs that feature pundits discussing the virtues and foibles of specific candidates. Most readers have come to expect newspaper editors and political talk show hosts to endorse specific candidates shortly before the election. Media endorsements and campaign coverage can have a significant impact on elections.

Attracting Coverage

Attracting media coverage requires planning and aggressiveness. Besides issuing streams of press releases, campaigns distribute copies of the candidate's schedule to correspondents, invite them to campaign events, and bend over backward to grant interviews. Candidates also submit themselves to interrogations by panels of newspaper editors with the goal of generating good press coverage or winning an endorsement.

Successful campaigns carefully play to the needs of different news media. Press releases that feature strong leads, have news value, provide relevant facts, and contain enough background information for an entire story are faxed to print reporters.[25] Advance notice of major campaign events, including information about predicted crowd size, acoustics, and visual backdrops, is given to television and radio correspondents with the hope that the event will be one of the few they cover.[26] Interpretive information is provided to all journalists, regardless of the media they work in, to try to generate campaign stories with a favorable "spin." News organizations routinely report stories based on materials distributed by campaigns; because few news organizations have adequate resources to research or even verify this information, most free press is uncritical.

Newspapers and radio stations are more likely to give candidates free media coverage than television stations. Television stations devote little time to covering congressional elections, particularly House races. Television news shows occasionally discuss the horse-race aspect of campaigns, cover small portions of campaign debates, or analyze controversial campaign ads, but few are willing to give candidates air time to discuss issues. Radio stations are more generous with air time. Many invite candidates to participate in "call-in" talk shows and candidate forums. Newspapers usually give the most detailed campaign coverage. Small, understaffed newspapers frequently print portions of candidates' press releases and debate transcripts verbatim.

Senate candidates attract more free media than do House candidates. Incumbents and open-seat contestants usually get more—and more favorable—press coverage than do challengers, regardless of whether the candidates are running for the House or the Senate. Inequities in campaign coverage are due to the professional norms that guide news journalists and to the inequalities that exist among candidates and campaign organizations. Journalists' preoccupation with candidates' personalities, qualifications, campaign organizations, and probable success are to the advantage of incumbents because they are almost always better known, more qualified, in possession of more professional organizations, and more likely to win than their opponents.[27]

Press coverage in House contests between an incumbent and a challenger is so unequal that veteran Democratic political adviser Anita Dunn believes "the local press is the unindicted co-conspirator in the alleged 'permanent incumbency.' "[28] As Dunn explains,

A vicious circle develops for challengers—if early on, they don't have money, standing in the polls, endorsements, and the backing of political insiders, they—and the race—are written off, not covered, which means the likelihood of a competitive race developing is almost nonexistent.[29]

The 1992 race between Republican incumbent Connie Morella and Democratic challenger Ed Heffernan in Maryland's 8th district demonstrates this point. Heffernan's name appeared in the *Washington Post* (the major newspaper serving the area) a mere ten times during the campaign season, and the coverage was consistently negative. During the primary phase of the election, the *Post* described Heffernan and the other candidates for the Democratic nomination as "chaff," an "embarrassment to the party," and "competing for the right to be underdog to Morella." During the general election, Heffernan was pronounced to be "largely unknown," "a bigger underdog than in the primary," and "facing long odds." Not surprisingly, the final mention of Heffernan's candidacy described him as being "handily defeated." [30]

Although many challengers can usually count on getting only four stories—their announcement, coverage of their primary victory, a candidate profile, and the announcement of their defeat—free media is still worth pursuing. Those few challengers who are able to make the case to journalists that they have the capacity to mount a strong campaign are able to attract significant media coverage, often enough to become known among local voters. Challengers who have held elective office or had significant unelective political experience, assembled professional campaign organizations, and raised substantial funds are in a better position to make this case than are those who have not. They typically receive extra press coverage, which in turn helps them raise more money, hire additional help, become more competitive, and attract even greater attention from the media.[31] A similar set of relationships exists for open-seat candidates, except it is usually easier for them to make the case that they are involved in a close contest.

Scandal can also help candidates attract more media coverage. Even underdogs are taken more seriously when their opponents have been accused of breaking the law or ethical misconduct. Republican challenger Peter Torkildsen, who defeated seven-term incumbent Nicholas Mavroules in the Massachusetts 6th district House race in 1992, is an example of an experienced challenger who took advantage of the heightened media exposure that resulted from scandal. Torkildsen, who had served six terms as a state representative and two years as the Massachusetts commissioner on labor and industries, mounted a highly professional and well-funded campaign effort. Under normal circumstances, neither he nor any Republican challenger in Massachusetts would have received much media coverage in a race against a long-time Democratic incumbent in a safe Democratic district. However, when Mavroules was indicted on federal charges of bribery, extortion, and tax evasion in August 1992, all sense of normalcy left the election. News correspondents began to devote significant coverage to the Republican congressional primary—an event often ignored in the state's Democrat-dominated politics—and later to Torkildsen's campaign to unseat Mavroules. The Torkildsen campaign fanned the flames of voter outrage over Mavroules's seventeen-count federal indictment by painting the incumbent as captured by the special interests; the campaign contrasted Mavroules's dependence on PAC money with Torkildsen's refusal to accept it. Torkildsen's ability to capitalize on the media opportunities provided by incumbent scandal enabled him to battle his way to a ten-point general election victory.[32]

Campaign Debates

Debates are among the few campaign activities that receive extensive press coverage and can place a challenger on equal footing with an incumbent. The decision to participate in a debate is a strategic one. Front-runners, who are usually incumbents, generally prefer to avoid debating because they understand that debates have the potential to do them more harm than good. Nevertheless, incumbents recognize that the public expects them to debate; to avoid being blasted for shirking their civic responsibility, they do so. Candidates who are running behind, usually challengers, have the most to gain from debating. They prefer to engage in as many debates as possible and to hold them when they will attract the most media coverage.

Before debates are scheduled, the candidates or their representatives negotiate a number of points. In addition to the number and timing of debates, candidates must agree on whether independent or minor-party candidates will participate, on the format that will be used, and on where the debate or debates will be held. All of these factors can influence who, if anyone, is considered the winner. Negotiations over debates can become heated but are almost always successfully resolved. Ninety-four percent of all House candidates and 96 percent of all Senate contestants debated their opponents in 1992.[33] Whether or not the candidates debate is one of the few questions in congressional elections that is usually decided in favor of challengers and candidates who are running behind.

Bias in the Press

Most House challengers and incumbents agree that the press does not cover elections evenhandedly.[34] More than half in each group believe that incumbents receive the lion's share of all press coverage (see Table 8-1). Democrats generally maintain that the press gives equal coverage to both campaigns, but Republicans typically report that their opponents received more press attention. More Democrats and incumbents than Republicans and challengers believe that the press covers elections fairly (see Table 8-2). To some extent these perceptions are a product of the

Table 8-1 Campaigners' Perceptions of the Distribution of Media Coverage in House Campaigns, 1992

Percent of respondents believing the media . . .	All	Party		Status			Competitiveness	
		Democrats	Republicans	Incumbents	Challengers	Open-seat candidates	Competitive	Uncompetitive
Gave more coverage to own campaign	29%	31%	28%	52%	13%	22%	28%	31%
Gave more coverage to opponent's campaign	34	28	40	10	53	39	32	36
Covered campaigns equally	37	41	32	37	34	39	40	33
(N)	(328)	(166)	(162)	(120)	(136)	(72)	(149)	(179)

Source: Question 25 of the 1992 Congressional Campaign Study.

Notes: Figures include responses from House general election candidates and campaign aides in major-party contested races, excluding those involved in incumbent-versus-incumbent races. Some columns do not add to 100 percent because of rounding.

Table 8-2 Campaigners' Perceptions of the Fairness of News Coverage in House Campaigns, 1992

Percent of respondents believing . . .	All	Party		Status			Competitiveness	
		Democrats	Republicans	Incumbents	Challengers	Open-seat candidates	Competitive	Uncompetitive
The media coverage was fair to both candidates	53%	60%	45%	73%	37%	46%	52%	53%
The media coverage favored candidate	7	6	7	8	5	8	8	5
The media coverage favored opponent	41	34	48	19	58	46	40	42
(N)	(323)	(164)	(159)	(120)	(131)	(72)	(147)	(176)

Source: Question 26 of the 1992 Congressional Campaign Study.

Notes: Figures include responses from House general election candidates and campaign aides in major-party contested races, excluding those involved in incumbent-versus-incumbent races. Some columns do not add to 100 percent because of rounding.

norms that guide journalists and the distribution of media endorsements—which favor incumbents, most of whom are Democrats (see Table 8-3). The perceptions also reflect a widely shared opinion among Republicans that the media corps is made up of members of the liberal establishment.[35] The large numbers of candidates and campaign aides of both parties who believe that the media are biased against them reflect the adversarial relationship that exists between politicians and the press.[36]

Field Work

Field work involves voter registration and get-out-the-vote drives, literature drops, and the distribution of yard signs and bumper stickers. It also includes candidate appearances at town meetings and in parades, speeches to Rotary Clubs and other civic groups, door-to-door campaigning, and other grass-roots activities. Field work is an important means of campaign communication and voter mobilization.

Field activities were the key to campaigning during the days of the old-fashioned political machines and they continue to play a role in modern House and Senate elections. Sophisticated targeting plans, similar to those used in direct mail, guide many field activities. Field work remains one of the most labor intensive, volunteer-dependent aspects of congressional elections.[37] Candidates, their supporters, and local party workers knock on doors to learn whether citizens intend to vote, whom they support, and if they have any specific concerns they would like the candidate to address. Supporters and potential supporters who express an interest in an issue, need to register to vote, indicate they could use help in getting to the polls, or are willing to work in the campaign typically receive follow-up contact.

Person-to-person contact is a highly effective means of political persuasion, especially when it takes place directly between the candidate and a voter. It also provides a campaign with useful feedback. Candidates routinely draw on conversations with individuals they meet along the campaign trail to develop anecdotes that humanize issues.

Field activities are relatively inexpensive because they can be carried out by volunteers. Local party activists, union members, and other volunteers can be called on to deliver campaign literature, register voters, or drive them to the polls. The development of the "coordinated campaign" has allowed many congressional candidates to rely in part on party organizations to carry out their field work.[38] Forty percent of all House campaigns reported that local party committees played a moderate-to-extremely important role in their registration and get-out-the-vote drives, and over half of the campaigns reported that local parties were a moderately-to-extremely important source of campaign volunteers.[39]

Table 8-3 Campaigners' Perceptions of Local Media Endorsements in House Campaigns, 1992

Percent of respondents reporting media endorsements received by . . .		Party		Status			Competitiveness	
	All	Democrats	Republicans	Incumbents	Challengers	Open-seat candidates	Competitive	Uncompetitive
Own candidate	33%	37%	29%	65%	6%	28%	27%	39%
Opponent	33	29	37	5	60	27	29	36
Both (by different outlets)	30	28	31	26	27	40	41	18
Neither candidate	4	6	3	5	7	4	3	7
(N)	(333)	(168)	(165)	(120)	(139)	(74)	(151)	(182)

Source: Question 27 of the 1992 Congressional Campaign Study.

Notes: Figures include responses from House general election candidates and campaign aides in major-party contested races, excluding those involved in incumbent-versus-incumbent races. Some columns do not add to 100 percent because of rounding.

The Importance of Different Communications Techniques

Congressional campaigns disseminate their messages through a variety of media, each having its advantages and disadvantages. Door-to-door campaigning is inexpensive but time consuming. Television advertising requires little commitment of the candidate's time, but it is rarely cheap. Radio advertising and direct mail require accurate targeting to be effective.

Most campaigners believe that television is the best medium for disseminating their messages (see Table 8-4).[40] Incumbents consider it to be more crucial than do challengers, reflecting the fact that more incumbents can afford to broadcast television commercials. But it is open-seat candidates who most consistently evaluate television as extremely important. The overwhelming majority of open-seat candidates can afford the high cost of broadcast time, and their races are usually competitive enough to warrant purchasing it.

Most House candidates and campaign aides also assess radio coverage and advertising, direct mail, and free media as very important. Campaign literature and speeches are rated slightly lower, but both are still considered moderately-to-very important ways of reaching voters. The differences in the evaluations of House campaigners are less pronounced for these media than they are for television. Republicans tend to place somewhat more emphasis on radio, direct mail, campaign literature, and speeches and rallies than do Democrats. Candidates involved in competitive contests, including open-seat contestants, place slightly higher significance on radio and direct mail than do others.

Most campaigns use candidate visits to shopping malls and workplaces, door-to-door canvasses, campaign debates, and newspaper advertisements to help get out their message, but they consider these to be only moderately important communication techniques. Neighborhood canvasses, billboards, surrogate campaigning, and other grass-roots activities are viewed less favorably by incumbents because they can afford to use television, direct mail, and other, more sophisticated approaches.

District characteristics and campaign strategy also have an impact on media usage patterns. Television is a more important communications medium for House campaigns in rural districts than it is for those conducted in urban and suburban settings, reflecting cost considerations and the mismatch between media markets and House seats in metropolitan areas (see Table 8-5). Greater population density allows campaigns waged in urban and suburban districts to make greater use of field activities, including distributing campaign literature and canvassing door-to-door, than campaigns waged in rural areas. Campaigns that target individuals who live in particular neighborhoods, work in certain occupations, or belong to specific segments of the population (such as women, the elderly,

Table 8-4 Campaigners' Perceptions of the Importance of Different Communications Techniques in House Campaigns, 1992

	All	Party		Status			Competitiveness	
		Democrats	Republicans	Incumbents	Challengers	Open-seat candidates	Competitive	Uncompetitive
Television (paid or free)	4.18	4.18	4.18	4.15	3.94	4.66	4.39	3.99
Radio (paid or free)	3.76	3.60	3.93	3.74	3.73	3.86	3.81	3.73
Newsletters and direct mail	3.68	3.53	3.83	3.77	3.50	3.87	3.79	3.59
Press releases and free media	3.67	3.67	3.66	3.69	3.74	3.49	3.70	3.63
Literature drops	3.50	3.40	3.61	3.27	3.65	3.60	3.41	3.58
Speeches and rallies	3.46	3.26	3.66	3.27	3.57	3.55	3.19	3.68
Candidate visits to shopping centers, factories, etc.	3.10	3.06	3.13	3.22	3.08	2.95	3.21	2.97
Door-to-door canvassing	3.10	3.10	3.11	2.81	3.26	3.29	3.08	3.13
Debates	3.06	2.84	3.28	2.70	3.10	3.57	3.06	3.06
Newspaper ads	3.00	3.06	2.94	2.96	3.06	2.94	3.06	2.94
Billboards and buttons	2.62	2.53	2.72	2.48	2.71	2.69	2.76	2.47
Surrogate campaigning	2.54	2.39	2.70	2.32	2.73	2.58	2.64	2.44
(N)	(325)	(164)	(161)	(118)	(133)	(74)	(149)	(175)

Source: Question 22 of the 1992 Congressional Campaign Study.

Notes: Candidates and campaign aides were asked to assess the importance of each technique on the following scale: 1 = not important or not used; 2 = slightly important; 3 = moderately important; 4 = very important; 5 = extremely important. The values listed are the arithmetic means of the scores. Figures include responses from House general election candidates and campaign aides in major-party contested races, excluding those involved in incumbent-versus-incumbent races.

Table 8-5 The Impact of Geography and Targeting Strategies on the Importance of Different Communications Techniques in House Campaigns, 1992

	District geography			Targeting strategy	
	Urban	Rural	Suburban or mixed	Group-based	Issue- or attitude-based
Television (paid or free)	4.17	4.50	4.13	4.25	4.12
Radio (paid or free)	3.77	3.72	3.76	3.78	3.75
Newsletters and direct mail	3.80	3.60	3.58	3.90	3.49
Press releases and free media	3.54	3.88	3.80	3.81	3.59
Literature drops	3.64	3.04	3.40	3.62	3.43
Speeches and rallies	3.46	3.48	3.44	3.47	3.44
Candidate visits to shopping centers, factories, etc.	3.02	3.25	3.22	3.12	3.08
Door-to-door canvassing	3.25	2.89	3.17	3.08	3.11
Debates	3.07	3.12	3.03	3.14	3.00
Newspaper ads	2.99	3.32	2.94	2.99	3.00
Billboards and buttons	2.71	2.68	2.50	2.69	2.57
Surrogate campaigning	2.54	2.40	2.57	2.60	2.50
(N)	(172)	(25)	(125)	(113)	(209)

Source: Questions 17 and 22 of the 1992 Congressional Campaign Study.

Notes: Districts are defined as urban (or rural) if 60 percent or more of the population lives in an urban (or rural) area; all others are classified as suburban or mixed. Targeting strategies are defined as group-based if campaigns focused on voters in specific geographic locations or demographic or occupational groups; targeting strategies are defined as issue- or attitude-based if they focused on issues, voters' party affiliations, persuadable voters, Perot supporters, or miscellaneous factors. Candidates and campaign aides were asked to assess the importance of each technique on the following scale: 1 = not important or not used; 2 = slightly important; 3 = moderately important; 4 = very important; 5 = extremely important. The values listed are the arithmetic means of the scores. Figures include responses from House general election candidates and campaign aides in major-party contested races, excluding those involved in incumbent-versus-incumbent races.

or members of an ethnic group) make greater use of direct mail than do campaigns that focus their efforts on less easily identifiable groups, such as single-issue voters.

Notes

1. Nielson Rating Service annual report and 1980 census data, cited in Frank I. Luntz, *Candidates, Consultants, and Campaigns* (Oxford: Basil Blackwell, 1988), 73.
2. Luntz, *Candidates, Consultants, and Campaigns,* 73; Thomas E. Patterson, *The Mass Media Election: How Americans Choose Their President* (New York: Praeger, 1980), 77-91.
3. See, for example, Darrell M. West, *Air Wars: Television Advertising in Election Campaigns, 1952-1992* (Washington, D.C.: Congressional Quarterly, 1993), especially chapter 6.
4. Quoted in Luntz, *Candidates, Consultants, and Campaigns,* 77.
5. This generalization is drawn from question 22 of the 1992 Congressional Campaign Study.
6. The figures for New York and Maine were provided by Will Robinson, vice president for production, Joe White and Company, personal interview, March 18, 1993.
7. Louis Sandy Maisel, *From Obscurity to Oblivion: Running in the Congressional Primary* (Knoxville: University of Tennessee Press, 1982), 111; Edie N. Goldenberg and Michael W. Traugott, *Campaigning for Congress* (Washington, D.C.: CQ Press, 1984), 116-119; John R. Alford and Keith Henry, "TV Markets and Congressional Elections," *Legislative Studies Quarterly* 9 (1984): 665-675; and Barbara G. Salmore and Stephen A. Salmore, *Candidates, Parties, and Campaigns: Electoral Politics in America,* 2d ed. (Washington, D.C.: CQ Press, 1989), 142.
8. Luntz, *Candidates, Consultants, and Campaigns,* 76.
9. Ibid., 85. For two excellent discussions of television campaign commercials see Luntz chapter 3 and Jamieson, *Dirty Politics, Deception, Distraction, and Democracy* (Oxford: Oxford University Press, 1992), passim.
10. Kim F. Kahn, Patrick J. Kenney, Tom W. Rice, "Ideological Learning in U.S. Senate Elections," paper presented at the annual conference of the American Political Science Association, Washington, D.C., September 2-5, 1993. See also Jay Bryant, "Paid Advertising in Political Campaigns," paper presented at the Conference on Campaign Management, The American University, Washington, D.C., December 10-11, 1992.
11. This generalization is drawn from question 22 of the 1992 Congressional Campaign Study.
12. Luntz, *Candidates, Consultants, and Campaigns,* 108.
13. Marty Stone, California field director, DCCC, personal interview, February 23, 1993.
14. See, for example, Frank Luther Mott, *American Journalism: A History of 250 Years, 1690 to 1940* (New York: Macmillan, 1947), 411-430.
15. This generalization is drawn from question 22 of the 1992 Congressional Campaign Study.
16. See, for example, Luntz, *Candidates, Consultants, and Campaigns,* 109-110.

17. This generalization is drawn from question 22 of the 1992 Congressional Campaign Study.

18. See, for example, R. Kenneth Godwin, *One Billion Dollars of Influence: The Direct Marketing of Politics* (Chatham, N.J.: Chatham House, 1988), especially chapters 1-3; Luntz, *Candidates, Consultants, and Campaigns*, 152; Jonathan Robbin, "Geodemographics: The New Magic," in *Campaigns and Elections*, ed. Larry J. Sabato (Glenview, Ill.: Scott Foresman, 1989), 105-124; and Sabato, "How Direct Mail Works," in *Campaigns and Elections*, ed. Sabato, 88-99.

19. See Salmore and Salmore, *Candidates, Parties, and Campaigns*, 86-87.

20. Stuart Rothenberg, "Pseudo-Newspapers and Other '92 Tales of Election Activity," *Roll Call*, November 23, 1992.

21. Ibid.

22. See Peter Clarke and Susan Evans, *Covering Campaigns: Journalism in Congressional Elections* (Stanford: Stanford University Press, 1983), chapter 6.

23. Xandra Kayden, *Campaign Organization* (Lexington, Mass.: D.C. Heath, 1978), 125.

24. See, for example, Clarke and Evans, *Covering Campaigns*, 60-62; Doris A. Graber, *Mass Media and American Politics*, 4th ed. (Washington, D.C.: CQ Press, 1993), 262, 268-270; Goldenberg and Traugott, *Campaigning for Congress*, 127.

25. A useful discussion of press releases is presented in Sallie G. Randolph, "The Effective Press Release: Key to Free Media," in *Campaigns and Elections*, ed. Sabato, 26-32.

26. Kayden, *Campaign Organization*, 126.

27. See, for example, Clarke and Evans, *Covering Campaigns*, 60-62; Goldenberg and Traugott, *Campaigning for Congress*, 127.

28. Anita Dunn, "The Best Campaign Wins: Coverage of Down Ballot Races by Local Press," paper presented at the Conference on Campaign Management, The American University, Washington, D.C., December 10-11, 1992.

29. Dunn, "The Best Campaign Wins."

30. Quoted in Dunn, "The Best Campaign Wins."

31. These generalizations are from an analysis that uses question 25 of the 1992 Congressional Campaign Study, the political experience measure developed in chapter 2, the campaign professionalism measure from the bottom of Table 3-1, and candidates' campaign receipts to demonstrate that political experience, campaign professionalism, and campaign receipts are positively related to the free media coverage that campaigns receive.

32. The material on the Torkildsen and Mavroules campaigns is from Gavin Sutcliffe, "The Price of Scandal: Legal Problems Defeat a Veteran Congressman in Massachusetts' Sixth District," unpublished paper, University of Maryland, 1992.

33. This generalization is drawn from question 22 of the 1992 Congressional Campaign Study.

34. The observations of candidates and campaign aides presented here are similar to the findings in a content analysis of the endorsements of local newspapers. See Clarke and Evans, *Covering Campaigns*, chapter 4.

35. On media bias see Michael J. Robinson, "Just How Liberal is the News? 1980 Revisited," *Public Opinion* 6 (1983): 55-60; William Schneider and I. A. Lewis, "Views on the News," *Public Opinion* 8 (1985): 6-11,58-59; S. Robert Lichter, Stanley Rothman, and Linda S. Lichter, *The Media Elite* (Bethesda, Md.: Adler and Adler, 1986); Herbert J. Gans, "Are U.S. Journalists Danger-

ously Liberal?" *Columbia Journalism Review* (November/December 1985): 29-33; and Times-Mirror Center for the People and the Press, "The People and the Press, Part 5: Public Attitudes Toward News Organizations."

36. See, for example, Lance W. Bennett, *News: The Politics of Illusion* (New York: Longman, 1983), 76-78; Austin Ranney, *Channels of Power: The Impact of Television on American Politics* (New York: Basic Books, 1983), 54-55.

37. See, for example, Will Robinson, "Campaign Field Work," paper presented at the Conference on Campaign Management, The American University, Washington, D.C., December 10-11, 1992, and Robbin, "Geodemographics," 105-124.

38. Paul S. Herrnson, "National Party Organizations and the Postreform Congress," in *The Postreform Congress,* ed. Roger H. Davidson (New York: St. Martin's Press, 1992), 65-66.

39. These generalizations are drawn from questions 30 and 35 of the 1992 Congressional Campaign Study.

40. The responses from campaigns that did not use one of the communications techniques in the table were recoded as 1 (meaning the specific technique was not important to their campaign) prior to calculating the figures in the table. For this reason, the figures underestimate the importance of certain communication techniques to the campaigns that used them but give a more accurate estimate of the overall importance of each technique to House campaigns in general. The major impact of recoding the data was to depress the estimates for the importance of television.

Chapter 9

Candidates, Campaigns, and Electoral Success

What separates winners from losers in congressional elections? How big an impact do candidate characteristics, political conditions, campaign strategy, campaign effort, party and interest group activities, and media coverage have on the percentage of the votes that House candidates receive? Do these factors affect incumbents, challengers, and open-seat contestants equally, or do these contestants need to do different things to win elections?

This chapter addresses these and other questions using the results of a statistical analysis that estimates the impact of these factors on the percentages of votes that candidates win. (Detailed descriptions of the statistical techniques are provided in the appendix.) It also discusses the differences in opinion among winners and losers over what determines the outcomes of House races. Finally, some comparisons are drawn between House and Senate campaigns.

Incumbent Campaigns

Incumbency has a tremendous impact on the kinds of campaigns that candidates mount, and it is the most important determinant of congressional election outcomes. Virtually all incumbents begin the general election with higher name recognition and voter approval levels, greater political experience, more money, and better campaign organizations than their opponents. Incumbents also benefit from the fact that most constituents and political elites in Washington expect them to win and act accordingly. For the most part, voters cast ballots, volunteers donate time, contributors give money, and news correspondents provide coverage in ways that favor incumbents. Most potential challengers also behave in ways that contribute to high incumbent success rates. Challengers who are most capable of waging strong campaigns generally wait until a seat becomes open rather than take on a sitting incumbent.

The big leads that most incumbents enjoy at the beginning of the election make defending those leads the major objective of their campaigns. Incumbent campaigns tend to focus more on reinforcing and mobilizing existing bases of support than winning new ones. As the campaign manager for one shoo-in House member explained,

> Our goals are to remind voters of [the candidate's] record, what he's done for the district, how he works hard on their behalf, and make sure they show up on Tuesday to give him their votes. If everyone does their part we should have no problem with this election.

The overwhelming advantages that incumbents possess make incumbency an accurate predictor of election outcomes in roughly nine out of ten House and three-quarters of all Senate races in which incumbents seek reelection.

Of course, not every incumbent is a shoo-in, and some challengers have realistic chances of winning. Incumbents who are implicated in a scandal, have cast roll-call votes that are out of sync with voters, or possess other liabilities need to mount more aggressive campaigns. These candidates must begin campaigning early to maintain their popularity among supporters, to remind voters of their accomplishments in office, and to set the campaign agenda. They also must be prepared to counter the campaigns of the strong challengers who are nominated to run against them. Many incumbents in jeopardy face experienced challengers, some of whom amass the financial and organizational resources needed to mount a serious campaign. A few of these challengers in each election are able to capitalize on their opponent's weaknesses and to win.

For the majority of House incumbents who begin with big leads over their opponents, there is little that can be done to increase their victory margins. All incumbents—Democrat or Republican, Caucasian or African American, old or young, male or female—have tremendously favorable odds of winning again. Few variables—indeed only the seven identified in Table 9-1—had a significant direct effect on the percentages of the vote that incumbents won in 1992. Such factors as gender, age, race, and occupation, which were so influential in separating House candidates from the general population, had no impact on incumbents' vote shares. Primary challenges from within their own party also did not significantly harm the reelection prospects of incumbents who defeated their primary opponents. Moreover, incumbents' targeting strategies, issues, and communications expenditures had no significant impact on their vote shares in the

Table 9-1   Significant Predictors of House Incumbents' Vote Shares, 1992

	Percent
Base vote	65.29
Partisan bias (per one-point advantage in party registration)	+0.08
Political scandal	−4.39
Significant independent or minor-party candidate	−9.65
Challenger spending on campaign communications (per $1,000)	−0.023
Party spending on behalf of challenger (per $1,000)	−0.12
Independent expenditures against incumbent (per $1,000)	−0.097
Media advantage favoring incumbent	+2.54

Sources: Questions 15, 20, 21, and 26 of the 1992 Congressional Campaign Study, Federal Election Commission data, various editions of *Congressional Quarterly Weekly Report,* and other sources discussed in the appendix.

Notes: Regression statistics are presented in Table A-2 in the appendix. The analysis includes general election candidates in major-party contested races, excluding those in incumbent-versus-incumbent races. N = 117.

general election. The campaign efforts that party committees and supportive PACs mounted on incumbents' behalf also had no impact.

The first figure in Table 9-1, labeled the base vote, represents the percentage of the vote that a House incumbent in a typical two-party contested race would have received if all of the other factors were set to zero.[1] A hypothetical incumbent who ran for reelection in a district that had equal numbers of registered Democratic and Republican voters, who had not been implicated in a scandal, who did not face minor-party opposition, who faced a challenger who spent no money and benefited from no party coordinated expenditures, who was not attacked by PACs, and who was not given preferential treatment by the press would have received roughly 65 percent of the vote.

Certain districts and states lend themselves to the election of particular kinds of candidates. Districts populated mainly by Democratic voters (often urban districts which are home to many middle-class, poor, or minority voters) typically elect Democrats; those populated by members of the GOP (frequently suburban districts inhabited by more affluent voters) usually elect Republicans. The partisan bias of the district (the difference between the percentage of registered voters who belong to a candidate's party minus the percentage of registered voters who belong to the opponent's party) has a positive impact on incumbents' electoral prospects.[2] As the second figure in the table indicates, for every one percent increase in the partisan advantage that incumbents enjoyed among registered voters in 1992, they received an additional .08 percent of the vote. Democratic incumbents who represented districts with 75 registered Democratic voters for every 25 registered Republicans typically won 4 percent (fifty-point advantage in party registration multiplied by .08) more of the vote than Democratic incumbents who ran in districts that were evenly split between Democratic and Republican registered voters. When this extra 4 percent is added to the base vote of 65 percent, these candidates' estimated vote shares increased to approximately 69 percent. Partisan bias is an important source of incumbency advantage because most House members represent districts that are populated primarily by members of their party.

Those few House members who represent districts in which the balance of voter registration does not favor their party are often in danger of losing reelection. Peter Kostmayer is an example of a House member who represented a marginal district and ultimately went down in defeat. Kostmayer, a fairly liberal Democrat, was first elected to represent Pennsylvania's 8th district in an open-seat contest in 1976. Anti-Republican sentiments brought on by the Watergate scandal contributed to his 1,312-vote victory. Kostmayer won reelection in 1978 by downplaying economic issues and emphasizing the environment, which was a major concern of many of his constituents.[3] In 1980, a year in which economic issues were at the center of public attention, Kostmayer lost to Republican James Coyne by a 2 percent vote margin. Kostmayer then defeated Coyne in the 1982 election 50 percent to 49 percent of the vote. He continued to hold tenuously to the seat through the 1980s, winning reelection with less than 52 percent of the vote twice and never amassing a reelection margin greater than 15 percent. In 1992, a year in which economic issues were once again at the center of the political agenda, Kostmayer lost to Republican state senator James Greenwood by 6 percent of the vote.

Members of Congress who are implicated in a scandal are also usually at risk. Those identified with salacious or highly publicized misbehavior frequently choose to retire rather than add the anguish of defeat to the humiliation associated with their ethical lapses. Nevertheless, some scandalized members of Congress attempt to remain in office. Many of them suffer at the ballot box. The 1992 House elections were notable for the huge number of members implicated in the House banking scandal.[4] Some had bounced only a few checks for insignificant sums, while others had bounced hundreds of checks for hundreds of thousands of dollars. Most voters are reasonable, have occasionally written a bad check, and would be willing to forgive a member of Congress who had a few overdrafts. Any House member who kited twenty-five or more checks at the House bank, however, had good reason to worry. The two House incumbents who were subjects of federal investigations—Nicholas Mavroules (D-Mass.) and Joseph McDade (R-Pa.)—also had reason to fear the effects of scandal. Voters' information about their elected representatives may be incomplete, but voters usually learn enough about a public official's ethical transgressions to put that person's career in jeopardy, as a number of House members learned in 1992. Incumbents who overdrafted twenty-five or more checks at the House bank or were the subject of some other major scandal were penalized by an average of nearly 4.4 percent of the vote.

One of the most important signs that a House incumbent might be in trouble is the emergence of a significant independent or minor-party candidate (one who garners 10 percent or more of the vote). These candidates usually run during periods of voter frustration or against incumbents who are perceived to be out of touch with their constituents or who are implicated in a scandal. Although they rarely win (Rep. Bernard Sanders of Vermont is the only one to serve in the House since 1955),[5] independent candidates can sometimes sufficiently alter the dynamics of a race as to affect its outcome. The main impact of independent and minor-party candidacies is to take away significant numbers of votes from incumbents. In 1992 House members who faced both major-party and minor-party opposition won almost 10 percent fewer votes than those who did not.

Because most House members begin the general election well known and liked by their constituents, few elements of incumbent campaigning have a significant impact on election outcomes. The targeting approaches that incumbents use, the themes and issues they stress, and whether or not they bash their opponents do not significantly affect the typical incumbent's vote margin.[6] Nor do the total dollars incumbents spend on campaign communications, the individual expenditures they make on direct-mail, television, radio, and newspaper advertising, or field work make a significant positive contribution to the percentage of the votes they win.[7]

Incumbent spending in 1992 followed the usual pattern of increasing in direct response to the closeness of the race.[8] Shoo-ins, such as David Price, who ran against underfunded challengers undertook fairly modest reelection efforts by incumbent standards, assembling relatively small organizations and spending moderate sums of money. Those who were pitted against well-funded challengers, however, followed Vic Fazio's lead and mounted very extensive campaigns. The average incumbent spent roughly $400,000 to communicate with voters and won 62 percent of the vote; the typical incumbent in jeopardy spent $523,000 on campaign communications and won just over 53 percent of the vote.

Although incumbents' communications expenditures and other campaign activities are not significantly related to higher vote margins, this does not mean they are inconsequential. A more realistic interpretation of incumbent campaigning is that it generally works to reinforce rather than expand a candidate's existing base of support. Incumbents who are in the most trouble—because they represent marginal districts, have been implicated in a scandal, failed to keep in touch with voters, or cast too many legislative votes that were out of line with constituents' views—usually spend the most. Most of these candidates either succeed in reinforcing their electoral bases or watch their share of the vote dip slightly from previous years. Others watch their victory margins become perilously low. The high-powered campaigns these incumbents wage might make the difference between winning and losing reelection. In a few cases, such as Mavroules's 10 percent loss to Republican challenger Peter Torkildsen, it is probable that no amount of incumbent spending would have made a difference. Scandal, poor performance, and some other factors simply put reelection beyond the reach of some candidates. Regardless of whether an incumbent in a close race wins or loses, that individual would undoubtedly have done worse absent an extensive campaign effort.

House challengers' expenditures, however, have a significant impact on incumbents' vote shares. For every $1,000 that challengers spent to communicate with voters in 1992, they deprived incumbents of roughly .023 percent of the vote. The typical challenger spent roughly $120,000 on voter contact, reducing the average incumbent's vote by nearly 3 percent to a total of 62.5 percent of the vote. Communications spending by hopeful challengers, which averaged $230,000, reduced the votes won by the typical incumbent in jeopardy by just over 5 percent to about 60 percent.

Party and interest group activity in House elections does more to harm than help incumbents' prospects. The coordinated expenditures that parties make on behalf of incumbents and the independent expenditures that PACs make to help them do not significantly improve most incumbents' already high prospects of reelection. This is largely so because parties and PACs get most involved when an incumbent is in trouble; therefore, those who attract the most party and PAC support often win by the smallest margins and sometimes lose.

The efforts that parties and PACs make on behalf of challengers, by contrast, do influence congressional elections. For every $10,000 a party spends on behalf of a challenger, it deprives the incumbent of 1.2 percent of the vote. Given that the average coordinated expenditure for challengers was roughly $16,000 in 1992, these expenditures cost the typical incumbent nearly 2 percent of the vote. When a party spent $55,000 in coordinated expenditures (the legal maximum) to assist its challengers, it helped those individuals drive down their opponents' vote shares by almost 7 percent. Similarly, for every $10,000 in independent expenditures that PACs make to defeat incumbents, they deprived them of about 1 percent of the vote. Because few PACs are willing to take the risks associated with making independent expenditures, however, their effect tends to be limited.

Media coverage has a significant impact on incumbents' reelection efforts. Incumbent campaigns that reported receiving more free media than their opponents or were the sole beneficiaries of media endorsements in 1992 won roughly 2.5 percent more of the vote than incumbents who did not enjoy such positive relations with the "fourth estate." The efforts that House candidates and their press secretaries make to cultivate news correspondents are clearly worthwhile.

Challenger Campaigns

Most challengers begin the general election at a disadvantage. Lacking a broad base of support, these candidates must build one. Challengers need to mount aggressive campaigns in order to become visible, build name recognition, give voters reasons to support them, and overcome the initial advantages of their opponents. Challenger campaigns also need to disseminate messages that will not only attract uncommitted voters but also convince some voters to abandon their pro-incumbent loyalties in favor of the challenger.

The typical House challenger is in a position similar to that of a novice athlete pitted against a world-class sprinter. The incumbent has experience, talent, professional handlers, funding, equipment, and crowd support. The challenger has few, if any, of these assets and has a monumental task to accomplish in a limited amount of time. Not surprisingly, most challengers end up eating their opponents' dust. Still, not every novice athlete or every congressional challenger is destined to suffer the agony of defeat. A strong challenger, who is able to assemble the money and campaign organization needed to devise and carry out a good game plan, may be able to win if the incumbent stumbles.

Even though the vast majority of challengers ultimately lose, the experience and resources that they bring to their races can have a notable impact on their abilities to win votes. In short, challenger campaigning matters. Table 9-2 demonstrates that challengers' targeting strategies, issue positions, and campaign expenditures as well as the amounts of party and interest group support they attract have small but significant effects on their vote shares. These generalizations hold regardless of a particular challenger's age, race, gender, or occupation.

A hypothetical challenger who runs in a district that is evenly split in terms of registered Republicans and Democrats, who is handed a major-party nomination without a primary fight, who does not use a group-based targeting strategy, who does not campaign on position issues, whose race is bereft of all candidate or party campaign spending, and who does not get more favorable media coverage than the incumbent will end the election with just 28 percent of the vote—a far cry from victory.

Table 9-2   Significant Predictors of House Challengers' Vote Shares, 1992

	Percent
Base vote	27.99
Partisan bias (per one-point advantage in party registration)	+0.13
Contested primary	+4.77
Group-based targeting	+1.95
Campaigned on position issues	+2.76
Challenger spending on campaign communications (per $1,000)	+0.009
Incumbent spending on campaign communications (per $1,000)	+0.005
Party spending on behalf of challenger (per $1,000)	+0.107
Media advantage favoring challenger	+3.28

Sources: Questions 13, 15, 17, 20, 21, and 26 of the 1992 Congressional Campaign Study, Federal Election Commission data, various editions of *Congressional Quarterly Weekly Report,* and other sources discussed in the appendix.

Notes: Regression statistics are presented in Table A-4 in the appendix. The analysis includes general election candidates in major-party contested races. N = 129.

Challengers who run under more favorable circumstances fare better. In most cases redistricting works to the advantage of incumbents, but a few 1992 challengers were fortunate enough to run in districts that were redrawn to favor their party. Challengers who ran in districts in which the balance of registered voters favored their party by 10 percent won 1.3 percent more votes than those who ran in neutral districts; those few challengers who ran in districts that favored their party by 20 percent won 2.6 percent more votes than others. Nevertheless, the typical challenger encountered a balance of party registration that favored the incumbent by 15 percent and won only 26 percent of the total vote.

Contested primaries, which only rarely have negative consequences in the general election for the incumbents who survive them, give challengers who emerge from them victorious significant electoral advantages over challengers who did not have to compete for the nomination.[9] It should be recalled from chapter 2 that opposing-incumbent primaries are often hotly contested when an incumbent is perceived to be vulnerable and are usually won by strategic candidates who know how to wage strong campaigns. The organizational effort, campaign activities, and media coverage associated with contested primaries provide the winners with larger bases of support and higher levels of name recognition than they would have enjoyed had the primary not been contested. The momentum that House challengers got from contested primaries in 1992 and the incumbent weaknesses that gave rise to those primaries in the first place gave those challengers who defeated one or more opponents in the primary nearly 5 percent more of the general election vote than challengers who were merely handed their party's nomination.

Political experience and campaign professionalism have indirect effects on challengers' abilities to win votes. Experienced challengers usually assemble organizations that are staffed by salaried professionals and purchase other campaign services from political consultants. As demonstrated in chapters 6 and 8, political experience and campaign professionalism help challengers raise money and attract free media. Experienced, well-staffed challenger efforts are also presumably better at developing and implementing targeting and communications plans than volunteer efforts waged by political amateurs.

House challengers who used group-based or segmented targeting strategies in 1992 won roughly 2 percent more votes than those who targeted on the basis of issues or voter attitudes. Challengers who ran on position issues, which presumably appealed to the groups they targeted, won an additional 2.8 percent. The combined effects of campaign targeting and message selection helped boost challengers' vote margins from 28 percent to nearly 33 percent.

Favorable media coverage can also help to boost a House challenger's performance. The 19 percent of all 1992 challenger campaigns that reported their candidate was either endorsed by the press or received the lion's share of free media coverage won over 3 percent more of the vote than the 81 percent that were not treated so favorably by the local media.

Campaign spending also has a significant impact on challengers' vote shares. For every $100,000 that 1992 House challengers spent on television, radio, newspaper, or direct-mail advertising or on campaign field work, they won an additional .9 percent of the vote on top of the base of 28 percent.[10] For every $10,000 a challenger's party spent on his or her behalf, that candidate won an additional 1 percent. Incumbent spending on campaign communications, which is largely a function of the closeness of the race and the efforts of strong challengers and their supporters, was also positively related to challengers' vote shares. Large communications expenditures by both candidates were strongly associated with closely decided incumbent-challenger races. Bill Richardson spent $564,000 on campaign communications and came within eleven percentage points of defeating Vic Fazio, who spent $1.2 million on communicating with voters. Peter Torkildsen and former representative Nicholas Mavroules spent $255,000 and $284,000, respectively, in a race that ended with Torkildsen unseating the seven-term member of Congress.[11] The fact that the typical House challenger spent only $120,000 on campaign communications helps to explain why so few of them won in 1992 and why challengers generally fare poorly.

How best to allocate scarce financial resources is a nearly constant concern for strategists in challenger campaigns. Are radio or television

Table 9-3   The Impact of Different Forms of Campaign Spending on House Challengers' Vote Shares, 1992

	Percent
Direct mail (per $1,000)	+0.030
Television ads (per $1,000)	+0.012
Field work (per $1,000)	+0.035
Radio ads (per $1,000)	Not significant
Newspaper ads (per $1,000)	Not significant

Sources: Questions 13, 15, 17, 20, 21, and 26 of the 1992 Congressional Campaign Study, Federal Election Commission data, various editions of *Congressional Quarterly Weekly Report,* and other sources discussed in the appendix.

Notes: Field work includes expenditures on get-out-the-vote drives, billboards and signs, campaign literature, and travel to and from campaign events. Regression statistics are presented in Table A-5 in the appendix. The analysis includes general election candidates in major-party contested races. N = 129.

commercials more effective than newspaper ads? How effective is direct mail at influencing voters compared with less precisely tailored and less well targeted forms of advertising? Is it worthwhile to invest any money in get-out-the-vote drives, handbills, or the grass-roots activities commonly referred to as campaign field work?

The estimates in Table 9-3 show the impact of different campaign activities on challengers' vote shares, while controlling for the effects of district partisanship, contested primaries, targeting strategies, issues, incumbent expenditures, party spending, and media coverage and endorsements.[12] They show that not all forms of campaign spending give House challengers a high rate of return. They also demonstrate that campaigns benefit from a variety of forms of campaign communications, including some that are highly targeted or technologically sophisticated and others that can be managed by volunteers or are intended to blanket an entire district.

Direct mail is one of the most effective campaign activities. Every $1,000 that challenger campaigns spend on mail is associated with a .03 percent increase in the votes they win. The typical challenger campaign spent just over $30,000 on mail in 1992, which helped it win an additional 1 percent of the vote. Some campaigns, however, spent considerably more and reaped greater rewards. The Richardson campaign spent nearly $290,000 on the *Valley Messenger* and other mailings. An expenditure of this magnitude was associated with a nearly 9 percent increase in the vote.

Television commercials are considerably more expensive and bring somewhat lower returns. The typical House challenger campaign spent

$42,000 on television ads, which was associated with an increase of one-half of one percent of the vote. Of course, campaigns which spent more on television, such as Richardson's, attracted considerably more votes.

Radio and newspaper advertisements play important roles in some challenger campaigns, but they do not have a significant impact on the numbers of votes that the typical challenger wins. Field work, which refers to get-out-the-vote drives, billboards and yard signs, campaign events, and the distribution of handbills and other literature, is a labor-intensive rather than capital-intensive form of electioneering. Thus, the $27,000 that the typical challenger spent on field work in 1992 does not perfectly represent that candidate's field operations, and the figure in the table cannot be interpreted in the same way as the others. Nevertheless, field work clearly emerges as an important component of challenger campaigns. Personal contact between candidates and voters and campaign activities that are often carried out by volunteers rather than professional consultants play a very important role in contemporary congressional elections.

In summary, most House challengers lose because the odds are so heavily stacked against them. Those few who run in competitive districts, target specific population groups, run on position issues, assemble the resources needed to communicate with voters, spend their money wisely, benefit from party and interest group campaigning, and curry favor with the media attract more votes than others, but they rarely win enough votes to defeat an incumbent. The preelection activities that incumbents undertake to cultivate the support of constituents and their successes in warding off talented and well-funded challengers are critical in determining the outcome of most incumbent-challenger races.

Yet, politics is a game that is often played at the margins. Not all House incumbents begin the general election as shoo-ins and go on to win. The few incumbents who run in marginal districts, commit ethical transgressions, draw both a strong major-party opponent and significant independent or minor-party opposition, are targeted for defeat by the opposing party and independent-spending PACs, or receive less than favorable treatment from the media often find themselves in a precarious position. Many of these candidates spend huge sums of money, sometimes to no avail. If the challengers who run against these incumbents are able to capitalize on the opportunities before them by assembling the money and organizational resources needed to wage a strong campaign, they can put their opponents on the defensive. Challengers who set the campaign agenda, carefully target groups of actual and potential supporters, tailor their messages to appeal to these groups, and communicate these messages through paid advertisements, free media, and strong field operations have reasonable prospects of winning. A victory by a challenger is typically the result of both incumbent failure and a strong challenger campaign. One-hundred thirteen House incumbents were in jeopardy during the 1992 general election, yet challengers defeated only twenty-four of them.

Open-Seat Campaigns

Elections for open seats are usually won by far smaller margins than incumbent-challenger races. Once a seat becomes open, a whole series of factors come into play. Because voters lack strong personal loyalties to either candidate, the partisanship of the district and the skills and resources that candidates and their organizations bring to the campaign have a bigger impact on open-seat elections than on incumbent-challenger races. Factors that are outside of the campaigns' control, such as national political trends, redistricting, and the mass media coverage that the candidates receive, can also have a big impact on open-seat elections. Table 9-4 lists the factors that had a significant effect on the outcome of open-seat House races in 1992.

National partisan tides clearly helped most Democratic open-seat contestants in 1992 despite President Clinton's short coattails (the Democrats suffered a net loss of ten House seats despite winning the White House). Voters who were dissatisfied with the state of the economy, uneasy about the nation's future, and displeased with President Bush's leadership appeared to be willing to give Clinton and some of his fellow Democrats a chance at governance. Democratic open-seat candidates were uniquely situated to benefit from partisan trends in two important respects. First, they could run as political outsiders and embrace the theme of change that was being championed by Clinton. Second, they did not have to defeat an incumbent to win. National partisan tides boosted the average Democratic open-seat candidate's vote share by 3.3 percent in 1992, to 47 percent.

Another advantage for many Democratic open-seat House candidates was that most House district boundaries were redrawn by Democratic state legislators and governors prior to the 1992 election. Although the courts ruled that some states had unfairly rigged the redistricting process to favor one party and required those states to redraw their House districts more evenhandedly, or redrew the districts themselves, the overall result of the redistricting process advantaged Democratic over Republican open-seat candidates. Democratic candidates further benefited from the creation of open-seat districts that were designed to promote minority representation because most of the voters who reside in these districts are Democrats.

Partisan, minority-related, and other considerations (including how the configuration of new open seats would affect the boundaries of other House districts), resulted in registered Democratic voters outnumbering registered Republicans by an average of 5.4 percent in House districts

Table 9-4   Significant Predictors of House Open-Seat Candidates' Vote Shares, 1992

	Percent
Base vote (constant)	43.76
Pro-Democratic national partisan tide	+3.31
Partisan bias (per one-point advantage in party registration)	+0.20
Media advantage favoring candidate	+3.70
Candidate spending on campaign communications:	
$100,000	+16.37
$200,000	+18.83
$300,000	+20.28
$400,000	+21.29
$500,000	+22.09
Opponent spending on campaign communications:	
$100,000	−15.02
$200,000	−17.28
$300,000	−18.60
$400,000	−19.54
$500,000	−20.27

Sources: Questions 2, 16, 20, 21, and 26 of the 1992 Congressional Campaign Study, Federal Election Commission data, various editions of *Congressional Quarterly Weekly Report,* and other sources discussed in the appendix.

Notes: The candidate and opponent spending figures are calculated from a regression equation that estimates the impact of the natural log of campaign spending on candidates' vote shares. Regression statistics are presented in Table A-6 in the appendix. The analysis includes general election candidates in major-party contested races. N = 70.

with open seats. The partisan bias of these districts contributed roughly 1.1 percent to the typical Democrat's share of the vote. Democrats who ran for open seats where the balance of voter registration was even more favorable to their party did even better: a Democrat who ran for an open seat in a district where Democratic voters outnumbered Republicans by 20 percent ended up winning an additional 4 percent of the vote as a result of district partisanship. Of course, Republicans who ran for open seats in districts where registered GOP voters outnumbered registered Democrats by 20 percent also got a 4 percent vote bonus. On balance, however, district partisanship favored Democrats. That partisan advantage, combined with national partisan tides, helped propel more than a few Democratic open-seat candidates into Congress.

The mass media also play an important role in open-seat House races. Experienced politicians who have strong campaign organizations and run for open seats in districts that are made up mostly of voters who belong to their party usually receive better treatment from the media than do their opponents. Open-seat candidates who attracted more media coverage than their opponents and won the endorsements of the local press picked up an extra 3.7 percent of the vote in 1992. They also may have enjoyed some indirect benefits from their preferential treatment by the media. Open-seat candidates who the media label as front-runners early in the race usually raise more money, are able to spend more on campaign communications, improve their name recognition, and create more momentum than their opponents.

Candidates in open-seat elections stand to make significant gains in name recognition and voter support through their campaign communications. In contrast to incumbent-challenger races, the communications expenditures made by both campaigns in open-seat elections have significant effects on the numbers of votes the candidates receive. A campaign's initial expenditures are particularly influential because they help voters become aware of a candidate and his or her message. Further expenditures, while still important, have a lower rate of return; as more voters learn about the candidates and their issue positions the effects of campaign spending diminish. In 1992 a hypothetical open-seat candidate who faced an opponent who spent no money would gain an additional 16.37 percent above the base vote of 43.76 percent for the first $100,000 spent communicating with voters. That same candidate would gain an additional 2.46 percent (a total increase to 18.83 percent) for the next $100,000 spent on campaign communications, and an additional 1.45 percent of the vote (a total increase to 20.28 percent) for the next $100,000. But such lopsided spending is unusual in open-seat contests; more often, these elections feature two well-funded campaigns. In situations where the campaigns spend nearly the same amount on voter contact, their expenditures largely offset one another. Democrat Corrine Brown spent roughly $290,000 on voter contact in her successful race in Florida's 3rd district in 1992, just $35,000 more than her opponent, Ron Weidner. Although Brown's spending advantage would be associated with only a 1.4 percent increase in the vote, it combined with her experience as a state legislator, her ability to attract favorable media coverage, the partisan bias and racial composition of Florida's 3rd district, and pro-Democratic national tides to help her achieve a 59 percent to 41 percent victory.

The amounts that open-seat campaigns spend on field work and direct-mail, radio, television, and newspaper advertising are all positively related to the vote shares that candidates receive, but the impact of each of these expenditures on election outcomes is difficult to evaluate because of the electoral and financial competitiveness of these races.[13] It is possible, however, to make some generalizations about the relative importance of each kind of campaign communication.[14] Newspaper ads are the best value, followed by field work. However, because campaigns budget relatively small amounts on these activities and because the impact of spending on them diminishes as it goes up, it is impossible to predict the impact that very large expenditures on newspaper advertising or field work would have on an open-seat candidate's vote share. Of those media that claim the largest portions of the typical open-seat campaign's communications budget, direct mail has the biggest impact on vote shares, followed by radio and television.

Claiming Credit and Placing Blame

Once the election is over, candidates and their campaign staffs have a chance to reflect on their contests. Their major interest, naturally, is what caused their election to turn out as it did. The opinions of losers provide useful insights into what can be done to increase the competitiveness of elections. The opinions of winners can also have implications for campaign reform, but more importantly they provide insights into the impact of elections on the governmental process.

Winners and losers have very different ideas about what factors influence congressional election outcomes. Some differences are obvious. With the exception of incumbents, losing candidates almost always obsess about money. If they had more funds they would have reached more voters and received more votes, virtually all agree. The four-to-one overall spending advantage that victorious House incumbents had over losing challengers in 1992 supports this point (see Figure 9-1). The nearly two-to-one advantage that successful open-seat candidates had over their opponents is not as big, but it also lends credence to the point that money matters. The fact that winning challengers, the only group of successful candidates who did not outspend their opponents, spent an average of $450,000 on their campaigns (in contrast to the average losing challenger who spent $136,000), suggests that there is a spending threshold that challengers must cross if they are to be competitive.

Once one gets beyond the obvious factor of money, other differences can be discerned as well. When asked to evaluate the determinants of their races, winners had a strong tendency to credit their victories to candidate attributes and factors that were largely under the control of their campaign. They considered the candidate's image to be the most important determinant of their election (see Table 9-5). Successful incumbents ranked their record in office next and claimed that the anti-incumbency mood that gripped the nation depressed their victory margins.

Winners ranked issues next, with their stances on national issues taking priority over local concerns. Many winners felt that they benefited from focusing on the economy, health care, and the other issues that formed the core of the national political agenda in 1992. They also considered the partisan loyalties of voters in their districts to be moderately important. Successful incumbents recognized the importance of

Figure 9-1   Average Campaign Expenditures of Winners and Losers, 1992

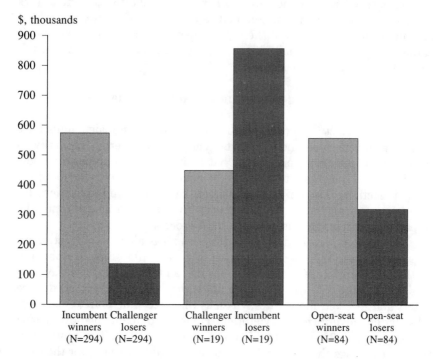

$, thousands

Source: Compiled by the author from Federal Election Commission data.
Note: Includes all general election candidates in major-party contested House races, excluding incumbent-versus-incumbent races.

officeholding, acknowledging the fund-raising, media relations, and name identification advantages it bestowed on them. Finally, winners considered campaign debates, newspaper endorsements, negative campaigning, scandals, and presidential and other elections to have had significantly less impact on the outcome of their contests.

The winners' opinions reflect a tendency to attribute their victories to their own efforts and the wisdom of voters.[15] These beliefs stand in stark contrast to political science theories that suggest congressional election outcomes are primarily a function of national conditions and events.[16]

Losers had a very different view of what caused their elections to end as they did. First and foremost, losing challengers pointed to the incumbent's perquisites of office, which they considered to have been extremely important. Next, most losers blamed voters' partisanship and the presidential election for their defeats. Many Republican losers linked their losses to that of President Bush. Losers of both parties felt that candidate imagery, issue positions, and debates were less important than these

Table 9-5 Winners' and Losers' Opinions of the Determinants of House Elections, 1992

	Winners	Losers
Candidate's image	4.48	3.34
Party loyalty	3.28	3.86
Local issues	2.89	2.49
National issues	3.69	3.20
Debates	2.24	2.16
Endorsements	2.40	2.55
Negative campaigning	2.36	2.58
Incumbent's record	4.13	2.70
Incumbency advantages	3.26	4.70
Anti-incumbency	3.31	2.16
Incumbent scandal	1.53	1.58
Presidential election	2.54	3.43
Perot campaign	2.07	2.54
U.S. Senate election	1.73	2.09
State or local elections	1.71	2.12
(N)	(160)	(164)

Source: Question 37 of the 1992 Congressional Campaign Study.

Notes: Candidates and campaign aides were asked to assess the importance of each factor on the following scale: 1=not important; 2=slightly important; 3=moderately important; 4=very important; 5=extremely important. The values listed are arithmetic means of the scores. Figures for incumbent's record, incumbency advantages, anti-incumbency, and incumbent scandal exclude responses from candidates and campaign aides from open seats. Figures include responses from House general election candidates and campaign aides in major-party contested races, excluding those involved in incumbent-versus-incumbent races.

other factors. They preferred to rationalize their defeats by blaming them on factors over which neither they nor their campaigns had any control.[17] The losers' views bear similarities to political science theories that downplay the importance of individual candidates and campaigns.

Senate Campaigns

The small number of Senate elections that take place in a given election cycle and the differences in the size and politics of the states in which they take place make it difficult to generalize about the impact of Senate campaigns. Nevertheless, a few generalizations are possible. Not surprisingly, chief among them is that incumbents possess substantial advantages over challengers. The advantages that incumbency in the Senate convey are similar to those for the House. Incumbents enjoy fund-raising advantages and higher levels of name recognition as well as greater political experience, particularly in running a statewide campaign.

Yet, the advantages that senators enjoy are not as great as those that House members have over their opponents. Most Senate challengers and open-seat candidates have previously served in the House, as governor, or in some other public capacity, and are more formidable opponents than are their House counterparts. Their previous political experience helps Senate challengers assemble the financial and organizational resources and attract the media coverage that are needed to run a competitive campaign.

One of the most important differences between Senate and House contests is the impact of incumbent expenditures on who wins. Though increased challenger spending has a negative effect on incumbents' margins in both Senate and House elections, it is only in Senate races that spending by incumbents is positively related to the number of votes they receive. Incumbent expenditures on campaign communications are not as important as are challenger expenditures, but the amounts spent by both sides are influential in determining the victor in Senate elections.

This difference is due to a number of factors. First, because Senate challengers are usually better qualified, Senate elections tend to be closer than House contests. Second, senators tend to have weaker bonds with their constituents than do representatives; senators' larger constituencies prevent them from establishing the kinds of personal ties that House members have with voters.[18] The greater diversity of their constituencies also means that senators are more likely to offend some voters when carrying out their legislative activities. Senators' six-year terms and greater responsibilities in Washington also discourage them from meeting as frequently with constituents as do House members. As a result of these differences, campaign spending and campaigning in general are more likely to affect the electoral prospects of Senate than House incumbents.

The dynamics of Senate elections bear other similarities to and differences from House contests. The partisan bias of the state and scandal have an impact on elections for both the upper and lower chambers. The quality of the opposition that an incumbent faces both in the primary and the general election has a bigger impact on the outcomes of Senate elections than House contests. Competitive primary contests are also harmful to Senate incumbents' general election prospects.[19]

Senate candidates also have a somewhat different view of what causes election outcomes than do House contestants. Both the winners and losers in the 1992 Senate contests emphasized factors that were largely under their control. Contestants across-the-board considered the images they projected to the voters to have been the number one determinant of the outcome of their elections. Winners typically considered candidate imagery to have been extremely important, while losers considered it to have been moderately important. Winners were more likely to emphasize the importance of issues, ranking them second only to imagery.

Losing challengers, on the other hand, considered the advantages of officeholding to be substantially more important. Winning and losing incumbents were equally likely to view incumbency as a two-edged sword, agreeing that the anti-incumbency mood of the nation had worked to reduce their vote margins.

Incumbents placed greater emphasis on the importance of their record in the Senate than did challengers, but both sets of candidates acknowledged that job performance was at least a moderately important determinant of the outcome of Senate elections. Both winners and losers also considered the partisan loyalties of state voters and the presidential election to have been moderately important. Such factors as debates, negative campaigning, the Perot campaign, local issues, and state and local elections, however, were considered to have been even less influential by Senate candidates than House contestants.

Notes

1. The analyses of incumbent, challenger, and open-seat campaigns are based on all two-party contests except incumbent-versus-incumbent House contests.
2. Detailed descriptions of the variables in this section and the following sections are presented in the appendix.
3. Michael Barone and Grant Ujifusa, *The Almanac of American Politics, 1988* (Washington, D.C.: National Journal, 1987), 1026.
4. On the effects of the check-bouncing scandal see Timothy Groseclose and Keith Krehbiel, "Golden Parachutes, Rubber Checks, and Strategic Retirements from the 102nd House," *American Journal of Political Science* 38 (1994): 75-99; Gary C. Jacobson and Michael A. Dimock, "Checking Out the Effects of Bank Overdrafts on the 1992 House Elections," *American Journal of Political Science* 38 (forthcoming 1994); and Michael A. Dimock and Gary C. Jacobson, "Checks and Choices: The Impact of the House Bank Scandal on Voting Behavior," paper presented at the annual meeting of the Midwest Political Science Association, Chicago, Ill., April 14-16, 1993.
5. The last third-party or independent candidate to be elected to the House was Henry Reams of Ohio, who served from 1951 to 1955. Phil Duncan, ed., *Politics in America, 1994* (Washington, D.C.: Congressional Quarterly, 1994), 1562.
6. These generalizations are similar to those reported in a study of the 1978 House elections. See Edie N. Goldenberg and Michael W. Traugott, *Campaigning for Congress* (Washington, D.C.: CQ Press, 1984), chapter 3.
7. See Table A-3 in the appendix for the impact of specific campaign expenditures on incumbents' vote shares. On the impact of campaign spending on congressional elections see especially Gary C. Jacobson, *Money in Congressional Elections* (New Haven, Conn.: Yale, 1980); Jacobson, "The Effects of Campaign Spending in House Elections: New Evidence for Old Arguments," *American Journal of Political Science* 34 (1990): 334-362; Jonathan S. Krasno and Donald Philip Green, "Salvation for the Spendthrift Incumbent," *American Journal of Political Science* 32 (1988): 844-907; Green and Krasno "Rebuttal to Jacobson's 'New Evidence for Old Arguments,'" *American Journal of Political Science* 34 (1990): 363-372.

8. Jacobson, *Money in Congressional Elections*, 113-123; Jonathan S. Krasno, Donald Philip Green, and Jonathan A. Cowden, "The Dynamics of Fundraising in House Elections," *Journal of Politics* 56 (1994): 459-474.

9. As noted earlier, running in a contested primary prior to the general election has no statistically significant relationship to incumbents' vote shares.

10. Communications expenditures exclude money spent on staff salaries, fundraising, polling, and other forms of research. Field work includes get-out-the-vote drives, the distribution of campaign literature, billboards and signs, and campaign travel.

11. Gavin Sutcliffe, "The Price of Scandal: Legal Problems Defeat a Veteran Congressman in Massachusetts' Sixth District," unpublished paper, University of Maryland, 1992; and Dwight Morris and Murielle E. Gamache, *Handbook of Campaign Spending* (Washington, D.C.: Congressional Quarterly, 1994), 333.

12. Each communications technique was tested individually because of the multicollinearity between them. That is, well-funded campaigns spend a great deal on all of them, and cash-poor campaigns spend very little, confounding estimates that are derived when all of the techniques are tested simultaneously.

13. When the expenditure made on any one form of communication is isolated from the others its impact is overridden by the total communications expenditures made by the opposing candidate.

14. These generalizations are drawn from Table A-7 in the appendix.

15. On the propensity of winners to "congratulate" themselves for the impact their efforts had on the election outcome and on the propensity of losers to blame their defeats on forces outside of their control see John W. Kingdon, *Candidates For Office: Beliefs and Strategies* (New York: Random House, 1968), especially chapter 2.

16. See especially Gerald Kramer, "Short-Term Fluctuations in U.S. Voting Behavior," *American Political Science Review* 65 (1971): 131-143; Edward R. Tufte, "Determinants of the Outcomes of Midterm Congressional Elections," *American Political Science Review* 69 (1975): 812-826; Howard S. Bloom and H. Douglas Price, "Voter Response to Short-Run Economic Conditions: The Asymmetric Effect of Prosperity and Recession," *American Political Science Review* 69 (1975): 1240-1254; Gary C. Jacobson, *The Politics of Congressional Elections* (New York: HarperCollins, 1993), chapter 6; Gary C. Jacobson, "Does the Economy Matter in Midterm Elections," *American Journal of Political Science* 34 (1990): 400-404; James E. Campbell, *The Presidential Pulse of Congressional Elections* (Lexington: University Press of Kentucky, 1993). For a contrary view, see Robert S. Erikson, "Economic Conditions and the Vote: A Review of the Macro Level Evidence," *American Journal of Political Science* 34 (1990): 373-399.

17. See Kingdon, *Candidates For Office*, especially chapter 2.

18. John R. Hibbing and John R. Alford, "Constituency Population and Representativeness in the United States Senate," *Legislative Studies Quarterly* 15 (1990): 581-598.

19. See also Alan I. Abramowitz and Jeffrey A. Segal, *Senate Elections* (Ann Arbor: University of Michigan Press, 1992), 109-115.

Chapter 10

Elections and Governance

"The election is over, and now the fun begins." Those were the words of one new House member shortly after being elected to the 103rd Congress. Others had more measured, if not more realistic, visions of what lay ahead. While getting elected to Congress is difficult, especially for those who have to topple an incumbent, staying there also requires great effort. The high reelection rates enjoyed by members of Congress are not a guarantee of reelection; they are the result of hard work and the strategic deployment of the resources that Congress makes available to its members.

This chapter examines the efforts that members of Congress make in order to stay in office, including the resources and strategies they use to shore up their electoral coalitions. The impact of elections on Congress as a policy-making institution is also reviewed. The analysis first places the member at the center of a large, personal organization that has a well-defined mission and abundant resources at its disposal. It then discusses the committees, issue caucuses, party organizations, and other groups that influence congressional activity. Finally, some comments are made about the policy-making process.

The Permanent Campaign

As locally elected officials who make national policy, members of Congress almost lead double lives. The main focus of their Washington existence is framing and enacting legislation, overseeing the executive branch, and carrying out other activities of national importance. Attending local functions, ascertaining the needs and preferences of constituents, and explaining their Washington activities are what legislators do at home. Home is where members of Congress acquire their legitimacy to participate in the legislative process and individual mandates to act. The central elements of legislators' lives in both locations are representing the voters who elected them, winning federally funded projects for their state or district, and resolving difficulties that constituents encounter when dealing with the federal government. The two aspects of a members' existence are unified by the fact that much of what representatives do in Washington is concerned with getting reelected, and a good deal of what they do at home has a direct impact on the kinds of policies and interests they seek to advance in the legislature.[1] In a great many respects, the job of legislator resembles a permanent reelection campaign.

Members of Congress develop home styles that help them to maintain or expand their bases of electoral support. One element of these home styles concerns the presentation of self. Members build bonds of trust between themselves and voters by demonstrating that they are capable of handling the job, have many things in common with constituents, and care about them. Legislators try to give voters the impression that they are whom they claim to be and are living up to their campaign promises.[2]

A second component of home style is concerned with discussing the Washington side of the job. Members describe, interpret, and justify what they do in the nation's capital to convey the message that they are working relentlessly in their constituents' behalf.[3] Many respond to the low opinion that people have of Congress by trying to separate themselves from the institution in the minds of voters. Members frequently portray themselves as protectors of the national interest locked in combat with powerful lobbyists and feckless colleagues.

Legislators and their staffs spend tremendous amounts of time, energy, and resources advertising the legislator's name among constituents, claiming credit for favorable governmental actions, and taking strong but often symbolic issue positions to please constituents.[4] Their offices provide them with abundant resources for these purposes. Each House member elected in 1992 received nearly $600,000 for staff, $185,000 for general office expenses, a postage account of just under $188,000, a travel budget of up to $67,000, five thousand square feet of office space, and virtually unlimited long-distance telephone privileges (see Table 10-1). Members who are assigned to certain committees, occupy committee chairmanships, or hold party leadership positions receive extra staff, office space, and operating funds. Senators are allowed even greater budgets, reflecting their larger constituencies and the greater responsibilities associated with representing an entire state. Senators' staffs, office space, and budget allocations are determined by their state's population and by their committee assignments.

Table 10-1 Congressional Allowances, 1993

	House	Senate
Salary[a]	$133,600	$ 133,600
Washington office		
Staff salaries	$557,400	$1,054,591-$1,914,144[b]
Committee legislative assistants	—[c]	$292,686
Interns	$2,420	—
General office expenses (average)	$185,000	$47,000-$200,000[b]
Telephone/telegraph	15,000 long-distance minutes to district	—[d]
Stationery	40,000 envelopes	1.8-27.2 million[b] sheets of paper
Office space	2,500 sq. ft.	4,800-8,000 sq. ft.[b]
Furnishings	—[d]	—[d]
Equipment	Provided	Provided
District/state offices		
Rental	2,500 sq. ft.	4,800-8,000 sq. ft.[b]
Furnishings/equipment	$35,000	$30,000-$41,744[b]
Mobile office	—	one
Communications		
Official mail allowance (average)	$187,719	—[b]
Automated correspondence	—	Provided by Senate computer center
Audio/video recordings, photography	—[d]	—[d]
Travel (by formula)	Min. $6,200; max. approx. $67,200	—[d]

Source: Roger H. Davidson and Walter J. Oleszek, *Congress and Its Members,* 4th ed. (Washington, D.C.: CQ Press, 1993), 149. © 1993 Congressional Quarterly Inc. Reprinted by permission.

Note: In some cases no dollar value is given because of the difficulty in determining the range of reimbursed costs—for example, travel and telephone reimbursements. Most of the 1993 allowances are transferrable from one account to another.

[a] Effective Jan. 1, 1993; leaders' salaries are higher.

[b] A sliding scale linked to the state's population.

[c] Provided for members of Appropriations, Budget, and Rules Committees.

[d] Covered within the "general office expenses" category. In most cases supplies and equipment are charged at rates well below retail levels.

Although few legislators consume all of the resources they are allocated, many come close. The average House member hires approximately seventeen staff assistants; the average senator hires about thirty-one.[5] Among these aides are administrative assistants (sometimes called chiefs of staff), legislative assistants, legislative correspondents, computer operators, schedulers, office managers, caseworkers, press secretaries, receptionists, staff assistants, and interns. Each performs a different set of functions, but nearly all are somehow related to building political support among constituents. Legislative correspondents, legislative assistants, and computer operators are highly conscious of the electoral connection when they send out franked mail—roughly 500 million pieces in 1992—to constituents.[6] Caseworkers help constituents resolve problems with the federal bureaucracy, knowing that their performance can directly affect their members' reelection prospects.[7] Receptionists, staff assistants, and schedulers are well aware that the tours they arrange for visitors to Washington contribute to the support their member maintains in the district. Those who forget that constituents come first are quickly reminded of this by the office's administrative assistant, who is responsible for making sure that the office runs smoothly and frequently serves as the chief political adviser to the member.

The most reelection-oriented staffers of all tend to be congressional press secretaries. Most members of Congress have at least one press secretary, and some have two or three deputy press assistants.[8] The press secretary usually acts as the chief public relations officer in a congressional office. Press aides write newsletters and press releases and are heavily involved in crafting the targeted congressional letters that legislators send to constituents. Press secretaries write scripts for radio and television spots, which they arrange to have aired over local stations. They help organize town meetings, arrange interviews with the local correspondents, and disseminate to the news media transcripts and videotapes of their boss's floor and committee speeches. A good press secretary is often able to arrange for local media outlets to print or air a legislator's remarks verbatim or with minimal editing.[9] In 1984 House members' press secretaries distributed an average of eighty-five press releases and thirty-five radio spots.[10] Since then many have expanded the scope of their activities to include new forms of communications, including the dissemination of video press releases and the use of satellite uplinks. These technologies have enabled members to gain air time on local television news programs and to beam live commentary on State of the Union addresses and other important political events. Senators' press operations are even more extensive and sophisticated.

The emergence of the press secretary as a key congressional aide is a fairly recent phenomenon. Like the growth in congressional staff in general and the practice of deluging voters with congressional mail, it is a development that points to how Congress has responded to its members' desire to function more effectively in Washington and to turn an elective position into a permanent career.[11] As recently as 1970, 84 percent of all House members reported having no person with press responsibilities working in their office. By 1986 the number of offices that had one or more persons assigned to deal with the press increased almost fivefold, to 76 percent.[12] The election of highly media conscious members in the mid-1970s, the increased role of television in congressional campaigns, the opening of Congress to greater media scrutiny, the growth in the size of the congressional press corps, and the availability of new communications technologies created both pressures and opportunities to increase the public relations side of congressional offices.[13] Congress, a highly resource rich institution, responded by allowing its members to hire specialized staff to cope with these pressures and opportunities. It gave legislators a valuable resource they could use to protect their political careers.

Congress has also allowed its members to exploit new computer technologies to firm up their relations with voters. Legislators use computerized databases to target large volumes of mail to specific audiences. Constituents who write or telephone their legislator about an issue are routinely entered into a computerized list that records their name, address, and the reason for their contact. They are then sent periodic communications that update them on what their member is doing in this area. Subsidized House and Senate recording studios and party-owned recording facilities also help legislators use the electronic media to reach voters. Many members use the studios to record radio shows and television briefings or to edit floor speeches that they deliver to local media outlets. Some make use of satellite technology to hold live "town meetings" with constituents located on the other side of the country.

A Decentralized Congress

Reelection Constituencies

The candidate-centered nature of congressional elections provides the foundation for a highly individualized, fragmented style of legislative politics. Members are largely self-recruited, are nominated and elected principally as a result of their own efforts, and know they bear the principal responsibility for ensuring they get reelected. Local party organizations, Washington-based party committees, PACs, and other groups and individuals may have helped them raise money and win votes, but politicians arrive in Congress with the belief that they owe their tenure to their own efforts.

Legislators owe their first loyalties to their constituents, and most organize their work in Washington to strengthen this relationship. Most staff their offices, decide which committee assignments to pursue, and choose areas of policy expertise with an eye to maintaining constituent support.

Campaign supporters, including those who live in a legislator's district or state and those who live outside of it, form another important constituency. Local elites and Washington-based PACs that provide campaign contributions, volunteer labor, or political advice routinely receive access to members of Congress, further encouraging legislators to respond to forces outside of the institution rather than within.[14] Other personal goals, including advancing specific policies, accruing more power in the legislature, or positioning themselves to run for higher office, also have a decentralizing effect on the legislative process.[15] Much of the work done to advance these goals—issue research, bill drafting, attending committee meetings, bureaucratic oversight, and meeting with constituents, campaign contributors, and lobbyists—is borne by staffers who owe their jobs and their loyalties to individual legislators more than to the institution.[16] This, in turn, makes their bosses less dependent on congressional leaders and encourages members to march to their own drums.

Congressional Committees

The dispersal of legislative authority among 22 standing committees and more than 120 subcommittees in the House, 17 standing committees and 86 subcommittees in the Senate, 4 joint committees, and a small number of select committees in each chamber adds to the centrifugal tendencies that originate from candidate-centered elections. Each committee and subcommittee is authorized to act within a defined jurisdiction. Each is headed by a chair and ranking member who are among the majority and minority parties' senior policy experts. Each also has its own professional staff, office, and budget to help it carry out its business. By giving expression to the differing views of representatives, senators, and their constituents, the committee system decentralizes Congress.

The committee system originally was designed to enable Congress to function more efficiently. It allows Congress to investigate simultaneously a multitude of issues and to oversee a range of executive branch agencies. Although committees and subcommittees are Congress's main bodies for making national policy, much of what they do revolves around local issues, the distribution of federal grants and programs, and the reelection of individual legislators. Most legislators serve on at least one committee or subcommittee with jurisdiction over policies of importance to their constituents. Members use their committee assignments to develop expertise in policy areas, to demonstrate they are actively promoting their constituents' interests, and to attract financial or volunteer support from PACs and the labor unions, corporations, trade associations, and other groups that sponsor them.

Congressional committees can be categorized according to the objectives they enable members to pursue: reelection, prestige, and policy.[17] The House Agriculture Committee and the Senate Agriculture, Nutrition, and Forestry Committee are "reelection committees" that enable their members, mostly legislators from farm states, to work directly on the policy areas that are most important to constituents. The House Public Works and Transportation Committee and the Senate Committee on the Environment and Public Works are reelection committees that allow virtually every member, regardless of where they are from, to build constituent support by authorizing the building of roads, bridges, or other federal facilities. Reelection committees usually rank highly among the assignments sought by new members of Congress. More than half of the 110 first-term House members elected in 1992 sought appointment to the public works committee, which was enlarged to accommodate 28 new members.[18]

"Prestige committees" give their members influence over legislative activities that are of extraordinary importance to their congressional colleagues. The House and Senate Appropriations Committees are the ultimate prestige or power committees. They are responsible for funding federal agencies and programs and have the ability to initiate, expand, contract, or discontinue the flow of federal money to projects located across the country. This gives their members the power to affect the lives of those who are the beneficiaries of these programs and the ability to influence the reelection prospects of legislators who represent them. The House Ways and Means and Senate Finance Committees' jurisdictions over tax-related matters, and particularly their ability to give tax breaks to various interests, give members of these panels sway with their colleagues. Members of prestige committees can act directly to help their constituents or indirectly by wielding their clout with other legislators. Membership on one of the appropriating or tax writing committees is particularly helpful when it comes to raising campaign funds from individuals and PACs associated with a wide array of economic interests.

In contrast with reelection and prestige committees, "policy committees," such as those that deal with criminal justice, education, or labor issues, are sought by legislators who have a strong interest in a particular policy area. These committees are among the most divisive because they are responsible for some highly charged issues, such as education, health insurance, and welfare reform, and many members use them to stake out conservative or liberal stands. Ambitious legislators who seek a career beyond Congress often use policy committees as platforms for developing a national reputation on salient issues.

Congressional Caucuses

Congressional caucuses—informal groups of members who share legislative interests—have a similar but less powerful decentralizing impact on Congress. They create competing policy leaders and alternative sources of information and they are additional sources of legislative decision-making cues.[19] Groups such as the Congressional Black Caucus and the Pro-Life Caucus are recognized as advocates for specific segments of the population or points of view. The Democratic Study Group and the Republicans' Wednesday Group are among the caucuses that are recognized for their research capacities. The Sunbelt Caucus, the Western States Senate Coalition, and other geographically based groups seek to increase the clout of legislators from particular regions.

Although they do not hold any formal legislative powers, most caucuses have staff, office space, elected officers, and by-laws. Many receive financial and staff support from private organizations. Congressional caucuses work to influence the legislative process by researching and publicizing issues, organizing meetings, planning strategies, and providing a framework for networking among legislators who have common interests. Virtually every member serving in the House or Senate during the early 1990s belonged to at least one of the 130 or so congressional caucuses.[20] Caucuses further add to the decentralization and fragmentation of Congress.

Interest Groups

Privately funded interest groups, which form an important part of the political environment with which Congress interacts, also have decentralizing effects on the legislative process. Like caucuses, interest groups are sources of influence that compete with congressional leaders for the loyalty of legislators on certain issues. Roughly 80,000 people work for trade associations, legal firms, and consulting agencies in the Washington area.[21] Not all of these people are lobbyists, but in one way or another they work to advance the political interests of some group, and Congress is their number one target.[22]

Interest groups work to influence the legislative process in a number of ways, and their collective effect is to fragment Congress. Some groups advertise on television, on radio, in newspapers, or through the mails to influence the political agenda or stimulate grass-roots support for or opposition to specific pieces of legislation. Their efforts often resemble election campaigns. The advertisements purchased by the health-care and insurance industries in opposition to President Clinton's health-care reform package in 1994 exemplify these, as do the advertising campaigns waged by unions and other groups in support of or opposition to the North American Free Trade Agreement (NAFTA) in 1993.

Most interest groups also advocate their positions in less visible ways that are designed to play to the legislative and electoral needs of individual members of Congress. Representatives of interest groups are frequently given the opportunity to testify at committee hearings. Group representatives contact legislators at their offices and often make informal contacts over dinners and lunches. Lobbyists use these and other forums to provide members and their staffs with technical information, impact statements of how congressional activity (or inactivity) can affect their constituents, and insights into where other legislators stand on the issue. Sometimes they go so far as to draft a bill or help design a strategy to promote its enactment.[23]

Many groups supplement these "insider" techniques with approaches that focus directly on the electoral connection. Trade and business groups ask local association members to contact their legislators. Unions, churches, and other large membership groups frequently organize telephone and letter-writing campaigns. The objective of these communications is to make the point that legislative decisions can have electoral consequences. They show members of Congress that important blocs of voters and their advocates are watching how the members vote on specific pieces of legislation.

Interest groups, congressional subcommittee members, and executive-branch officials form collegial decision-making groups that are frequently referred to as "iron triangles," "issue networks," or "policy subgovernments."[24] These issue experts often focus on the minutiae of arcane, highly specialized areas of public policy. Because they form small governments within a government, they further contribute to the decentralization of Congress.

Political Parties: Centralizing Agents

Unlike these other structural, organizational, and political factors which work to decentralize Congress, political parties act as a glue (albeit a weak one) to bond members together. They socialize new members, distribute committee assignments, set the legislative agenda, coordinate congressional activities, disseminate information, and carry out other tasks that are essential to Congress's law-making, oversight, and representative functions. Although they are not the central actors in elections, parties do help legislators with their campaigns and carry out communications designed to whip up public support for their candidates' positions or undermine support for the opposition. Parties also work to rally their members to vote for legislation that is at the core of their partisan agenda.

The leadership organizations of America's congressional parties are structured similarly to those of legislative parties in other countries. The Democrats and Republicans are each headed by one leader in each chamber—the Speaker and minority leader in the House and the majority and minority leaders in the Senate. Each party has several other officers and an extensive whip system to facilitate communications between congressional party leaders and rank-and-file legislators. Legislative parties convene caucuses and task forces to help formulate policy positions and legislative strategy. Congressional party leaders' ability to provide campaign assistance, give out committee assignments and other perks, set the congressional agenda, structure debate, and persuade legislators that specific bills are in the best interests of their constituents and the nation are important tools for building coalitions.

Nevertheless, party leaders have less control over the policy-making process than do their counterparts in other democracies.[25] The persuasive powers of party leaders are usually insufficient to sway members' votes when party policy positions clash with those of legislators' constituents and campaign supporters. Recognizing the primacy of the electoral connection, party leaders generally tell legislators to respond to constituents rather than "toe the party line" when the latter could endanger their chances of reelection. The efforts of congressional party leaders are probably less of a factor in explaining how party members cast their roll-call votes than are commonalities in political outlook or similarities among legislators' constituents.[26] Party leaders are most able to overcome the forces that work to fragment Congress when they seek to enact policies that possess widespread bipartisan support or when the majority party possesses many more seats than the opposition and proposes popular legislation that advances its core principles.

Responsiveness, Responsibility, and Public Policy

In representative democracies elections are the principal means of ensuring that governments respond to the will of the people and promote their interests. Voters, through elections, hold public officials accountable for their actions and for the state of the nation as a whole. Elections serve as sounding boards that voters can use to register their approval or dismay with the individual performances of those whom they have put in office. They are a blunt instrument of control that allows people to inform their individual representatives or the government as a collectivity about how recent political action or inaction has affected the quality of their lives. Other avenues of influence, such as contacting members of Congress or giving campaign contributions, are usually used to advance narrower goals, are more demanding, and are in practice less democratic.

Individuals whose public service is contingent on getting reelected often straddle the fuzzy line that demarcates responsiveness and responsibility in government. On some occasions, legislators are highly responsive, functioning as delegates who advance their constituents' views. On others, they take the role of trustee, relying on their own judgment to protect the welfare of their constituents or the nation.[27] Responsible legislators must occasionally vote against their constituents' wishes in order to best serve the interests of the nation.

Election Systems and Public Policy

Election systems have a big impact on the responsiveness and responsibility of elected officials and entire governments because they determine to whom public officials are accountable. Nations with parliamentary systems which feature party-focused elections, such as Great Britain, tend to hold elected officials accountable to national political majorities.[28] Members of Parliament (MPs) perform casework and are attentive to their constituents, but their inclinations are to vote for legislation that is fashioned to please national rather than local constituencies. MPs support party initiatives because they know their prospects for reelection are closely tied to their party's ability to enact its legislative program.

The candidate-centered nature of the American system encourages elected officials to be highly responsive to the desires of constituents and organized groups that support their campaigns, sometimes in opposition to their party's leadership. Candidates who pledge to protect local interests while campaigning have strong incentives to focus their attention on advancing those interests once in office. Candidates who rely on the financial support of PACs are similarly motivated to consider the views of the Washington-based lobbyists who represent these groups. The framers of the Constitution looked favorably upon a certain level of parochialism in government. They also believed that allowing organized interests to petition the government would protect the rights of individuals.[29]

The separation of powers reinforces legislators' predispositions to "vote the district first" when casting their legislative roll-call votes. Even when one party controls the White House and both chambers of Congress, it may have difficulty unifying legislators because they can disagree with one another without fear of losing control of the government. Members of the majority party in Congress cast their roll-call votes secure in the knowledge that they will remain in office for their full two- or six-year terms even if their party suffers a major legislative defeat. In parliamentary systems, by contrast, majority-party members understand that a major policy defeat may be interpreted as a vote of no confidence in their party and may force an election that could turn them out of office in less than a month. The separation of powers also affects the behavior of legislators who are in the minority party. They have little incentive to vote against legislation that could benefit their constituents just because it was sponsored by the majority party since even a smashing legislative defeat would not force a "snap" election.

President Clinton's close victory on NAFTA demonstrates the difficulties that congressional parties face when they try to overcome the centrifugal forces influencing members of Congress. NAFTA was opposed by many congressional Democrats whose constituents thought they would lose manufacturing jobs as a result of the relaxation of trade barriers with Canada and Mexico. The treaty forced many legislators to choose between remaining loyal to their party's national leaders or pleasing their constituents. Most members, regardless of seniority, placed their constituents' interests and their own views above those of party leaders, who were themselves divided. Among those who opposed NAFTA were House majority leader Richard Gephardt (D-Mo.), House majority whip David Bonior (D-Mich.), and the chairs of several House committees. These leaders, who were selected by their congressional colleagues to advance core party policies, used the prestige, staff, and other resources of their leadership offices to oppose a policy that was advanced by President Clinton, who is their party's titular leader.

The separation of powers, bicameralism, federalism, and a fixed-date system of elections make it difficult for legislators to enact long-term, nationally focused policies. Members of Congress who believe that their individual images, policy positions, and public records were decisive to their elections are less likely than legislators in party-centered democracies to sacrifice the short-term interests of constituents or to compromise on salient issues to enact policies advocated by party leaders. House members, who must run for reelection every two years, respond particularly strongly to parochial concerns.

The effects of parochialism are most apparent in distributive politics, which provide tangible benefits to private individuals or groups. These benefits usually come in the form of government subsidies for roads, bridges, or other forms of infrastructure. They also include the establishment of military bases, grants for universities, and financial support for museums, libraries, and other activities.

Building coalitions in support of spending on public programs is relatively simple in a decentralized legislature such as the U.S. Congress. Bill sponsors can add new programs and projects in order to win enough legislative supporters to pass their plan.[30] A farm advocate who is hoping to subsidize northern sugar beets, for example, might build support for this cause by expanding the number of subsidized crops in a piece of legislation to include sugar cane, rice, corn, wheat, and even tobacco, thereby expanding support that began with representatives from Minnesota to include colleagues from Hawaii, Massachusetts, virtually every southern state, and the states of the Midwest.[31] Subsidies for ostrich farmers can be left out because they will not draw many legislative votes, but food stamps can be added to attract the support of legislators from poor urban districts.[32] Trading subsidies for votes is a simple example of logrolling. Other deals are cut over tax breaks, budget votes, and even appointments to the federal judiciary.[33]

Logrolling and other forms of compromise usually do not allow individual legislators to get all of the federal "pork" they would like for their constituents. Nevertheless, these compromises enable most legislators to insert enough pork into a bill to claim credit for doing something to help their constituents. A broadly supported distributive bill is an easy candidate for congressional enactment because, like a Christmas tree decorated by a group of friends, everyone can see his or her handiwork in it and find something to admire in the finished product.

Distributive politics are problematic because they are practiced with both eyes focused on short-term gains and little attention toward long-range consequences. Broadening programs that were originally intended to provide benefits to one group to include others usually causes the programs to become ineffectively targeted, watered down, and overly expensive. When large sums are spent to benefit many groups, overall spending is increased, and fewer funds remain available to help the group that was originally targeted for assistance. This does little to promote the original goals of a piece of legislation and leads to deficit spending.[34] Pork-barrel spending and logrolling, which are at the heart of distributive politics, have contributed heavily to the over $4 trillion national debt the U.S. government reported in 1992. Distributive politics are a prime example of what happens when independently elected officials seek to promote the interests of their constituents and campaign supporters without giving much thought to the impact of their collective actions on the nation.

Policy Gridlock and Political Cycles

Parochialism also leads to a reactive style of government and incremental policy making. Congress is better at making short-term fixes than at developing long-term initiatives. When their party lacks control of the White House, congressional leaders find it particularly difficult to develop a vision for the future. During the 1980s, House Democrats undertook a number of steps to outline, publicize, and act on a partisan agenda. Parts of this effort were successful, but many were not. Differences in legislators' political philosophies, the diversity of their constituencies, and the limited resources available to party leaders undermined efforts to develop and implement a Democratic game plan for the nation's future.[35] When Republican congressional leaders undertook similar efforts after the 1992 elections, they encountered similar obstacles.

Under most circumstances, election outcomes, constituent demands, interest group pressures, and White House initiatives support the continuation of the status quo or suggest only small changes in public policies. When pressure for change exists Congress generally initiates limited reform, but only after a period of some delay. Even when legislators receive information suggesting the existence of enduring problems, public policies are rarely subject to anything beyond incremental change.

On some occasions, however, the federal government does enact comprehensive programs that have a major impact on people's lives. Major policy change is most likely to occur during periods of crisis and is frequently associated with partisan realignments. Partisan realignments are accompanied by sweeping changes in the philosophies that underlie government activity. They occur when a critical event polarizes voters on a major issue, the two major parties take clear and opposing stands on that issue, and one party succeeds in capturing the White House and large majorities in both the House and Senate. Then, that party is in a position to use its electoral mandate to enact major policy change.[36]

The events leading up to and continuing through Franklin D. Roosevelt's presidency exemplify federal policy making during a period of crisis. The seeds of Roosevelt's New Deal programs were sewn in the Great Depression of the 1930s. Republicans controlled the White House, the House of Representatives, and the Senate when the stock market crashed in 1929. The GOP was blamed for the crash and for the depression that followed. The Democrats made the Republicans' failure to initiate economic reforms to reverse the depression a major campaign issue. After winning the White House and both chambers of Congress, Roosevelt and congressional Democrats used their electoral mandate to replace laissez-faire economics with Keynesian policies, which relied on government intervention to revive the economy. Other partisan and policy realignments took place during the late 1820s, the Civil War era, and the 1890s.

Some major policy changes have been instituted in the absence of partisan realignments, but most of these were less sweeping than those that followed critical elections. The civil rights and Great Society programs of the 1960s and the American withdrawal from Vietnam are examples of major policy changes that occurred in the absence of a partisan realignment. These changes were similar to Roosevelt's New Deal in that they were responses to widespread public demands for a solution to a salient national problem.

Congress can overcome its normal state of decentralization when there is a widespread consensus for change among the American people. Widespread consensus enables congressional leaders to centralize power. Using the committee system, whip structures, and other institutions, they are able to pass legislation that initiates fundamental change. Once public support for sweeping change erodes, however, the centrifugal forces that normally dominate Congress reassert themselves, and the legislature returns to its normal, incremental mode of policy making. The parochialism of members of Congress, bicameralism, the internal decentralization of the House and the Senate, and other centrifugal forces promote political cycles marked by long periods of incremental policy making followed by short periods of major policy change.

Notes

1. For an excellent discussion of the constituent-oriented and Washington-oriented aspects of legislators' jobs and the impact that they have on Congress see Roger H. Davidson and Walter J. Oleszek, *Congress and Its Members,* 4th ed. (Washington, D.C.: CQ Press, 1994).
2. Richard F. Fenno, Jr., *Home Style: House Members in Their Districts* (Boston: Little Brown, 1978), 54-61.
3. Ibid., 153.
4. David R. Mayhew, *Congress: The Electoral Connection* (New Haven: Yale University Press, 1974), 49-68.
5. Davidson and Oleszek, *Congress and Its Members,* 148.
6. It should be noted that in 1992 franking was at its lowest election-year point in twelve years. Davidson and Oleszek, *Congress and Its Members,* 152.
7. In the late 1970s, House members estimated their average caseload at slightly more than 10,000 cases per year, senators from small states averaged between 1,000 and 2,000 cases, and senators from large states averaged from 8,000 to 70,000 cases. House Commission on Administrative Review, *Final Report,* I:655; and Janet Breslin, "Constituent Service," in *Senators: Offices, Ethics, and Pressure,* Senate Commission on the Operation of the Senate, 94th Congress, 2nd session, 1977 committee print, 21. Both are cited in Davidson and Oleszek, *Congress and Its Members,* 146,160.
8. Timothy E. Cook, *Making Laws and Making News: Media Strategies in the U.S. House of Representatives* (Washington, D.C.: Brookings Institution, 1989), 71.
9. See, for example, Ben H. Bagdikian, "Congress and the Media: Partners in Propaganda," *Columbia Journalism Review* (January-February 1974): 5.
10. Cook, *Making Laws and Making News,* 103.
11. See, for example, Glenn R. Parker, "Home Styles—Then and Now," in *Congressional Politics,* ed. Christopher J. Deering (Chicago, Ill.: Dorsey Press, 1989), 51.
12. Cook, *Making Laws and Making News,* 72-73.
13. Ibid., 2, 3, 37, 90.
14. Laura I. Langbein, "Money and Access: Some Empirical Evidence," *Journal of Politics* 48 (1986): 1052-1062; John R. Wright, "PAC Contributions and Lobbying," *Journal of Politics* 51 (1989): 713-729.
15. Richard F. Fenno, Jr., *Congressmen in Committees* (Boston: Little Brown, 1973), 13.
16. Harrison W. Fox and Susan Webb Hammond, *Congressional Staffs: The Invisible Force in American Lawmaking* (New York: The Free Press, 1977), 121-124; Kenneth Kofmehl, *Professional Staffs of Congress* (West Lafayette, Ind.: Purdue University Press, 1977), 147-163; Michael J. Malbin, *Unelected Representatives: Congressional Staff and the Future of Representative Government* (New York: Basic Books, 1980), 33-35.
17. Fenno, *Congressmen in Committees,* 1-14.
18. Kenneth J. Cooper, "The House Freshmen's First Choice," *Washington Post,* January 5, 1993, A13.
19. Susan Webb Hammond, Daniel P. Mulhollan, and Arthur G. Stevens, Jr., "Informational Congressional Caucuses and Agenda Setting," *Western Political Quarterly* 38 (1985): 583-605; Davidson and Oleszek, *Congress and Its Members,* 307-312.
20. Davidson and Oleszek, *Congress and Its Members,* 307.

21. "80,000 Lobbyists? Probably Not, but Maybe," *New York Times,* May 12, 1993, A13.
22. Kay Lehman Schlozman and John T. Tierney, *Organized Interests and American Democracy* (New York: Harper and Row, 1986), 272.
23. Ibid., 289-310.
24. See, for example, Douglas Cater, *Power in Washington* (New York: Random House, 1964); Randall B. Ripley and Grace A. Franklin, *Congress, the Bureaucracy, and Public Policy* (Homewood, Ill.: Dorsey Press, 1976); Gordon Adams, *The Iron Triangle* (New York: Council on Economic Priorities, 1981), 175-180; Hugh Heclo, "Issue Networks and the Executive Establishment," in *The New American Political System,* ed. Anthony King (Washington, D.C.: American Enterprise Institute, 1978), 87-124.
25. See, for example, Leon D. Epstein, *Political Parties in Western Democracies* (New York: Praeger, 1967), 340-348.
26. See, for example, Herbert F. Weisberg, "Evaluating Theories of Congressional Roll Call Voting," *American Journal of Political Science* (1978): 554-577.
27. See especially Hannah Pitkin, *The Concept of Representation* (Berkeley: University of California Press, 1967).
28. For an excellent comparison of the operations of the British Parliament and the U.S. Congress see Bruce Cain, John Ferejohn, and Morris Fiorina, *The Personal Vote: Constituency Service and Electoral Independence* (Cambridge, Mass.: Harvard University Press, 1987).
29. James Madison, *Federalist* Nos. 10 and 46.
30. See, for example, R. Douglas Arnold, "The Local Roots of Democracy," in *The New Congress,* ed. Thomas E. Mann and Norman J. Ornstein (Washington, D.C.: American Enterprise Institute, 1981), 250-287.
31. Edwin J. Derwinski, "The Art of Negotiation Within Congress," in *The Art of Negotiation Within Congress,* ed. Diane B. Bendahmane and John W. McDonald, Jr. (Washington, D.C.: Foreign Service Institute, U.S. Department of State, 1984), 9, cited in Davidson and Oleszek, *Congress and Its Members,* 375-376.
32. John Ferejohn, "Logrolling in an Institutional Context: A Case Study of Food Stamp Legislation," in *Congress and Policy and Change,* ed. Gerald C. Wright, Jr., Leroy N. Rieselbach, and Lawrence C. Dodd (New York: Agathon Press, 1986), 223-253.
33. Davidson and Oleszek, *Congress and Its Members,* 374-378.
34. It should be noted that in recent congresses legislation has had to stay within a set of overall budgetary limits in order to limit growth of the federal deficit.
35. Paul S. Herrnson and Kelly D. Patterson, "Agenda Setting and Coalition Building in the House: Toward a More Programmatic Democratic Party?" *Polity,* forthcoming.
36. On critical elections and realignments see V. O. Key, Jr., "A Theory of Critical Elections," *Journal of Politics* 17 (1955): 3-18; Walter Dean Burnham, *Critical Elections and the Mainsprings of American Politics* (New York: W. W. Norton, 1970); James L. Sundquist, *Dynamics of the Party System: Alignment and Realignment of Political Parties in the United States* (Washington, D.C.: Brookings Institution, 1973); Everett Carll Ladd, Jr., with Charles D. Hadley, *Transformations of the American Party System* (New York: W. W. Norton, 1978).

Chapter 11

Campaign Reform

Congress has come under assault in recent years both for its inability to solve some of the nation's most pressing problems and for its failure to keep its own house in order. Gridlock, deficit spending, scandal, and the foibles of its members have led many to champion congressional reform. Reformers have called for a variety of changes, ranging from tinkering with the committee system to term limits, which would restructure members' and would-be members' political careers and drastically transform the operations of Congress. Campaign reform falls somewhere in between these two extremes. This chapter identifies aspects of the system that should be considered for reform, presents some reform proposals, and discusses the prospects for meaningful reform to be enacted.

The Case for Reform

Numerous arguments can be made for reforming Congress: some focus on the outcomes of congressional elections, some on the processes that produce those outcomes, and others on the impact that elections have on the political process. Those arguments that fall in the first category dwell on the fact that incumbents almost always win. They frequently discount or ignore that incumbents' successes are largely the result of legislators' efforts to serve their constituents prior to the election season, the weak competition they encounter once the campaign has begun, and inequalities in the campaign resources available to different kinds of candidates. Critics also ignore the fact that many incumbents choose to retire rather than face a strong challenge.

Shotgun Approaches to Reform

Many of those who build their case for reform on the outcomes of congressional elections rather than on the process that produces those outcomes are willing to embrace fairly radical changes. Some advocate mandating turnover in Congress through term limits, which would force even popular and effective legislators to retire. Others argue that a balanced budget amendment or presidential line-item veto—which they herald as foolproof solutions to the nation's deficit problem—would prevent legislators from using pork-barrel spending to build support for reelection. Still other reformers are so fed up with government gridlock that they want to bypass the electoral connection altogether. These champions of direct democracy prescribe using initiatives and referenda as the means for overcoming what they consider to be an unresponsive and irresponsible Congress.

These radical reforms have been embraced by some because they are frustrated with economic decline, rising crime, increased taxes, and reduced government services and because they believe the desires of the average taxpayer are being sacrificed by a government that panders to special interests. Reform movements are often headed by defeated congressional challengers and other frustrated politicians, some of whom even served in Congress. Some reform efforts, including those focused on term limits, are sponsored by business and pro-Republican groups that are frustrated by the Democrats' seemingly ironclad hold over the House. Laws that limit the number of terms a legislator may serve, impose restrictions on government spending, or make government decisions subject to direct popular approval tap into Americans' traditional ambivalence toward politics and distrust of politicians. Those who favor term limits argue that a regular rotation of public-spirited amateur legislators in and out of Congress would result in the enactment of laws that would solve the nation's most pressing problems.

Such positions are naive and often based on a superficial understanding of the political process. Term limits might encourage greater rotation among national legislators, but those nonincumbents with the best prospects of getting elected would continue to be experienced politicians who have the ability to assemble the organizational and financial resources needed to communicate to voters, not the public-spirited "citizen legislators" that some reformers have in mind. Putting a cap on the number of terms a legislator can serve would also strengthen the congressional and executive branch aides and "inside-the-beltway" lobbyists who are part of the permanent Washington establishment. Turning members of Congress into "lame ducks" at the end of a fixed number of terms would also probably make legislators more concerned about courting new employers than responding to constituent interests or governing responsibly.

Moreover, term limits would probably reduce electoral competition and incumbent accountability because strategic nonincumbents who are capable of waging strong campaigns would probably wait until a seat in Congress became open rather than challenge an incumbent.

A balanced budget amendment would also have major shortcomings. Although it might temporarily limit the growth of government spending, it would more than likely result in the development of new techniques of creative accounting. Moreover, if rigid budgetary constraints were possible, they could prevent the federal government from coping with national emergencies, ensuring the nation's military preparedness, or making long-term investments in schools, roads, or other forms of infrastructure that are needed to keep our nation safe and economically competitive. A constitutional amendment to balance the budget is no substitute for the political will of citizens and their elected representatives.

The line-item veto poses a different set of problems. Rather than encourage members of Congress and the president to build widespread support for a budget through compromise, as they presently do, it would give presidents the power to pick and choose the parts of the budget they prefer and eliminate the rest. A budget is a government's strongest statement of its policy priorities. By virtue of its being the nation's most representative institution Congress should have a major role in the budgetary process. Their recognition of this fact led the framers of the Constitution to require that all revenue bills originate in the House of Representatives and be accepted by majorities in both the House and the Senate before being submitted to the president for approval. During the 1970s, President Nixon's failure to spend federal money on the projects for which Congress had appropriated funds led to the passage of the Congressional Budget and Impoundment Control Act, which returned the balance of power over budgeting closer to that embraced by the framers. The line-item veto would do more than reverse the effects of the act. It would give the president far more power in determining the nation's immediate and long-term priorities than was originally envisioned or is appropriate for a chief executive in a representative democracy.

Initiatives and referenda, which require citizens to make decisions on complex policies, are also a patently bad idea. Most Americans are not interested enough in politics or public policies to research major program initiatives. Few can be counted on to educate themselves adequately to cast an informed vote on health-care reform, the federal budget, criminal justice policy, or any of the other major issues on the national agenda. Governing a large, heterogeneous nation is far more difficult than running a large business. Yet, while many reformers are willing to defer to expertise in areas of commerce, they seem to forget that expertise is also needed in public affairs. Political decision making in a democracy requires specialized knowledge, but even more important, it requires an ability to form coalitions from groups of individuals who have disparate goals and values. The framers understood that the vast majority of individuals in a democratic polity would lack the desire, interest, or time to rise above their personal affairs and tend the affairs of the nation. Those advocating government by initiatives and referenda appear to have forgotten this important lesson. These reformers and those who advocate term limits, the balanced budget amendment, the line-item veto, or any one of a number of other "false solutions" to the nation's problems are likely to do more harm than good, despite their best intentions.

Analyzing the Issues

Reform proposals designed to make congressional elections more competitive have the potential to improve the political system. Rather than altering the principles of republican government, which are the foundation of American democracy, these proposals have the potential to improve the system's capacity to live up to those principles. Real reform must contribute to the competitiveness of congressional elections by encouraging a larger number of experienced and well-qualified candidates to run. The best way to accomplish this is to even the playing field, particularly in incumbent-challenger contests. The fact that most incumbents begin and end both the campaign for resources and the campaign for votes far ahead of their opponents discourages the best would-be challengers from running. The advantages associated with incumbency cannot be completely eliminated by campaign reform, but reform is needed to encourage more qualified challengers to run and to give those who do run a fighting chance.

Even though reformers raise the issue of campaign costs more often than they discuss electoral competition, the complaint that campaigns cost too much has little foundation in reality. The amount of money spent on congressional elections has risen in recent years, but not inordinately so when one takes into consideration the rate of inflation and the growth in advertising costs imposed by television, radio, and direct-mail companies.[1] The price that candidates pay for political campaigns is minuscule compared with the price that corporations pay to advertise consumer products. The state of American advertising is such that companies such as Coca-Cola, which spend billions of dollars a year repeating the names of products that are already household terms, drown out candidate communications. This is particularly harmful to House challengers. As veteran Democratic media consultant Will Robinson has commented:

> Our challengers not only have to compete with an incumbent congressman, they also have to compete with that damned 'Energizer Bunny!' They need more, not less, money.

The resources committed to educating citizens about candidates and elections, which are critical to the functioning of a representative democracy, ought to be increased. Raising, not reducing, campaign expenditures has the potential to increase the knowledge that voters have about candidates, issues, and campaigns. Moreover, if ceilings on expenditures are set too low, challengers will have less opportunity to communicate with voters and elections will become less competitive. Critics of spending limits are correct in their assertion that legislation limiting the amounts that challengers can spend would be tantamount to an incumbent protection act.[2] Spending limits in open-seat races and incumbent-challenger contests would also work to the advantage of candidates who belong to the majority party in their state or district.

Related to the issue of costs are concerns over where campaign money originates. Complaints that wealthy and well-organized elements of society play too big a role in funding campaigns have been around for a long time and have been addressed by various pieces of legislation.[3] The Federal Election Campaign Act of 1974 and its amendments ban businesses and unions from making contributions and limit individuals to contributions of $1,000 and PACs to contributions of $5,000 per candidate during each phase of the election. The law has not eliminated the role of wealthy individuals in campaign finance but it has forced candidates to turn to a broader array of financial sources and it has reduced the impact that any individual or small group of contributors can have on an election. The number of individuals who are involved in the financing of campaigns should be further increased.

One of the unintended side effects of the FECA, however, has been to increase the efforts that candidates have to make when campaigning for resources. The amount of time and money that candidates spend chasing contributions is a major shortcoming of the system which drew a great deal of attention during the Keating Five scandal. Former senator Alan Cranston (D-Calif.) pinpointed the root of the problem when, in responding to the reprimand he received from the Senate Ethics Committee, he stated that "a majority of Senators feel it is necessary to raise money all the time. Campaigns [for the Senate] go on for 6 years."[4]

Another unintended result has been the growth in the importance of professional fund-raisers and others who are tapped into networks of wealthy individuals and PACs located in Washington and other major cities. The fact that candidates raise money from national fund-raising constituencies should be of somewhat lesser concern because members of Congress remain highly responsive—perhaps too much so—to their states and districts despite the fact that they and other candidates reach beyond these boundaries when raising money.

Changing the way campaigns are financed is not likely to make members of Congress less attentive to Washington-based lobbyists because legislators depend on them for much more than campaign money. Legislators rely on lobbyists for technical and political information about legislation and executive agency performance. Moreover, as national policy makers, members of Congress should pay attention to representatives of organized interests that are heavily affected by congressional action even if those interests are not located in their states or congressional districts. Lobbyists and those whom they represent know the strengths and weaknesses of existing and proposed policies better than most individuals. Interest group representatives have a strong case for access to members of congressional committees who write and oversee the implementation of federal policies that affect them, regardless of their geographic connection to these lawmakers.

Nevertheless, some reformers maintain that the way congressional elections are presently funded raises questions about the institution's political legitimacy. In situations where money matters, primarily in close races, reformers are correct in their assertion that those who make contributions have a greater impact on elections than those who do not. By providing their preferred candidates with some of the money needed to communicate with voters, wealthy individual contributors and political action committees, like the hundreds of thousands of professionals and volunteers who work on campaigns, increase their impact on the electoral process.

The sums that any one individual or group can contribute to a candidate, however, are too small to have a determining impact given the hundreds of thousands of dollars that are spent in most House contests and the millions of dollars spent in many Senate and some House campaigns. What individuals and groups usually get for their contributions is the opportunity to meet with members of Congress and their staffs, not the power to tell them how to govern.[5] Representatives and senators consider an array of factors when making policy decisions, including the views of constituents, committee chairs, party leaders, other legislators, and executive branch officials.[6] Legislators also strive to keep their roll-call votes consistent with those they have cast on related issues.[7] Reformers who focus on the role of money underestimate the importance of these other factors.

Soft money contributions, however, pose unique problems. These contributions, which frequently exceed $100,000, do have the potential to increase greatly the volume at which an individual or organization speaks. Yet, not all soft money is the same. Party soft money expenditures are used to help a large, rather than a small, group of candidates. Because party soft money is given to and spent by party committees, not candidates, it does not create "IOUs" between contributors and legislators. Finally, parties can be held accountable for much of their soft money finances because national party soft money transactions must be reported to the Federal Election Commission (FEC), which publicizes them. Contrary to what some reformers argue, party soft money is not likely to corrupt the political system.

Soft money that is given to private voter-mobilization groups created to promote the reelection of one or a small number of candidates is another matter. Large gifts to these groups contradict the intent of current campaign finance law because they establish a relationship between the candidate and the contributor. Often, this relationship is hidden from the public because neither the contributors nor the recipients of the money are required to disclose these transactions. As the Keating Five scandal demonstrates, soft money contributions to these organizations can corrupt the political process and should be outlawed. At the very least, rules governing the reporting and disclosure of the soft money transactions of private, nonparty voter-mobilization groups should be strengthened.

Low voter turnout is a more serious problem that is raised less frequently by reformers than either political money or electoral competition. Only 55 percent of all eligible Americans turned out to vote in the 1992 congressional elections, and this constitutes a recent record. Turnout-related issues are important because one can question the political legitimacy of elected officials who received the votes of less than half of all eligible voters. Congress sought to address this issue in 1993 when it enacted the "motor voter" bill, which mandated that Americans be able to register to vote when registering their cars or transacting other business with national, state, or local governments. More efforts should be taken to encourage people to vote and to participate in other areas of politics. Increased spending in congressional elections might bolster political participation because voter turnout increases when elections become more competitive.[8] As the 1992 elections showed, vigorous debate over salient issues also stimulates electoral participation.

The content of campaign messages is rarely discussed by reformers, but 84 percent of the general public is bothered by what politicians say to get elected.[9] Candidates campaign in slogans and sound bites mainly because short communications are cheaper than long ones. Candidates and campaign aides also believe that repetition is preferable to detail because their audiences have limited attention spans. Meeting the needs of the journalists who cover campaigns and controlling the flow of campaign information are two other objectives that encourage candidates to disseminate short, symbolic statements. The fact that many voters cast their ballots on the basis of candidate imagery and qualifications rather than on a detailed understanding of the issues further encourages many candidates, particularly incumbents, to campaign on valence issues rather than focus on concrete solutions to major problems. Reforms that provide candidates with free or subsidized postage, radio time, or television time could improve the quality of campaign communications.

The fact that many candidates from the major parties campaign on similar positions is a complaint raised by Marxists and other radicals, who comprise a tiny part of the population. They argue that the narrow range of positions is caused by the way elections are financed; Democrats and Republicans, they say, raise money from similar sources. While their charge is undeniable, their explanation is wrong. The narrow breadth of dialogue in American elections is caused by the fundamental agreement among most voters on the issues; it is not caused by the need to raise campaign money. Candidates of both major parties often seek to become associated with valence issues in order to attract voter support. Nothing short of restructuring American political, economic, and educational institutions is likely to broaden substantially the dialogue of American politics. Enacting ballot access or campaign finance reforms designed to strengthen minor parties or increase their number might slightly influence the nation's political debate, but it is very doubtful that enacting these reforms would break the fundamental consensus that exists on major issues.

Reformers should not be overly optimistic about the impact that campaign reform would have on voters' confidence in their elected representatives, Congress as an institution, or the entire political system. Congress has never been looked upon with much favor by the American public, and changing the way that its members are elected is unlikely to alter this fact. Conversely, it can be argued that the last set of campaign finance reforms to be passed had the opposite effect. The FECA's reporting requirements greatly improved the regulation of federal elections, particularly in the area of disclosure; they made available more information than ever before about the flow of political money. This information increased press coverage and public awareness of the role of money in politics, but it has done little to increase the level of confidence that the American people have in the political system. Instead, it has probably had the opposite effect.

Recommendations

Campaign reform should be founded on an understanding that elections are primarily fought between candidates and campaign organizations that devise strategies, accumulate and distribute resources, take issue positions, communicate images, and carry out grass-roots activities in order to win voter support. Party committees, PACs, and other groups play important supporting roles in the election process. Reformers need to appreciate the different goals and resources that individuals and groups bring to elections and need to consider how their proposals will affect these groups.

Campaign reform should be predicated on the assumption that

highly participatory, competitive elections are desirable because they are the best way to hold elected officials accountable to voters. Reform should make congressional elections more competitive by encouraging more experienced candidates to run and by improving the abilities of candidates, particularly nonincumbents, to communicate with voters. Campaign reform should also seek to increase the number of people who vote and give campaign contributions. The recommendations that follow are not a comprehensive reform package but are a series of proposals that would improve congressional elections and instill greater public confidence in the political system.

Free or Subsidized Communications

Free or subsidized campaign communications—whether they come in the form of postage, television or radio time, or communications vouchers—would be important vehicles for improving congressional elections because they would give candidates, particularly challengers, the opportunity to present their messages to the public. The promise of free or heavily discounted communications resources has the potential to encourage better candidates to run for Congress because it would give them the knowledge that should they win their party's nomination, they would be guaranteed access to some of the resources needed to campaign.[10] By encouraging the entry of better candidates and providing those who win a nomination with resources, this proposed reform would lead to more competitive congressional campaigns.

The availability of communications resources also has the potential to encourage greater electoral competition indirectly. Congressional challengers and open-seat candidates who use these resources effectively are in a position to attract the attention of local journalists, thereby helping challengers communicate more effectively with citizens and helping citizens base their voting decisions on more information. Because campaign communications help stimulate public interest in elections, reforms that ensure both candidates have adequate communications resources would probably increase voter information and turnout. A perception of greater competitiveness may also encourage some PACs and wealthy individuals to contribute to challengers, though most will likely continue to employ access or mixed strategies, which dictate contributing primarily to incumbents.

Free or subsidized mailings would give candidates opportunities to present targeted, detailed information about their qualifications, issue positions, and political objectives. Giving major-party House candidates free postage for three or four first-class mailings—including postage for one or two six-to-ten-page newsletters—is a simple reform that would improve the quality of the information that voters receive and increase electoral competitiveness. Giving Senate candidates amounts of free postage based on the number of registered voters in their states is a simple way to improve Senate elections.

Parties should also be offered free postage to mobilize current supporters and attract new ones. Minor parties and their candidates, as well as candidates who run as independents, could be given free postage if they convince a threshold number of voters to register under their label prior to the current election or if their candidates received a minimum number of votes in the previous contest. Minor parties and candidates could also be reimbursed retroactively for postage if they reached some threshold level of votes in the current election. Extending free postage to candidates and parties is justified by the fact that it would contribute to the education of citizens—the same arguments that are used to justify congressionally franked mail and reduced postage for party committees and nonprofit educational groups.

Giving candidates access to radio and television broadcast time is more complicated because of disparities in rate charges and the fact that congressional districts and media markets often do not match one another.[11] One solution is to require local broadcasters to provide Senate candidates with free television time and to require local radio stations to give free radio time to both House and Senate candidates. Congress could require broadcasters to issue back-to-back, prime-time segments to opposing candidates. Candidates could be issued five-minute blocs of time early in the campaign season, which they could use to air "infomercials" similar to those aired by Ross Perot in the 1992 presidential contest. These time-slots would be lengthy enough for candidates to communicate some information about their personal backgrounds, political qualifications, issue positions, and major campaign themes. Later in the campaign season, two- or one-minute advertisements could be distributed so that candidates could reinforce the images and campaign themes they introduced earlier. Thirty- or fifteen-second advertisements could be made available during the summation stage of the election for candidates to pull together their campaign messages and rally their supporters.

This system of structured, free media time would give candidates the opportunity to communicate substantive messages. It would also encourage voters to compare those messages. The differences in requirements for each chamber reflect the fact that television is an efficient and heavily used medium in virtually all Senate elections but is less practical and less frequently used in House contests, especially those held in major metropolitan areas.

The Democratic and Republican national committees should also be given free blocs of time on the national networks so that each can remind voters of its party's accomplishments, philosophies, and objectives. Giving each party an opportunity to present its views during (and after) the election has the potential to introduce more collective responsibility into the political system.[12] Minor parties and candidates should be given free blocs of radio and television time on terms similar to those described in connection with the provision of free postage.

Requiring local broadcasters to provide free political advertisements is justifiable because the airwaves are public property and one of the conditions of using them is that broadcasters "serve the public interest, convenience, and necessity." [13] The United States is the only major industrialized democracy that does not require broadcasters to contribute air time to candidates for public office—a distinction that should be eliminated.[14] Cable television operators should also be required to distribute advertising time to House and Senate candidates and parties with the justification that much of what is viewed on cable television passes through the public airwaves or over publicly maintained utility poles.

An alternative to providing candidates and parties with communications resources is to have the government distribute communications vouchers. This would allow campaigners to exercise more freedom in designing their communication strategies. Campaigns that feel the need to allocate more resources to setting the agenda could use their vouchers to purchase mass media ads. Campaigns that wish to focus on mobilizing specific population groups could devote a greater portion of their vouchers to direct mail. One of the trade-offs of the voucher option is that it imposes fewer costs on broadcasters and greater costs on taxpayers. One way to ease slightly the burden on the public treasury is to require all radio, television, and cable companies to sell candidates and parties prime-time advertising space at nonpreemptible lowest unit rates.[15] Another way to allay campaign costs is to require all candidates who accept communications vouchers to turn over any portion of their campaign treasury that remains after the election to a federal election campaign fund that would be used to help provide vouchers in the ensuing election.[16]

The preceding proposals would not provide communications resources to primary candidates or general election contestants from parties lacking widespread political support. This is both a cost-saving measure and a way to discourage the declaration of trivial candidacies. Reforms that place free or subsidized communications resources at the disposal of candidates have the potential to reduce the importance of money in politics as well as lower campaign costs and increase the competitiveness of congressional elections.

Voter Registration Initiatives

One of the major shortcomings of congressional elections, and American elections in general, is low voter turnout. Voter turnout in congressional elections has not exceeded 56 percent since 1968, and it has not exceeded 40 percent in any midterm election since 1970. Citizen apathy and disenchantment with the political system are probably responsible for some voter abstention, but voter registration laws are believed to depress turnout by about 9 percent.[17] The motor voter bill has eased some barriers to voting. Another step that should be taken is to require all states to include a check-off on their tax returns that enables citizens to register to vote when they complete their annual tax forms. The federal government should require the states (which administer elections) to mail a simple postcard-sized form to all unregistered voters that informs them of how to register easily with their state or county board of elections. Measures that shift the onus for registering from citizens to the government will not cause a groundswell in voter turnout, but they should increase it. These measures have the added benefit of allowing candidates and parties to focus more of their field activities on communicating with and mobilizing rather than registering voters.

Contributions and Expenditures

The amounts that individuals and groups can contribute to campaigns should be reviewed periodically in light of the roles that each set of contributors plays in the electoral process. The limits on individual and PAC contributions to candidates should remain at $1,000 and $5,000, respectively, for the primary and the general election because most persons and groups who give the legal maximum follow access or mixed strategies and give most of their contributions to incumbents. The aggregate limit for individual contributions to all federal candidates and party committees and PACs that participate in federal elections should be raised from $50,000 to $66,000 per year to reflect the impact of inflation. This change would increase the total amount of money spent in federal elections without increasing the influence that wealthy individuals can have on any one congressional race.

A limit of $50,000 should be imposed on contributions that candidates (and their families) make to their own campaigns to discourage the trend toward millionaire candidacies. Although outright limits on what candidates and their families can spend are likely to be interpreted by the courts as an infringement on free speech, candidates might voluntarily abide by these limits in return for communications subsidies.

Expenditures by House and Senate candidates' campaign organizations should remain unlimited. Money is essential to communicating with voters under the current cash-based campaign system. Spending limits have the potential to reduce the communications that candidates have with citizens and could deprive voters of the information they need to cast informed ballots. Spending limits would be especially harmful to challengers' campaigns.

Limiting the amounts that candidates' organizations can spend would also increase the influence of interest groups, parties, and the media. Independent expenditures made by PACs and wealthy individuals and party coordinated expenditures, generic advertisements, and field activities are no substitute for the unfiltered communications that candidates disseminate to voters. The same is true of news stories published in local newspapers or over the airwaves. The goal of campaign reform should be to increase, not decrease, the communications resources that candidates have at their disposal. Should Congress decide to enact spending limits for candidates who accept communications subsidies (or for some other reason), it needs to make sure that the limits are high enough to enable candidates to disseminate their messages, respond to their opponent's attacks, and counter communications expenditures that may be made by outside groups.

The amounts that parties can spend on behalf of candidates should be increased by 50 percent to allow party organizations to play a bigger role in congressional elections. Increasing the level of party activity in elections could enhance their competitiveness because parties strive to focus most of their resources on close contests, including those of challengers. Greater party expenditures would have an indirect effect on the competitiveness of some campaigns in that they would help candidates attract resources and attention from other contributors and the press. By enabling parties to pledge more support to potential candidates, this reform could help the parties encourage strategic politicians who are weighing the pros and cons of entering a race for Congress to decide in favor of running. This reform has an advantage over increasing party contribution limits because these expenditures encourage more coordinated activity among candidates and parties.

Parties should also be allowed to continue to collect soft money contributions, but a ceiling should be set on the amounts that party organizations can raise from any one source. I recommend the ceiling be equal to the aggregate limit for hard money contributions. Placing a high ceiling on soft money contributions to parties would enable party organizations to continue to use soft money for research, generic advertising, voter mobilization, and other campaign activities while forcing them to broaden their base of soft money donors.

These activities are important for several reasons. First, they contribute to the competitiveness of congressional and other elections. Second, they stimulate local political activism, thereby strengthening state and local party organizations and improving the farm teams from which congressional candidates emerge. Third, they help build bridges among elected officials who serve in different branches and levels of government.

Finally, many party soft money programs are designed to register and mobilize new voters. This distinguishes them from candidates' voter mobilization efforts, which are mostly targeted at citizens who have a previous voting history. Because party soft money programs help stimulate democratic activity, they are worth preserving so long as disclosure requirements continue to hold the parties accountable for their receipts and disbursements.

Most privately run, nonparty groups and their backers do not share the parties' electoral motives, and they are not subject to the same kind of accountability or institutional checks as are parties, PACs, and candidates.[18] Because nonparty groups usually seek to curry favor with individual officeholders and candidates, they should be banned from collecting or spending soft money in direct connection with federal elections. It would be difficult to fashion legislation that promotes this goal without infringing on the rights to organize and engage in free speech, but Congress ought to attempt to regulate these expenditures. Perhaps it could alter the tax code in ways that would discourage the formation of private voter mobilization groups funded by soft money contributions.

Reforms should not impose a complete ban on contributions by PACs or wealthy individuals. These contributors currently have other avenues of access or influence to which they can turn, and if their contributions were limited, they would undoubtedly create new avenues. Some might set up private, independent expenditure groups or create new organizations that would reside in some other loophole in the law. Others might return to the practice of delivering large, clandestine cash contributions as was customary prior to the Watergate scandal.

Wealthy individuals and groups that bundle contributions, host receptions, or provide other forms of fund-raising assistance, however, should have these activities count toward the contribution limits set by law. Reforms designed to prohibit individuals and groups from encouraging friends and colleagues to give contributions to specific candidates are unworkable and probably in violation of the right to free speech. But, because these fund-raising activities have the potential to increase an individual's or group's influence beyond that which would accrue from merely voting or making a cash contribution, they should be treated as "in-kind" contributions and assigned a cash value by the Federal Election Commission.

Tax Incentives

Tax incentives should be used to broaden the base of campaign contributors and to offset the impact of funds collected from wealthy and well-organized segments of society. Prior to the tax reforms introduced in 1986, individuals were able to claim a tax credit of $50 if they contributed $100 or more to federal candidates. (Couples who contributed $200 could claim a tax credit of $100.) While a significant number of taxpayers took advantage of these credits, the credits themselves were not sufficient to encourage many citizens to give campaign contributions.[19]

A system of graduated tax credits similar to those used in some other Western democracies might accomplish this goal.[20] Individuals who are eligible to claim a 100 percent tax credit for up to $100 in campaign contributions would be more likely to make them. Credits of 75 percent for the next $100 and 50 percent for the following $100 would encourage further contributions. Tax credits would encourage candidates and parties to pursue more aggressively small contributions and increase the number of taxpayers who give them. Using taxpayer dollars to increase the number of individuals who give money to federal candidates is an expensive proposition but it would probably be the most effective way to increase the number of people who participate in the financing of congressional elections. Increasing the base of small contributors is the best way to offset the influence of individuals and groups that make large contributions while maintaining a tie between a candidate's level of popular and financial support.

The Federal Election Commission

The Federal Election Commission should be strengthened so that it can better administer the law. The commission is currently unable to investigate all of the complaints brought before it, has a backlog of cases that is several years old, and has been criticized for its failure to dispense quickly with frivolous cases and pursue more important ones. Some of these shortcomings are caused by the fact that it is often micromanaged by its oversight committees in Congress and is severely underfunded. Other shortcomings are due to the FEC's structure—it has three Democratic and three Republican commissioners—which lends itself to indecision and stalemate. Finally, the agency should increase the speed with which it dispenses information about the receipts and expenditures of individual campaigns, party committees, and PACs. Providing these organizations with accounting and reporting software would accomplish this goal and ease the burden of disclosure.

Prospects for Reform

Enacting legislation that improves the quality of the candidates who run for Congress, enhances candidates'—especially nonincumbents'—abilities to communicate with voters, and enables campaigns to turn out more of their supporters would not be an easy task. Campaign reform is a highly charged issue. Candidates and parties often try to portray themselves as reformers while advocating changes that reflect their own self-interest. Incumbents are heavily preoccupied with protecting elements of the system that work to their advantage. Challengers are just as vocal about doing away with those advantages, at least until they become incumbents. Democrats, who are in control of Congress, are more favorably disposed toward spending limits, which would work to the disadvantage of challengers. Republicans oppose these and advocate an increase in existing limits on party spending, which would enable them to take advantage of their superior fund-raising prowess.

Inter-chamber differences also exist, with members of the Senate advocating the elimination of PAC contributions and House members defending PACs. These differences reflect the greater dependence of members of the lower chamber on PAC funds. Other differences of opinion reflect the demands that campaigning makes on different kinds of candidates from varied districts. Women, African Americans, and members of other traditionally underrepresented groups, who depend heavily on large national donor networks, have preferences that differ from those of most white male candidates. The views of candidates from wealthy, poor, urban, rural, or suburban districts on campaign finance reform often vary according to their fund-raising and spending needs. Of course, not all differences are grounded in personal or partisan advantage. Philosophical differences also divide politicians and parties.

The diversity of views and the complexity of the issue make it difficult to find the common ground needed to pass meaningful campaign reform. The sometimes questionable reform recommendations and inflammatory public relations campaigns of Common Cause and other self-styled citizens' lobbying groups have made it difficult for members of Congress to move beyond public posturing and engage in serious reform efforts. During the 1980s and early 1990s, House members and senators of both parties introduced comprehensive packages that they knew would never be adopted by their respective chambers, survive a conference committee, and be signed into law by the president. Their efforts were geared largely toward providing political cover for themselves rather than toward enacting campaign finance reform.

During the 103rd Congress, the House and the Senate approved two extremely different bills that were subjected to spirited negotiations. Both bills contained some useful provisions, including some of the recommendations discussed in the previous section.

H.R. 3, which was passed by the House on November 22, 1993, contained provisions for $200,000 in publicly funded communications vouchers that would be given to House candidates who accepted a "voluntary" spending limit of $600,000.[21] The limit would be increased if a candidate won a primary by 20 percent or less or had to compete in a runoff. The bill retained the existing $5,000 limit on PAC contributions, and it imposed an aggregate limit of $200,000 on PAC contributions to each congressional candidate per election cycle. An extra $66,000 in PAC contributions would be allowed for candidates who won their primaries by 20 percent of the vote or less, and an additional $100,000 would be allowed for candidates involved in run-off elections.[22] H.R. 3 also banned bundling by PACs that have parent organizations but allowed bundling by nonconnected groups such as EMILY's List and the WISH List. The bill allowed members of Congress to continue to operate the PACs that some use to contribute to and increase their clout with their fellow members.

S. 3, which the Senate passed on June 17, 1993, also established voluntary limits on campaign spending. These were based on the size of state populations. The ceilings for the general election ranged from $1.2 million in the smallest states to $5.5 million in California. Candidates were to be allowed to spend the equivalent of 67 percent of their state's ceiling in the primary and an extra 20 percent if they competed in a runoff. In contrast with the House bill, the Senate bill only provided public support to candidates whose opponents exceeded the voluntary spending limits. The Senate bill also differed from the House measure in that it sought to abolish PACs. It contained back-up provisions that would have gone into effect in the event the Supreme Court declared the ban on PAC contributions unconstitutional. These provisions limited PAC contributions to candidates to $1,000 and allowed candidates to accept no more than 20 percent of their total contributions from PACs.

The two bills had a few points in common. Both retained the existing $1,000 limit on individual contributions to candidates but raised the aggregate limit on individual contributions to candidates, parties, and PACs to $60,000 per election. Both also proposed to tighten restrictions on soft money by prohibiting federal candidates from raising it and restricting parties from using it for purposes that promoted the election of federal candidates. The bills also would have provided candidates with funds to counter independent expenditures made by individuals or PACs. Because the House bill established higher spending ceilings and distributed communications resources, it would have enhanced the competitiveness of congressional elections more than its Senate counterpart.

Differences between the bills made reconciliation impossible. Their different treatment of PACs proved to be the biggest sticking point.[23] Disagreements over public funding and how to raise the estimated $90 million to $200 million needed to finance it were others.[24] The House passed its bill by a straight party-line vote, with 255 Democrats voting yea and 175 Republicans voting nay. The Senate bill passed by a vote of 60 to 38, and the Democratic leadership had to rely on the support of seven moderate Republicans to bring the debate to cloture. The views of these seven GOP members weighed as heavily as those of House and Senate Democrats, as Democratic leaders sought to iron out the differences between the two bills. Their failure to broker an acceptable compromise resulted in the latest round of campaign reform dying before a conference committee was convened.

Reformers might have been wiser to have shunned comprehensive packages such as H.R. 3 and S. 3 in favor of an incremental approach to reform. More progress would probably have been made if Congress had first enacted changes that enjoyed widespread support and then worked to build bipartisan coalitions on the more divisive issues. Incrementalism offers the additional advantage of enabling Congress to adjust the law to offset the unintended consequences that routinely emerge as the result of regulatory change.

Reform often occurs in response to the public outcry for change that follows a major political scandal. The Federal Election Campaign Act of 1974, the most important piece of campaign finance legislation enacted in American history, was passed after the Watergate scandal focused public attention on the break-in at Democratic National Committee headquarters and the financing of presidential elections. The Keating Five, House Post Office, and House banking scandals and the general frustrations that many Americans vented at the 103rd Congress did not generate enough pressure to result in reform.

Conclusion

The rules and norms that govern congressional elections resemble those that structure any activity: they favor some individuals and groups over others. In recent years the number of Americans who believe that the electoral process is out of balance and provides too many advantages to incumbents, PACs, wealthy individuals, and other "insiders" has grown tremendously. Their views are reflected in the growing distrust that citizens have in government, the sense of powerlessness expressed by many voters, and their willingness to follow the leads of insurgent candidates and reformers without scrutinizing their qualifications or issue positions. These are signs that the prestige and power of Congress are in danger. They are also signs that meaningful campaign reform is in order.

Campaign reform should make congressional elections more competitive and increase the numbers of citizens who participate in them, both as voters and as financial contributors. Campaign reform should also enable candidates to spend less time campaigning for resources and more time campaigning for votes. The campaign finance reform legislation that has been debated by Congress during the last few years would succeed in accomplishing some, but not all, of these goals.

Without major campaign reform, incumbency will remain the defining element of most congressional elections. Challengers, particularly those running for the House, will continue to struggle to raise campaign funds and attract the attention of voters. The dialogue that occurs in House incumbent-challenger contests will remain largely one-sided, while that in open-seat contests and Senate races will continue to be somewhat more even. Congress, elections, and other institutions of government will remain targets for attack both by those who have a sincere wish to improve the political process and those seeking short-term partisan gain.

Elections are the most important avenues of political influence that are afforded to the citizens of a representative democracy. They give voters the opportunity to hold public officials accountable and to reject politicians with whom they disagree. Respect for human rights and political processes that allow for citizen input are what make democratic systems of government superior to others. Yet all systems of government have their imperfections, and some of these are embodied in their electoral processes. There are times when these imperfections are significant enough to warrant major change. Such change should bring the electoral process closer in line with broadly supported notions of liberty, equality, and democracy as well as the other values that bind a nation. The current state of congressional elections demonstrates that change is warranted in the way in which Americans elect those who serve in Congress.

Notes

1. See, for example, Frank J. Sorauf, *Inside Campaign Finance* (New Haven, Conn.: Yale University Press, 1992), 231.
2. Gary C. Jacobson, *Money in Congressional Elections* (New Haven, Conn.: Yale University Press, 1980), especially 48-49, 211-214; Jacobson, "The Effects of Campaign Spending in House Elections: New Evidence for Old Arguments," *American Journal of Political Science* 34 (1990): 334-362; Ruy A. Teixeira, "Campaign Reform, Political Competition and Citizen Participation," in *Rethinking Political Reform: Beyond Spending and Term Limits,* ed. Ruy A. Teixeira, L. Sandy Maisel, and John J. Pitney, Jr. (Washington, D.C.: The Progressive Foundation, 1994), 8, 13-14. For a slightly different point of view, see Donald P. Green and Jonathan S. Krasno, "Salvation for the Spendthrift Incumbent: Reestimating the Effects of Campaign Spending in House Elections," *American Journal of Political Science* (1988): 884-907.
3. See, for example, Herbert E. Alexander, *Financing Politics: Money, Elections, and Political Reform* (Washington, D.C.: CQ Press, 1992), 23-26.
4. U.S. Congress, Senate, *Congressional Record,* daily ed., 102nd Cong., 2nd sess., November 20, 1992, S17182.
5. On the limited impact of PAC contributions on congressional roll-call votes see John R. Wright, "PACs, Contributions, and Roll Calls: An Organizational Perspective," *American Political Science Review* 79 (1985): 400-414; "PAC Contributions, Lobbying, and Representation," *Journal of Politics* 51 (1989): 714-729; and Janet M. Grenzke, "PACs and the Congressional Supermarket: The Currency is Complex," *American Journal of Political Science* 33 (1989): 1-24. For an alternative viewpoint see John Frendreis and Richard Waterman, "PAC Contributions and Legislative Behavior: Senate Voting and Trucking Deregulation," *Social Science Quarterly* 66 (1985): 401-412.
6. John W. Kingdon, *Congressmen's Voting Decisions* (New York: Harper and Row, 1981).
7. Aage R. Clausen, *How Congressmen Decide* (New York: St. Martin's, 1973).

8. Gary W. Cox and Michael C. Munger, "Closeness, Expenditures, and Turnout in the 1982 U.S. House Elections," *American Political Science Review* 83 (1989): 217-231.

9. "Poll Finds Public Sour on Congress, Seeking More Bi-Partisanship on Issues and Reform, Uncertain and Divided on Details of Reform," press release, Conference on Campaign Reform, Committee for the Study of the American Electorate, July 29, 1994.

10. L. Sandy Maisel, "Competition in Congressional Elections: Why More Qualified Candidates Do Not Seek Office," in *Rethinking Political Reform,* ed. Teixeira, Maisel, and Pitney, 29.

11. The idea of giving candidates free television and radio broadcast time has been around for many years. See, for example, Twentieth Century Fund Commission on Campaign Costs, *Voters' Time* (New York: Twentieth Century Fund, 1969); and Campaign Study Group, "Increasing Access to Television for Political Candidates" (Cambridge, Mass.: Institute of Politics, Harvard University, 1978).

12. See, for example, Larry J. Sabato, *Paying for Elections: The Campaign Finance Thicket* (New York: Twentieth Century Fund, 1989), 29-34.

13. See, for example, Doris A. Graber, *Mass Media and American Politics,* 4th ed. (Washington, D.C.: CQ Press, 1993), 53-55.

14. Sabato, *Paying for Elections,* 31.

15. Currently, the law requires broadcasters to make preemptive time available at the lowest unit rate; most candidates choose the more expensive nonpreemptible time slots.

16. Subsidized or free communications can also be used to induce additional sorts of behavior. Candidates could be offered communications subsidies in exchange for participating in campaign debates or abiding by spending limits, for example.

17. Raymond E. Wolfinger and Stephen J. Rosenstone, *Who Votes?* (New Haven, Conn.: Yale University Press, 1980), 61-88.

18. Sorauf, *Inside Campaign Finance,* 185.

19. See Ruth S. Jones and Warren E. Miller, "Financing Campaigns: Macro Level Innovation and Micro Level Response," *Western Political Quarterly* 38 (1985): 190, 192.

20. A number of countries and some American states offer citizens the opportunity to obtain tax credits for political contributions. See the case studies in *Campaign and Party Finance in North America and Western Europe,* ed. Arthur B. Gunlicks (Boulder, Colo.: Westview Press, 1993).

21. For a useful summary of H.R. 3 and S. 3 see Joseph E. Cantor and L. Paige Whitaker, "Comparison of Current Law with H.R. 3 and S. 3 As Passed by the House and Senate in the 103rd Congress" (Washington, D.C.: Congressional Research Service, Library of Congress, December 29, 1993). A cogent analysis of the reforms is provided by Herbert E. Alexander, "White Paper on Election Reform: A Critique and Commentary on S. 3 and H.R. 3 103rd Congress" (Los Angeles: Citizens' Research Foundation, March 1994).

22. All of these limits would be adjusted for inflation.

23. Helen Dewar and Kenneth J. Cooper, "Campaign Finance Mired in Gulf Between House and Senate," *Washington Post,* May 28, 1994, A8.

24. Tim Curran, "Footing the Bill for Campaign Reform," *Roll Call,* May 26, 1994, 3, 22.

Appendix

Methodology

My goal in writing this book was to evaluate systematically and comprehensively congressional election campaigns. Seven objectives were pursued in the course of the research: 1) to learn about the kinds of individuals who compete for and win a major-party nomination and general election; 2) to describe the organizations that candidates assemble to mount their campaigns; 3) to analyze the goals, decision-making processes, and resources of parties, PACs, and other campaign contributors; 4) to examine how candidates campaign for the support of these groups; 5) to discuss the strategies and communications techniques that candidates use to campaign for votes; 6) to discuss the impact of elections on the operation of Congress and the larger political system; and 7) to make some recommendations for campaign reform.

Data Sources

Addressing the first five objectives required a major data collection effort. I conducted roughly twenty semistructured personal interviews with congressional candidates and campaign aides in 1992 to learn about specific campaign strategies. This information was supplemented with materials that students in my fall 1992 undergraduate honors seminar on congressional elections collected from an additional twenty-four campaigns while researching their course projects. Each student tracked both the Democratic and Republican campaigns conducted in one House election. In the course of their research, they interviewed candidates, campaign managers, and other campaign aides and systematically collected press clippings, issue papers, and other materials that were relevant to the elections they researched. All of the interviews were guided by a common questionnaire.[1] The 1992 materials were supplemented by interviews conducted and materials collected in the 1984, 1986, and 1988 congressional elections.

The information on party strategy is based mainly on about thirty interviews that I conducted over the course of the 1992 election. National party officials were interviewed about their organizations' goals, expectations, and strategies on several occasions between January 1991 and January 1993. Several members of the DCCC's and NRCC's political staffs were interviewed five times over the course of the election cycle. The interviews enabled me to record how these organizations formulated their initial strategies and adjusted their tactics in response to changing conditions. As was the case with the information collected from candidates and campaign aides, this information was supplemented with materials collected during prior elections.

The information on PAC decision making is based on interviews that I and twenty colleagues and graduate students conducted over the course of the 1992 election cycle as part of a related study of PACs.[2] We each conducted at least three personal interviews (most conducted four or more) with the managers of twenty-one PACs using a common questionnaire.[3]

Other information was gathered from newspapers, periodicals, and discussions with a wide range of political operatives with whom I spoke at conferences, fund-raising events, and other informal occasions. As the study progressed, parts of the research were made available to many of the participants, allowing for the establishment of a continuing dialogue. Feedback from the participants was occasionally used to illuminate or reinterpret some of the observations I had made earlier. The information collected from the interviews and informal conversations enabled me to describe congressional elections from the perspectives of the individuals who are most deeply involved in the electoral process.

I turned to a variety of sources for information about different aspects of congressional election campaigns. Information on candidates' backgrounds was culled from issues of *Congressional Quarterly Weekly Report*. These data were supplemented with information from files kept by various party organizations and PACs. The National Committee for an Effective Congress provided data on the composition of congressional districts and the candidates' racial backgrounds. Political scientists David Canon, Matthew Schousen, and Patrick Sellers provided additional information on African American candidates. Campaign finance data were supplied by the Federal Election Commission.

A questionnaire that was mailed to congressional candidates and campaign aides who competed in the 1992 House and Senate elections was an important source of information on congressional candidates, their campaign organizations, budgets, strategies, and related topics (see Figure A-1). The questionnaire was sent to the campaign headquarters of every major-party House or Senate candidate who faced major-party opposition in the 1992 general election. Questionnaires were also sent to congressional candidates who did not face major-party opposition in the general election and to roughly a dozen minor-party candidates who appeared likely to garner a significant share of the vote. The responses from these campaigns and those from incumbent-versus-incumbent House campaigns were later eliminated from the sample to make the study as representative as possible of typical two-party contested congressional elections.

The mailing was timed so that the questionnaires would arrive two days after the election, thereby ensuring that the campaign would be fresh in the minds of the respondents and that the respondents would have the time to provide accurate answers to the questions. Second and third copies of the questionnaire were sent to campaigns that did not return previous copies. Each questionnaire was accompanied by a cover letter that was personally addressed to the campaign's manager or some other high-ranking campaign aide. This individual was asked to complete the questionnaire or give it to the candidate or someone else who had a broad knowledge of their campaign. Prior to and after mailing the questionnaires, post cards were sent to alert the addressees of the questionnaires' impending arrival and to request that they return their completed questionnaire as soon as possible.[4]

This process netted a total of 334 usable questionnaires for the House and 28 for the Senate. The response rates were 42 percent and 41 percent, respectively. Some of the completed questionnaires were accompanied by descriptive narratives and other information about the campaigns. The House sample was representative of the underlying population on such key variables as party affiliation, incumbency, and election outcome (see Table A-1). The Senate sample is much smaller and somewhat less representative of the underlying population than is the House sample. It does not readily lend itself to the same level of detailed, rigorous analysis. For these reasons and for the reasons discussed in the text, the generalizations developed from the Senate data were advanced more tentatively. Wherever possible, these generalizations were checked against similar data collected from Senate campaigns that took place during the 1984, 1986, and 1988 election cycles. Many of the generalizations developed from the 1992 House data were also compared to those from a study of the 1984 elections.[5]

No distinctions were drawn between the responses of candidates, campaign managers, treasurers, and other campaign aides.[6] There are several reasons for treating these responses equally. First, since campaign decision making is a cooperative endeavor involving a small group of decision makers, these individuals can be expected to have similar percep-

Figure A-1   The 1992 Congressional Campaign Study Questionnaire

Form no._____

THE 1992 CONGRESSIONAL CAMPAIGN STUDY

The University of Maryland regularly surveys voters, political candidates, and elected officials to learn about important issues and political processes. Congressional election campaigns are one of our major interests.

This is a CONFIDENTIAL SURVEY. Please DO NOT SIGN the questionnaire. Once your completed questionnaire is received, the responses will be entered into a computer. It will then be impossible to associate them with your name. The number at the top of the page is only a mechanical device that will be used to determine the response rate and to send follow-up letters to individuals who have not returned their questionnaires by NOVEMBER 21st.

PLEASE TAKE THE 20 MINUTES NEEDED TO COMPLETE THE SURVEY. Your cooperation will help those interested in elections learn more about campaigning for Congress. Thank you for your time and assistance.

PLEASE CIRCLE THE ANSWERS THAT BEST DESCRIBE YOUR OPINIONS. (Feel free to provide additional comments on extra sheets of paper.)

1. What was your position in the campaign?
   1) Candidate 2) Campaign Manager 3) Treasurer 4) Press Aide
   5) Other: _____

2. What was your candidate's party affiliation?
   1) Democrat 2) Republican 3) Independent 4) Other: _____

3. How competitive was your candidate's primary?
   1) Very competitive 2) Moderately competitive 3) Slightly competitive
   4) There was no primary opposition

4. What was your candidate's position in the general election?
   1) Incumbent 2) Challenger 3) Open seat 4) Incumbent vs. Incumbent

5. How did your candidate do in the general election?
   1) Won 2) Lost

6. How many times has your candidate run for Congress?
   1) 1st time 2) 2nd time 3) 3-5 times 4) More than 5 times

7. How much does the present district resemble the district that existed in 1990?
   1) Exactly the same 2) Similar 3) Somewhat different 4) Very different
   5) A completely new district

Figure A-1 (continued)

8. Compared to most registered voters in your district, would you say that your candidate's views are:
   1) More liberal 2) More conservative 3) About the same

9. What do you think were your candidate's basic strengths in the campaign?

   Greatest strength: _____ Others: _____

10. What do you think were your candidate's basic weaknesses in the campaign?

    Greatest weakness: _____ Others: _____

11. What do you think were your opponent's basic strengths in the campaign?

    Greatest strength: _____ Others: _____

12. What do you think were your opponent's basic weaknesses in the campaign?

    Greatest weakness: _____ Others: _____

13. What do you think were the most important issues in your campaign? (You may list local and/or national issues)

    Most important issue: _____ Others: _____

14. How important were each of the following in helping you LEARN ABOUT VOTERS' OPINIONS on major issues? Circle the appropriate choice for each.

	Not	Slightly	Moderately	Very	Extremely
Mail from voters	1	2	3	4	5
Newspaper, radio, & TV stories	1	2	3	4	5
Public opinion surveys	1	2	3	4	5
Local party leaders & activists	1	2	3	4	5
National party leaders	1	2	3	4	5
National party publications & briefings	1	2	3	4	5
Personal contacts with voters	1	2	3	4	5
Other: _____	1	2	3	4	5

15. Approximately what percentage of the registered voters in your district would describe themselves as... (Fill in your answers, which should total 100%).

    ____% Democratic   ____% Independent

    ____% Republican   ____% Others: _____

16. Which of the following groups of voters did your campaign specifically target? Circle as many responses as you think are appropriate.
    1) Members of your party 2) Independents 3) Members of opponent's party
    4) Others:_____ 5) Focused on all voters equally

Figure A-1 (continued)

17. Did your campaign concentrate on any demographic, occupational, geographic, or issue groups? If yes, list those targeted most heavily.

    Most targeted group: _____ Others: _____

18. How important do you believe each of the following groups were in INFLUENCING YOUR CANDIDATE'S DECISION TO RUN FOR CONGRESS? Circle the most appropriate choice for each.

	Not	Slightly	Moderately	Very	Extremely
Family & Friends .	1	2	3	4	5
City &/or County Parties	1	2	3	4	5
State Party .	1	2	3	4	5
National Party Committee (DNC or RNC)	1	2	3	4	5
Cong. Campaign Committee (DCCC or NRCC)	1	2	3	4	5
Labor Unions	1	2	3	4	5
Other Interest Groups .	1	2	3	4	5
Political Action Committees	1	2	3	4	5
Issues &/or Ideology .	1	2	3	4	5
A Desire to Improve Government .	1	2	3	4	5
A Desire to be a Political Leader	1	2	3	4	5

19. For each of the following activities, did your campaign rely on salaried campaign staff, paid consultants, party staff, union members, unpaid volunteers, the assistance of some other group, or did the campaign not carry out the activity? Circle the appropriate choice(s) for each.

	Campaign Staff	Paid Cons.	Party Staff	Union Mbrs.	Unpaid Vols.	Other Groups	Not used
Campaign management .	1	2	3	4	5	6	7
Media advertising . .	1	2	3	4	5	6	7
Press relations . .	1	2	3	4	5	6	7
Issue & opposition research	1	2	3	4	5	6	7
Polling . . .	1	2	3	4	5	6	7
Fundraising . .	1	2	3	4	5	6	7
Get-out-the-vote activities	1	2	3	4	5	6	7
Legal advice . . .	1	2	3	4	5	6	7
Accounting/Filing FEC Reports	1	2	3	4	5	6	7

20. Approximately what percentage of your campaign's TOTAL BUDGET was spent on each of the following? Fill in your answers, which should total 100%.

    Staff salaries . . ____%

    Research . . . ____%

    Polling . . . . ____%

    Direct mail . . . ____%

    Travel . . . . ____%

    Get-out-the-vote activities ____%

    Media and advertising ____%

    Other:_____ ____%

Figure A-1 (continued)

21. Approximately what percentage of your campaign's MEDIA BUDGET was spent on each of the following? Fill in your answers, which should total 100%.

Radio ads   .   .   .   ____%

Television ads   .   .   ____%

Newspaper ads   .   .   ____%

Campaign literature   .   ____%

Billboards and yard signs   ____%

Other:_____   ____%

22. How important were the following techniques in CONVEYING THE CANDIDATE'S MESSAGE TO VOTERS? Circle the appropriate choice for each technique.

	Not	Slightly	Moderately	Very	Extremely	Not Used
Radio (paid or free) . .	1	2	3	4	5	6
Television (paid or free) .	1	2	3	4	5	6
Literature drops . . .	1	2	3	4	5	6
Speeches and rallies . .	1	2	3	4	5	6
Newsletters and direct mail .	1	2	3	4	5	6
Newspaper ads . . .	1	2	3	4	5	6
Press releases and free media	1	2	3	4	5	6
Campaign debates . . .	1	2	3	4	5	6
Billboards, buttons, etc. .	1	2	3	4	5	6
Surrogate campaigning . .	1	2	3	4	5	6
Door-to-door canvassing .	1	2	3	4	5	6
Candidate visits to shopping centers, factories, etc. .	1	2	3	4	5	6
Other:_____ .	1	2	3	4	5	6

23. Which of the techniques listed in Question 22 do you think your campaign utilized... (Fill in your answers below)

a) Most effectively:_____ b) Least effectively:_____

24. Which one of the following did your campaign advertising primarily focus on?
    1) Your candidate's image
    2) Your candidate's issue positions
    3) Opponent's image
    4) Opponent's issue positions
    5) Other: _____

25. Which campaign received more news coverage?
    1) Your campaign   2) Opponent's campaign   3) Both were covered equally

26. Do you believe the news media covered the campaign fairly?
    1) Yes, the media coverage was fair to both candidates
    2) No, the media coverage favored your candidate's campaign
    3) No, the media coverage favored the opponent's campaign

Figure A-1 (continued)

27. Did the local media endorse any candidates in the general election?
    1) Yes, your candidate was endorsed
    2) Yes, the opponent was endorsed
    3) Both candidates received endorsements from different media outlets
    4) No candidates were endorsed

28. Did your campaign or your opponent's campaign use negative advertising?
    1) Your campaign did 2) Opponent's campaign did 3) Both campaigns did
    4) No negative advertising was used by either campaign

The next eight questions are concerned with the kinds of assistance your campaign received from different groups. All of the questions use exactly the same format. Circle the number associated with the most appropriate choice for each group.

29. How important were the following groups in providing your campaign with INFORMATION ABOUT VOTERS (survey data, demographic data, targeting assessments)?

	Not	Slightly	Moderately	Very	Extremely
City &/or County Parties	1	2	3	4	5
State Party	1	2	3	4	5
National Party Committee (DNC or RNC)	1	2	3	4	5
Cong. Campaign Committee (DCCC or NRCC)	1	2	3	4	5
Labor Unions	1	2	3	4	5
Other Interest Groups	1	2	3	4	5
Political Action Committees	1	2	3	4	5

30. How important were the following groups in assisting your campaign with REGISTERING VOTERS and GETTING THEM TO THE POLLS ON ELECTION DAY?

	Not	Slightly	Moderately	Very	Extremely
City &/or County Parties	1	2	3	4	5
State Party	1	2	3	4	5
National Party Committee (DNC or RNC)	1	2	3	4	5
Cong. Campaign Committee (DCCC or NRCC)	1	2	3	4	5
Labor Unions	1	2	3	4	5
Other Interest Groups	1	2	3	4	5
Political Action Committees	1	2	3	4	5

31. How important were the following groups in providing your campaign with MASS MEDIA ADVERTISING and DEVELOPING THE CANDIDATE'S PUBLIC IMAGE?

	Not	Slightly	Moderately	Very	Extremely
City &/or County Parties	1	2	3	4	5
State Party	1	2	3	4	5
National Party Committee (DNC or RNC)	1	2	3	4	5
Cong. Campaign Committee (DCCC or NRCC)	1	2	3	4	5
Labor Unions	1	2	3	4	5
Other Interest Groups	1	2	3	4	5
Political Action Committees	1	2	3	4	5

Figure A-1 (continued)

32. How important were the following groups in assisting your campaign with
FUNDRAISING, including introductions to potential campaign contributors
and direct-mail fundraising?

	Not	Slightly	Moderately	Very	Extremely
City &/or County Parties	1	2	3	4	5
State Party	1	2	3	4	5
National Party Committee (DNC or RNC)	1	2	3	4	5
Cong. Campaign Committee (DCCC or NRCC)	1	2	3	4	5
Labor Unions	1	2	3	4	5
Other Interest Groups	1	2	3	4	5
Political Action Committees	1	2	3	4	5

33. How important were the following groups in assisting your campaign with
ISSUE RESEARCH AND DEVELOPMENT?

	Not	Slightly	Moderately	Very	Extremely
City &/or County Parties	1	2	3	4	5
State Party	1	2	3	4	5
National Party Committee (DNC or RNC)	1	2	3	4	5
Cong. Campaign Committee (DCCC or NRCC)	1	2	3	4	5
Labor Unions	1	2	3	4	5
Other Interest Groups	1	2	3	4	5
Political Action Committees	1	2	3	4	5

34. How important were the following groups in providing your campaign with
OPPOSITION RESEARCH?

	Not	Slightly	Moderately	Very	Extremely
City &/or County Parties	1	2	3	4	5
State Party	1	2	3	4	5
National Party Committee (DNC or RNC)	1	2	3	4	5
Cong. Campaign Committee (DCCC or NRCC)	1	2	3	4	5
Labor Unions	1	2	3	4	5
Other Interest Groups	1	2	3	4	5
Political Action Committees	1	2	3	4	5

35. How important were the following groups in providing your campaign with
VOLUNTEER WORKERS?

	Not	Slightly	Moderately	Very	Extremely
City &/or County Parties	1	2	3	4	5
State Party	1	2	3	4	5
National Party Committee (DNC or RNC)	1	2	3	4	5
Cong. Campaign Committee (DCCC or NRCC)	1	2	3	4	5
Labor Unions	1	2	3	4	5
Other Interest Groups	1	2	3	4	5
Political Action Committees	1	2	3	4	5

Figure A-1 (continued)

36. How important were the following groups in assisting with <u>CAMPAIGN
    MANAGEMENT</u>, including the formulation of campaign strategy?

	Not	Slightly	Moderately	Very	Extremely
City &/or County Parties . . .	1	2	3	4	5
State Party	1	2	3	4	5
National Party Committee (DNC or RNC)	1	2	3	4	5
Cong. Campaign Committee (DCCC or NRCC)	1	2	3	4	5
Labor Unions	1	2	3	4	5
Other Interest Groups	1	2	3	4	5
Political Action Committees . .	1	2	3	4	5

37. How important do you believe the following factors were in determining
    the <u>OUTCOME OF THE ELECTION</u>?

	Not	Slightly	Moderately	Very	Extremely
Candidate image & personality . .	1	2	3	4	5
Traditional party loyalties . .	1	2	3	4	5
Local issues	1	2	3	4	5
National issues	1	2	3	4	5
Debates	1	2	3	4	5
Newspaper endorsements . . .	1	2	3	4	5
Incumbent's advantages of office .	1	2	3	4	5
Incumbent's record in Congress . .	1	2	3	4	5
Negative Campaigning	1	2	3	4	5
Anti-incumbency mood among voters .	1	2	3	4	5
Influence of the presidential election	1	2	3	4	5
Influence of Ross Perot's campaign .	1	2	3	4	5
Influence of a U.S. Senate election .	1	2	3	4	5
Influence of state or local elections	1	2	3	4	5
Political scandal	1	2	3	4	5

38. In your own words, did any unusual circumstances or major events
    influence the election? (Please feel free to use additional sheets of
    paper.)

---

tions of the important factors in and determinants of the campaign.[7] Second, during pretests of the questionnaire, several members of the same campaign provided responses that were nearly identical. Third, in about a dozen cases a copy of the survey was received from a candidate and a campaign adviser of the same campaign, and, as was the case in the pretests, the responses of the two campaigners mirrored each other closely.[8]

Quantitative Data Analysis

The data analyzed in chapter 2 were for all major-party primary contestants. Descriptive statistics, including sums, means, and percentages,

Table A-1 The Representativeness of the House and the Senate Samples

	House		Senate	
	Sample	Population	Sample	Population
Democrats	50%	50%	61%	50%
	(168)	(397)	(17)	(34)
Republicans	50%	50%	39%	50%
	(166)	(397)	(11)	(34)
Incumbents	36%	39%	39%	38%
	(121)	(313)	(11)	(26)
Challengers	41%	39%	32%	38%
	(138)	(313)	(9)	(26)
Open-seat candidates	23%	21%	29%	24%
	(75)	(168)	(8)	(16)
Winners	48%	50%	57%	50%
	(162)	(397)	(16)	(34)
Losers	52%	50%	43%	50%
	(172)	(397)	(12)	(34)
Total N	(334)	(794)	(28)	(68)

Notes: The samples consist of all 1992 campaigns that returned mail questionnaires; they include general election campaigns in major-party contested races, excluding incumbent-versus-incumbent House races. The populations consist of all general election campaigns in major-party contested races, excluding incumbent-versus-incumbent House races.

provide the foundation for most of the data analysis in chapters 2 through 8. The analyses in chapters 3 through 9 are based on major-party general election campaigns except for incumbent-versus-incumbent House races.

Following standard practice, all current officeholders were classified as incumbents, candidates who ran against them were classified as challengers, and the rest were classified as open-seat candidates. This means that challengers who defeated incumbents during the primary phase of the election were classified as challengers during their primary races and as open-seat candidates during the general election. Similarly, their general election opponents were also classified as open-seat candidates.

Competitive campaigns include all winning and losing campaigns in which the victor defeated the second-place finisher by 20 percent or less of the vote; the rest are classified as uncompetitive. This is a fairly large victory margin, but it is appropriate given the heightened level of uncertainty that initially surrounded the 1992 election and persisted throughout most of the campaign season. A narrower competitiveness measure, such as a 15 percent margin, would have eliminated campaigns that were competitive for part of the election but were ultimately decided by more than 15 percent of the vote. The 20 percent measure enabled me to contrast the campaign organizations, budgets, strategies, and contributions received by campaigns that were competitive at some point during the election with those that were never competitive. Slightly changing the boundaries for the competitiveness measure does not significantly change the results.[9]

Tables 9-1 through 9-4 were created using ordinary least-squares (OLS) regressions. The full regression equations are presented in Tables A-2 through A-7. The equations are the product of an extensive model-building process that tested the impact of numerous variables using a variety of statistical techniques. The variables that were tested in earlier versions of the models include candidates' background characteristics and political experience, their party affiliations, the professionalism of their campaign organizations, party and PAC campaign services and expenditures, the percentage of current voters who lived in the district prior to redistricting (to control for the redrawing of House seats), and the ideological match between the candidate and the district. Numerous OLS regressions, two-stage least-squares regressions, and logistic regressions (which dichotomized the dependent variable as win/lose) were tested prior to selecting the final equations. The model-building process tested numerous variables, including many that recorded information about both of the candidates and campaigns that were involved in a particular election. Some of the models used transformed variables, including the natural log of the campaign spending variables. The final models were selected for reasons of statistical fit, parsimony, and ease of interpretation. They are statistically robust; adding, subtracting, or transforming the variables does not lead to major changes in the results or the generalizations they support.

Predictors of House Incumbents' Vote Shares

Table A-2 presents the OLS regression that was used to generate the results that appear in Table 9-1. That regression predicts the impact of incumbent campaign activity on incumbents' vote shares while controlling for preexisting political conditions (the partisan bias of the district, political scandal, and the presence of a minor-party candidate) and for many of the campaign activities of the challenger. The information for incumbents' campaigns, district conditions, and mass media coverage is drawn from questionnaires received from incumbents. The information for challengers' spending on campaign communications was drawn from the mail questionnaires returned by challengers or was estimated in cases where the challenger did not return a completed questionnaire. The candidates' characteristics and many of the campaign organization, strategy, and communications variables discussed in chapters 2, 3, 7, and 8 were not included in the incumbent equation because they did not approach statistical significance. The variables for party and interest group cam-

Table A-2 OLS Regression Estimates of House Incumbents' Vote
Shares, 1992

	b	Se b
Base vote (constant)	65.292	—
Partisan bias (per one-point advantage in party registration)	0.084***	0.033
Political scandal	−4.391***	1.510
Significant independent or minor-party candidate	−9.648**	4.641
Incumbent spending on campaign communications (per $1,000)	−0.001	0.003
Challenger spending on campaign communications (per $1,000)	−0.023****	0.006
Party spending on behalf of challenger (per $1,000)	−0.120****	0.032
Independent expenditures against incumbent (per $1,000)	−0.097**	0.044
Media advantage favoring incumbent	2.540*	1.453

Sources: Questions 15, 20, 21, and 26 of the 1992 Congressional Campaign Study, Federal Election Commission data, various editions of *Congressional Quarterly Weekly Report,* and other sources discussed elsewhere in the appendix.

Note: The sample includes general election candidates in major-party contested races, excluding those in incumbent-versus-incumbent races.

N = 117
Adjusted R^2 = .42
*p ≤ .10; **p ≤ .05; ***p ≤ .01; ****p ≤ .001 (two-tailed test).

paign services discussed in chapters 4 and 5 were dropped because of multicollinearity with the party and PAC spending variables. Party affiliation was not included in the final model because neither Democratic nor Republican incumbents derived any benefits from national partisan tides; the only significant effects of party affiliation resulted from the partisan bias of congressional districts. The operationalization of the independent variables is as follows:

> *Partisan bias:* the percentage of registered voters of the incumbent's party minus the percentage of registered voters of the challenger's party. This information was collected in question 15 of the 1992 Congressional Campaign Study (see Figure A-1).
> *Political scandal:* a dummy variable that was coded 1 for all candidates who had twenty-five or more overdrafts at the House bank or were under federal indictment and 0 if otherwise. This information was collected from *Roll Call* and memos prepared by congressional aides.
> *Significant independent or minor-party candidate:* coded 1 for all candidates who faced a minor-party or independent candidate who won 10 percent or more of the vote and 0 if otherwise.
> *Incumbent spending on campaign communications (per $1,000):*

spending on direct-mail, radio, television, and newspaper advertising and field activities (get-out-the-vote drives, campaign literature, billboards and yard signs, and travel to and from campaign events). This figure was calculated by multiplying the percentages that respondents specified in response to questions 20 and 21 by their total campaign expenditures.[10]

Challenger spending on campaign communications (per $1,000): calculated using the formula that was used to calculate incumbent spending on campaign communications unless a challenger campaign did not return a questionnaire. In the latter case, challenger spending was estimated by multiplying the average amount that challengers spent on campaign communications by each challenger's total campaign expenditures.

Party spending on behalf of the challenger (per $1,000): the total coordinated expenditures that party committees made on behalf of the challenger, as reported to the FEC.

Independent expenditures against the incumbent: the total independent spending that PACs made advocating an incumbent's defeat, as reported to the FEC.

Media advantage favoring the incumbent: coded 1 if the incumbent's campaign reported that their candidate received more news coverage than the challenger (response 1 to question 25) or if the incumbent's campaign reported that their candidate received the endorsement of the local media (response 1 to question 27) and 0 if otherwise.

Some researchers have found that the log of total incumbent expenditures and the log of total challenger expenditures are better predictors of incumbents' vote shares than are untransformed spending figures.[11] Substituting the logs of incumbent and challenger spending on campaign communications for the untransformed figures does little to improve the fit of the model (the adjusted R^2 improves by only .01), needlessly complicates the interpretation of the results, and does not alter the generalizations that were developed from the incumbent equation. For these reasons, the untransformed measures are used.

Table A-3 confirms that when incumbent expenditures are disaggregated, none of them has a positive statistically significant impact on incumbents' vote shares. The operationalization of the independent variables is largely self-explanatory. Direct mail (per $1,000), for example, stands for the expenditures made on this campaign activity. The variables were calculated by multiplying the percentages that respondents specified in questions 20 and 21.[12]

Predictors of House Challengers' Vote Shares

Table A-4 presents the OLS regression that was used to generate the results that appear in Table 9-2. It predicts the impact of challenger cam-

Table A-3 OLS Regression Estimates of the Impact of Different Forms of Campaign Spending on Incumbents' Vote Shares, 1992

	b	Se b
Direct mail (per $1,000)	0.005	0.006
Radio ads (per $1,000)	0.008	0.016
Television ads (per $1,000)	−0.009*	0.005
Newspaper ads (per $1,000)	0.025	0.028
Field work (per $1,000)	−0.004	0.011

Sources: Questions 15, 20, 21, and 26 of the 1992 Congressional Campaign Study, Federal Election Commission data, various editions of *Congressional Quarterly Weekly Report,* and other sources discussed elsewhere in the appendix.

Notes: The coefficients were estimated while controlling for the impact of the other variables listed in Table A-2 (excluding incumbent expenditures on campaign communications). Separate equations were used to estimate the impact of each form of campaign communication because of multicollinearity between the campaign activities. Field work includes expenditures on get-out-the-vote drives, billboards and signs, campaign literature, and travel to and from campaign events. The sample includes general election candidates in major-party contested races, excluding those in incumbent-versus-incumbent races.

N = 117
*p ≤ .10; **p ≤ .05; ***p ≤ .01; ****p ≤ .001 (two-tailed test).

paign activity (including challenger campaign strategies) on challengers' vote shares while controlling for preexisting political conditions (the partisan bias of the district and whether the challenger was involved in a contested primary prior to receiving the nomination) and the campaign activities of the incumbent. The information is drawn from similar sources as the information used in the incumbent equation. Information about incumbent spending on campaign communications was drawn from mail questionnaires returned by incumbents or was estimated if the incumbent did not return a completed questionnaire. As in the incumbent equation, many of the variables discussed in preceding chapters were not included in the challenger equation because they did not approach statistical significance or because of multicollinearity. The operationalization of the independent variables is as follows:

Partisan bias: see the operationalization used in the incumbent equation.
Contested primary: coded 1 if a challenger had to compete with one or more primary opponents for the party nomination and 0 if otherwise.
Group-based targeting: coded 1 if a campaign targeted voters on the basis of demographic traits (gender, age, race, or ethnicity), occupation, or geography and 0 if otherwise.
Campaigned on position issues: coded 1 if a campaign responded to question 13 that one or more of the following were important cam-

Table A-4   OLS Regression Estimates of House Challengers' Vote Shares, 1992

	b	Se b
Base vote (constant)	27.993	—
Partisan bias (per one-point advantage in party registration)	0.134****	0.027
Contested primary	4.770****	1.150
Group-based targeting	1.951*	1.126
Campaigned on position issues	2.761*	1.601
Challenger spending on campaign communications (per $1,000)	0.009**	0.004
Incumbent spending on campaign communications (per $1,000)	0.005**	0.002
Party spending on behalf of challenger (per $1,000)	0.107****	0.031
Media advantage favoring challenger	3.279**	1.453

Sources: Questions 13, 15, 17, 20, 21, and 26 of the 1992 Congressional Campaign Study, Federal Election Commission data, various editions of *Congressional Quarterly Weekly Report,* and other sources discussed elsewhere in the appendix.

Note: The sample includes general election candidates in major-party contested races.
N = 129
Adjusted R^2 = .57
*p ≤ .10; **p ≤ .05; ***p ≤ .01; ****p ≤ .001 (two-tailed test).

paign issues: gun control, abortion, prayer in school and other religion-based issues, illegal immigration, family values, social entitlement programs, civil rights and racial issues, senior citizens' issues, policy toward Cuba, the preservation of endangered species, nuclear power, and other environmental issues and 0 if otherwise.

Challenger spending on campaign communications (per $1,000): spending on direct-mail, radio, television, and newspaper advertising and field activities (see the formula used for incumbent spending in the incumbent equation).

Incumbent spending on campaign communications (per $1,000): calculated using the formula that was used for incumbent spending in the incumbent equation unless the incumbent campaign did not return a questionnaire. In the latter case, incumbent spending was estimated using the formula used to estimate challenger spending in the incumbent equation.

Party spending on behalf of the challenger (per $1,000): see the operationalization in the incumbent equation.

Media advantage favoring the challenger: see the operationalization in the incumbent equation.

Once again, untransformed measures of spending on campaign communications were used. Substituting the logs of incumbent and chal-

Table A-5 OLS Regression Estimates of the Impact of Different Forms of Campaign Spending on House Challengers' Vote Shares, 1992

	b	Se b
Direct mail (per $1,000)	0.030	0.014***
Radio ads (per $1,000)	0.009	0.014
Television ads (per $1,000)	0.012	0.007*
Newspaper ads (per $1,000)	0.037	0.053
Field work (per $1,000)	0.035	0.016**

Sources: Questions 13, 15, 17, 20, 21, and 26 of the 1992 Congressional Campaign Study, Federal Election Commission data, various editions of *Congressional Quarterly Weekly Report*, and other sources discussed elsewhere in the appendix.

Notes: The coefficients were estimated while controlling for the impact of the other variables listed in Table A-4 (excluding challenger expenditures on campaign communications). Separate equations were used to estimate the impact of each form of campaign communication because of multicollinearity between the campaign activities. Field work includes expenditures on get-out-the-vote drives, billboards and signs, campaign literature, and travel to and from campaign events. The sample includes general election candidates in major-party contested races.

N = 129
*p ≤ .10; **p ≤ .05; ***p ≤ .01; ****p ≤ .001 (two-tailed test).

lenger spending on campaign communications does not significantly improve the fit of the model (the adjusted R^2 improves by a mere .02).

Table A-5 shows the regression coefficients and standard errors that were used to generate the results that appear in Table 9-3. The estimates are for the impact of different challenger expenditures on campaign communications while controlling for other relevant independent variables. The operationalization of the independent variables is the same as that used in the incumbent equation.

Predictors of House Open-Seat Candidates' Vote Shares

Table A-6 presents the OLS regression that was used to generate the results that appear in Table 9-4. It predicts the impact of an open-seat campaign's election activity while controlling for preexisting or national political conditions (the partisan bias of the district, pro-Democratic national partisan tides) and the campaign activities of others. The information on candidate spending on voter communications, district conditions, and mass media coverage is drawn from questionnaires submitted by the campaigns whose vote shares are being predicted. Information about the opposing campaigns' spending on campaign communications was drawn from mail questionnaires when they were available or estimated in cases where the opponents did not return completed questionnaires. Again,

Table A-6 OLS Regression Estimates of House Open-Seat Candidates' Vote Shares, 1992

	b	Se b
Base vote (constant)	43.761	—
Pro-Democratic national partisan tide	3.314*	1.734
Partisan bias (per one-point advantage in party registration)	0.201****	0.039
Ln-candidate spending campaign communications (per $1,000)	3.555****	0.895
Ln-opponent spending on campaign communications (per $1,000)	−3.261****	0.957
Media advantage favoring candidate	3.699**	1.631

Sources: Questions 2, 16, 20, 21, and 26 of the 1992 Congressional Campaign Study, Federal Election Commission data, various editions of *Congressional Quarterly Weekly Report,* and other sources discussed elsewhere in the appendix.

Notes: The candidate and opponent spending figures are natural logs. The sample includes general election candidates in major-party contested races.

N = 70

Adjusted R^2 = .72

*p ≤ .10; **p ≤ .05; ***p ≤ .01; ****p ≤ .001 (two-tailed test).

many of the variables discussed in preceding chapters were not included in the open-seat equation because they did not approach statistical significance or because of multicollinearity. The operationalization of the independent variables is as follows:

Partisan bias: see the operationalization in the incumbent equation.

Pro-Democratic national partisan tides: coded 1 if the candidate is a Democrat and 0 if otherwise.

Ln-Candidate spending on campaign communications (per $1,000): the natural log of candidate spending on direct-mail, radio, television, and newspaper advertising and field activities. This figure was calculated by first multiplying the percentages campaigns specified in questions 20 and 21 by their total campaign expenditures,[13] and then taking the log of that figure.

Ln-Opponent spending on campaign communications (per $1,000): calculated using the preceding formula for candidate spending, unless the opponent's campaign did not return a questionnaire. In the latter case, opponent spending was estimated by first using the approach used to estimate challenger spending in the incumbent equation,[14] and then taking the log of that figure.

Media advantage favoring the candidate: see the operationalization in the incumbent equation.

Table A-7 OLS Regression Estimates of the Impact of Different Forms
of Campaign Spending on House Open-Seat Candidates'
Vote Shares, 1992

	b	Se b
Ln-Direct mail (per $1,000)	1.360**	0.555
Ln-Radio ads (per $1,000)	1.126**	0.053
Ln-Television ads (per $1,000)	0.941**	0.460
Ln-Field work (per $1,000)	1.690***	0.644
Ln-Newspaper ads (per $1,000)	2.221***	0.699

Sources: Questions 20 and 21 of the 1992 Congressional Campaign Study, Federal Election
Commission data, various editions of *Congressional Quarterly Weekly Report*, and other
sources discussed elsewhere in the appendix.

Notes: The coefficients are bivariate OLS estimates that regress candidate vote shares on
the natural log of the expenditures for each campaign activity. Separate equations were
used to estimate the impact of each form of campaign communication because of
multicollinearity between the campaign activities. Field work includes expenditures on get-
out-the-vote drives, billboards and signs, campaign literature, and travel to and from campaign events. The sample includes general election candidates in major-party contested
races.

N = 70
*p ≤ .10; **p ≤ .05; ***p ≤ .01; ****p ≤ .001 (two-tailed test).

The analysis of open-seat candidates' vote shares uses natural logs
of spending on campaign communications because transforming the
data significantly changes the results. Substituting the logs of candidate
and opponent spending on campaign communications significantly improves the fit of the model (the adjusted R^2 improves by over .07). As
the retransformed figures in Table 9-4 demonstrate, expenditures on
campaign communications have diminishing returns in open-seat contests.

Table A-7 estimates the impact that different amounts of spending
on campaign communications have on open-seat candidates' vote shares.
The operationalization of the independent variables is the same as that
used in connection with the incumbent and challenger campaigns except
that natural logs of the campaign expenditures are used to control for
their diminishing impact on the candidates' vote shares. Unlike the estimates in Tables 9-3, A-3, and A-5, the estimates in Table A-7 were gener-
ated without controlling for the opposing campaign's expenditures on
campaign communications, district bias, and other relevant variables.
These controls were eliminated from the analysis because they (mainly
the opponent's total campaign expenditures) overwhelmed the impact of
the money that campaigns spent in any one area.

Senate Campaigns

The analytical techniques that were used to examine Senate campaigns were constrained by the small sample size and the other factors discussed above. The data analysis for the Senate was conducted along the same general lines as that for the House, but bivariate tests were often substituted for the multivariate tests used for the House. The analysis of the 1992 Senate campaigns was replicated using data collected from previous elections.[15] Wherever possible, the statistical findings for the Senate were compared to those reported in other studies of Senate elections. Because of the limitations of the data, the generalizations developed for Senate campaigns were advanced tentatively and received less coverage than those for the House. Most of the discussion of Senate campaigns is comparative and is meant to highlight similarities and differences between campaigns for the upper and lower chambers of Congress.

Notes

1. The interview questionnaire was very similar to the mail questionnaire in Figure A-1 but featured many more open-ended questions and probes and fewer close-ended questions.
2. See Robert Biersack, Paul S. Herrnson, and Clyde Wilcox, eds., *Risky Business? PAC Decisionmaking in Congressional Elections* (Armonk, N.Y.: M. E. Sharpe, 1994).
3. Denise Baer, Martha Bailey, Mary Bendyna, Anne Bedlington, Robert Biersack, Joseph Ferrara, James Gimpel, Roland Gunn, Robyn Hicks, Barbara Levick-Segnatelli, Robert Mutch, Candice Nelson, William Pierce, John J. Pitney, Jr., Craig Rimmerman, Jack Rossotti, Ronald Shaiko, Julia Stronks, Sue Thomas, and Clyde Wilcox participated in the project. I am thankful for having had the opportunity to incorporate their findings into this book.
4. The process used to develop the questionnaire is similar to that described in Don A. Dillman, *Mail and Telephone Surveys: The Total Design Method* (New York: John Wiley and Sons, 1978).
5. Paul S. Herrnson, *Party Campaigning in the 1980s* (Cambridge, Mass.: Harvard University Press, 1988).
6. The respondents to the House survey identified themselves as follows: 40 percent candidates, 46 percent campaign managers, 4 percent press aides, 2 percent treasurers, and 9 percent other. The respondents to the Senate survey identified themselves as follows: 71 percent campaign managers, 4 percent press aides, 4 percent treasurers, and 21 percent other.
7. See, for example, Robert Agranoff, *The Management of Election Campaigns* (Boston: Holbrook Press, 1972), 176-211; and Xandra Kayden, *Campaign Organization* (Lexington, Mass.: D.C. Heath, 1978), 147-148.
8. If a questionnaire was not received from a campaign before the date of the follow-up mailing, and if the original questionnaire and the follow-up ques-

tionnaire were then both completed and returned, the questionnaire that was received first was included in the sample and the second questionnaire was excluded.

9. Other competitiveness measures were considered. Measures based on previous election margins were rejected because many congressional districts had undergone significant change in 1992 as a result of redistricting. Measures based on the lists of competitive elections compiled by party organizations, the NCEC, other lead PACs, publications such as *Congressional Quarterly Weekly Report* and *Roll Call,* and various political newsletters were rejected because of the differences among them. Lists that were compiled early in the election cycle—when candidates, parties, and PACs were making some important strategic and contribution decisions—classified more campaigns as competitive than those that were published later.

10. Prior to calculating the spending figures, the percentages specified in question 21 were adjusted to reflect their share of the total campaign budget.

11. Gary C. Jacobson, *Money in Congressional Elections* (New Haven, Conn.: Yale University Press, 1980); Jacobson, "The Effects of Campaign Spending in House Elections: New Evidence for Old Arguments," *American Journal of Political Science* 34 (1990): 334-362; and Donald Philip Green and Jonathan Krasno, "Salvation for the Spendthrift Incumbent: Reestimating the Effects of Campaign Spending in House Elections," *American Journal of Political Science* 32 (1988): 884-907.

12. See note 10.

13. See note 10.

14. See note 10.

15. For a description of these data see Herrnson, *Party Campaigning in the 1980s,* appendix A.

Index